What readers are saying about
Take the Step: The Bridge Will Be There

"Every page offers you nourishment for your soul. I was deeply touched by Grace's passionate and profound honesty." —Dr. Wayne W. Dyer, author of *10 Secrets for Success & Inner Peace*

"I am so touched, so warmed, and so elated by the words in *Take the Step: The Bridge Will Be There*. . . . Her words hug my opened heart, and I feel connected to God's own wisdom-filled love. . . . I know that thousands of people's lives will be changed forever by this sparkling book. Grace Cirocco is a unique Uplifter of Humanity—an angel, sent here on special assignment. Thank you, God, for her." —Neale Donald Walsch, author of *Conversations with God*

"Grace has unique insights, great passion, and a heart that bursts with understanding and love. She has done for me, through her impressive and inspirational writing, what I do for others. It is a gift to have her voice at hand. Buy this book and invite Grace to be your guide as you venture forth; better yet, keep it with you and refer to it often, to find out how good you can be." —Dr. Blaine Lee, Senior Vice President, FranklinCovey, and author of *The Power Principle*

"This is a wonderful book that will invite you to stretch in every direction—to make your life large, to make your heart whole. Kindhearted and daring, it will allow you to trust that, whatever the step you're longing to take, the bridge will surely be there." —Daphne Rose Kingma, author of *The Future of Love*

"A wonderful, warm, moving book, full of ideas and insights to deepen your reflections and raise you to new heights of self-understanding and self awareness." —Brian Tracy, author of *Create Your Own Future*

"This book will comfort, guide and inspire you. With Grace's support you can lay claim to your uniqueness and true creativity." —Pragito Dove, author of *Lunchtime Enlightenment*

"Grace is a guide in the truest and most ancient sense of the word. She reaches out, and with the touch of her magic wand, she awakens the passion that lies in every seeking soul. . . . Her book is an irresistible call to participate in our own dreams." —Michelle Tocher, author of *Brave Work: A Guide to the Quest for Meaningful Work*

"This is one of the most courageous books I've ever read. I admire you so much. . . . Grace is a perfect name for someone who has the effect on other people that you do." —Denise Bissonnette, author of *The Wholehearted Journey*

"Grace, it was a blessing to receive your guidance, wisdom and insights. I've asked for a leave of absence and know now that I need to leave behind a 22-year career in education. . . Your book had that much of an impact. My angels led me to you and now they will lead me to my life's mission." —Anne-Marie Melanson

"I read your book from cover to cover in a few hours, and have read it a second and a third time, going further on my journey, grieving, forgiving, healing, forging the bridge to my dreams. Thank you for being my inspiration and for bringing so much light to the world." —Anne Godin

"I had felt this terrible isolation and yearned for a sense of purpose. I was a ship lost at sea. Your book was the catalyst. I finally felt 'understood' and valued as a human being with all my frailties. Most of all I felt loved, nurtured and guided. Your words of encouragement and inspiration continue to be a guiding force in my life. You have been such a gift." —Linda Moras

"Grace Cirocco has the gift of helping others 'get it,' move forward and change their lives. On the subject of personal growth and development, this book represents the best thinking of our times. It is a treasure that is loaded with insight, examples, methods and resources." —Theril Andrews

"Your book is the salve today's troubled souls so desperately need. . . . I am recommending it as a must-read for all who are authentic in their quest towards the inner self." —John McCormick

"Grace, your book . . . is very thorough and full of wisdom. I was moved to tears, inspired and challenged." —Michael McFarlane

"Grace, I want to tell you that your book got me motivated and I was able to fulfill a lifelong dream. . . . Nothing is going to stop me now!" —Tony Sciliberto

"As soon as I started reading [your book] I was overwhelmed with amazement—I really found what I was looking for. . . . I would like to thank you from the bottom of my heart for writing this great book. . . . It really helped me in so many ways." —Sana Bokhari

"Grace, you have touched my heart and soul. . . . There were so many moments when I remember I had to simply close the pages and hold your book in silence against my heart. There were so many special parts. . . . We need you, Grace. I'm a teacher and I know that educators need you." —Lucy Rinaldi

"*Take the Step* is not a rehash of old material. It has insights about familiar topics that made many lightbulbs come on for me. I read it during a week when I attended two funerals. . . . I was searching for a life lesson and your book helped provide it for me—a lesson that has changed my life forever!" —Herald McLellan

"Thanks for a wonderfully inspiring book, written so down-to-earth and straight from the heart. The world desperately needs more people like you, Grace, to touch the hearts of those who are struggling to find out who they truly are." —Terri Palmer

"I have been studying and practising the principles in your book for some time, and found your stories, advice and wisdom poignant and inspiring. A close friend and I read chapters of *Take the Step* to each other to help keep our dreams alive and our minds and hearts aligned to our purpose." —Elaine McManus

"My dream was to open a health food store with holistic therapies after leaving the security of a nursing career. Well, I did it! I opened my store April 1, 2002. . . . I am living my dream, Grace. . . . I was scared taking this step but I'm so glad I did it. Your book . . . helped me live my dream." —Lynn Lindberg

"Your wonderful words have filled all the nooks and crannies within me. . . . I feel a surge of joy just below my heart when I think of the 'bridge' that your phrase "Whatever you want, give it away first" has connected with me and my wife and the world around us. For this I am eternally grateful. I see you as a light of courage because you write the right thing rather than the popular one. . . . Your book has the right balance of personal stories, insights, quotes and metaphors. . . . I sense your book as an extension of your soul, an emotional print that you have so graciously put in words." —Jeff Lapointe

"I remember shuffling my way into the bookstore one evening ready to throw in the towel. I purchased your book and my life will never be the same. Your words are God-sent. I have taken the step and I am about to share my poetry with the world. You have been instrumental as a mentor and a woman who moves fearlessly in a world teaching all who wish to remember the divine gifts of the Spirit." —Bonnie Lynn Morris

"As fate would have it, I was in a bookstore a couple of days later and there it was, sitting on the shelf staring me in the face. I knew the copy was mine! In the days that followed, having brought my relationship to an end, *Take the Step* would become a grounding force for me, helping me through the low points. There have been moments of reflection, tears and laughter as I've read your words and worked through the beginning exercises in the past week. I'm nowhere being done the book, so it will be my close companion for a while yet. In the meantime, I'm recommending it to special people in my life. I thank you for your time and for inspiring others (and me!) to take the step." —Claudette Lachance

"I have read more self-help, spiritual, shamanism, psychology and inspirational books than anybody I know. Reading has been my best source of enjoyment for the last forty years. This is the biggest compliment I could ever give anybody: Your book *Take the Step* is exactly the book I would have written. But now, I don't have to write that book anymore—it's been done. Thanks for limiting my choices. . . . I can move on to my other passion: healing! Congratulations! Your book truly is a precious gift . . . the way you wrote it, it flows really smoothly—and makes sense of a very complicated topic: the human experience." —Sylvie Paquette

To read more testimonials visit
www.gracecirocco.com/step.html

Grace Cirocco

Take the Step:
The Bridge Will Be There

INSPIRATION AND GUIDANCE
FOR MOVING YOUR LIFE FORWARD

Blessings, love as you take your step!

♡ Grace

Collins

Take the Step: The Bridge Will Be There
Copyright © 2001, 2011 by Grace Cirocco. All rights reserved.

Published by Collins, an imprint of HarperCollins Publishers Ltd

First published in a hardcover edition by HarperCollins Publishers Ltd: 2001
First paperback edition: 2003
This revised Collins paperback edition: 2011

HarperCollins books may be purchased for educational,
business, or sales promotional use through our Special Markets Department.

HarperCollins Publishers Ltd,
2 Bloor Street East, 20th Floor,
Toronto, Ontario, Canada M4W 1A8

Library and Archives Canada Cataloguing in Publication information is
available upon request

ISBN 978-1-44340-911-7

Printed and bound in the United States
RRD 9 8 7 6 5 4 3 2

For my mother Concetta Cirocco,
whose compassionate heart taught me faith.

For my father Matteo Cirocco,
whose courageous spirit taught me action.

And for Santo, Jasper & Kajsa,
who teach me faith and action everyday.

We shall not cease from exploration
And the end of all our exploring
Will be to arrive where we started
And know the place for the first time.

T.S. ELIOT

The average person does not know what to do with his
life, yet wants another one which will last forever.

ANATOLE FRANCE

Contents

A Note from the Author

Since the first edition of *Take the Step: The Bridge Will Be There* was published in 2001, I have received many communications from people who have been transformed and touched by my stories and message. It's very gratifying to know that so many readers continue to derive benefit from my work, so I'm extremely pleased that HarperCollins Canada has decided to produce this very special 10th anniversary edition.

For over twenty years, I have spoken to large groups of people and worked with men and women individually as well as in small groups. For a person who revels in helping others in a real and tangible way, writing this book was an opportunity to spread my message to a wider audience. In the ten years since *Take the Step* was first published, I have seen many miracles occur: People who thought they were at the end of their rope managed not only to hang on but also to gradually pull themselves up to safety and into a much more dynamic, satisfying life. Others who were stuck either personally or professionally found the motivation and courage to take bold steps. If you are one of these people, I am confident that the book you now hold in your hands will inspire you to take the necessary steps that will change your life for the better. You too can learn to use faith (belief) and action in your life to achieve whatever changes you wish, for your own benefit and that of your family and your community.

In the past few years, we have seen exciting new discoveries in the fields of biology (epi-genetics) and neuroscience. We now know that beliefs do change our biology and that the brain is plastic and capable of dramatic change. These findings support the core message of my book and have encouraged me to keep doing this work that I love. But more than that, it has been my admiration for the many participants in my women's Intensives and couple's retreats that has fuelled my work; the courage these people have shown in making the terrifying journeys that I have guided them along has been truly inspirational. It has been a joy and a privilege for me to witness their transformations, and it is my hope that *Take the Step* will offer up the bridge to many new participants. To these new readers and to my faithful ones of years past, I wish you courage and strength as you negotiate through the sometimes thorny paths of your own lives. May you keep dancing across your bridge to endless possibilities.

Tashi Deley

Introduction

I was supposed to scale a vertical wall. It was smooth, shiny and hard. It was made of black marble and went straight up. Climb this with my bare hands? Impossible, I thought, but I knew that at least one other person had done it, a Chinese acrobat. She was tiny and athletic. I had to get up the wall because I had to solve a computer problem of national importance on the other side. I was the only one who had the answer to the problem, yet I couldn't get over that darn wall. I tried and tried. Each time I slid right down to the bottom. There was nothing to hold on to.

"This is impossible," I thought, a bit annoyed. "It must be some sort of trick." I made all sorts of excuses why I couldn't do it. "I don't have the right body type. I'm not strong enough. Besides, I know nothing about computers." This went on for some time. Then I got tired of all the excuses. Some deep part of me knew that if I really wanted to, I could climb that slippery surface. But how? I had never done anything like that before.

I closed my eyes, took a deep breath and said to myself, "I can do this." I began to repeat, "I can do it, I can do it, I can do it," over and over again to myself until it became a mantra. All the while, I was focusing on the marble wall. And then eight words appeared out of nowhere. *Take the step — the bridge will be there*. The words were there at the top of wall, beckoning me to go up.

"Take the step . . . Okay. The bridge will be there? What bridge?" There was no bridge. Just a wall. I needed to go over that wall. Okay, relax. Take a deep breath. Focus. Visualize. "Grace, you can do it! Grace, you can do it! *Just do it!*"

I opened my eyes — miraculously, I had climbed the wall. I was at the top. All I could think was, "Gee, was that ever easy!" I was exhilarated for a moment. "Wow, I did it!" And then the doubt came. "Yes, but could I do it again?" I needed to know, so I slid back down the wall. That was a risk!

I closed my eyes and saw the same eight words: *Take the step — the bridge will be there*. "Okay, I get it. *Do it with faith!*" Then I was climbing again, except this time it was even easier. I began thinking, "Maybe I should tell others about this."

Then I woke up.

Two years before I had that dream, I had left a secure, well-paying job to start my own training and consulting company. That was in the early 1990s; everywhere I looked, organizations were restructuring and re-engineering — and laying people off. Nobody wanted to hire an unknown when huge training companies with proven records were competing for work. With two toddlers, mounting debts and a husband who also freelanced, I felt I could no longer afford to pay someone to watch my children while I went to my office to stare at the telephone. After two years of spinning my wheels, I made the decision to give up the call of my soul and get a "real" job.

And that's when I had the dream. Sometimes our souls send us messages just as we're about to turn our backs on our true path. That dream inspired me. It helped me believe in myself again. I wrote *Take the step – the bridge will be there* in huge black letters and stuck them on my office wall. Those words became my compass whenever I felt lost. They gave me courage to keep following my heart's desire and stay true to my soul's calling. Eventually I designed a workshop called "Take the Step – The Bridge Will Be There," and over the past eight years I have helped tens of thousands of people take that step toward their dreams.

Action ("take the step") and faith ("the bridge will be there") are the two most important ingredients for achieving anything you want in your life. Typically the problem is that if we want to take action, we don't move forward because we don't believe in ourselves. Or if we do believe in our abilities, we're too afraid to act. Rarely do we display both faith and action at the same time and in the right mix.

TAKING ACTION

My soul does not find itself unless it acts. Therefore it must act. Stagnation and inactivity bring spiritual death.

– THOMAS MERTON

There are people who have plenty of faith, or so it would seem. They say they believe in themselves; they claim they can do anything. They appear confident and self-assured, and they talk constantly about all the things they're going to do – someday. These people can't move their lives forward because they don't move their feet. They procrastinate, they complain, they postpone their lives. They suffer from analysis paralysis. These people will unfortunately never know whether their faith is real or not because they never test it by taking action. The truth is, you will never know whether you can really do something until you actually try it. Faith without action is not really faith. Only action makes faith real.

It is said that knowledge is power, but knowledge that lies dormant in your brain will not move your life forward. It's what you do with what you know that will make the difference in your life. The moment your brain sends the message "Move" to your feet is the moment when you walk across the bridge and change your life forever. What will it take for you to finally act?

Taking action builds bridges to possibilities. Action nurtures self-esteem and self-respect. When we stare down fear and take action, our lives can be transformed from ordinary to extraordinary.

In Part One of this book we will discuss how you can do the necessary groundwork for taking action in your life. You'll have an opportunity to ask yourself, "What do I really want? What brings me joy? What vision do I hold of my life and how can I get there? What have I been postponing? What am I waiting for?" You'll have an opportunity to address what is still undone in your life.

The paradox is this: In order to take action and *do*, we must first learn how to *be*. The gateway to action is the powerful states of being that I will discuss in the next five chapters. Yes, you must act, but you must align your compass with what is most sacred to you. That can be done only by exploring who you are.

NURTURING FAITH

At your most daring moments you believe that what is going on
is the ultimate human work – the shaping of a soul.
The power of life comes from within; go there; pray; meditate.
Reach for those luminous places in your Self.

– ARDIS WHITMAN

All of us personally know some "action heroes" – people who are doers, who have no trouble taking the step. They appear to be fearless and dynamic. They have lots of projects on the go, but somehow they don't seem to get any of them done. Many people end up feeling stuck. They can't move their lives forward because they don't have the necessary faith in themselves. They lack the connection to their magnificence, to their authenticity.

That is what happened to me. I took action – I registered a business, rented office space and sent out hundreds of packages outlining my services. But deep down I didn't really believe I could make a living from doing work that I loved.

Even though we're taking action on the outside, on the inside we may feel like imposters. Doubts, fears and demons from the past rear their ugly heads. We lack the internal authority to silence the doubt and say, "Yes, this is possible. I can do it!" Consequently, the action we take is often miscalculated, off target or not effective. Your body can't go where your mind has never been. What we need to do first is convince ourselves that we can do it, nurture faith in ourselves, and *then* take the step.

In Part Two of the book, I discuss ways you can nurture faith – in yourself, in each other and in our world. So many of us feel we can't cross the bridge because we don't have the right credentials or the proper background. We feel that we may be "too much" or not enough. We believed the naysayers when they said, "It's too difficult" or "It's never been done before." Why would we challenge all those years of programmed beliefs? The path of least resistance is to believe what we're told. It's never what you *are* that holds you back – it's what you *think you're not*. That's why we need to grow faith if we are to achieve our goals.

When I speak about faith, I mean the faith we need to believe in our gifts, our talents, our dreams, our desires and our highest purpose. Nurturing faith in yourself is therefore nurturing faith in the vision you have of your life. It is growing the belief that you can do it, whatever "it" is for you. With faith, all is possible – even miracles.

Faith is like the tides; it is not always constant. There are days when we feel we can slay any dragon, and other days when we might as well offer ourselves up as the dragon's next meal. The only way to keep your faith "tuned up" is to be true to your spiritual journey. Turn your eyes inward toward the Spirit that you are. See the Light. See the Love. We are reflections of the universal Love. See that which is holy and pure. Remember who you were just before you were born. You were Spirit, and that's where you will return to.

THE SPIRITUAL JOURNEY

The conditions of a solitary bird are five:
the first, that it flies to the highest point;
the second, that it does not suffer for company,
not even of its own kind;
the third, that it aims its beak to the skies;
the fourth, that it does not have a definite color;
the fifth, that it sings very softly.

— SAN JUAN DE LA CRUZ

There has been so much outward change in the world that it has forced many of us to begin an inner dialogue. In our effort to awaken to the beauty in our lives, many of us have embarked on a spiritual journey. This journey has taken us through "the dark nights of the soul" and the fires of transformation. This journey invites us to lead authentic lives and asks us to open our hearts to faith, hope and love.

The spiritual journey is not always easy. Our fears can seem insurmountable. And as we attempt to cross the bridge we can come face to face with the demons of the past. "Go back!" they shout. "The chasm will swallow you whole," they warn, but we press on.

We take the step – and with each step we grow our souls. And as we cross the bridge, Spirit helps us welcome miracles into our lives.

Miracles happen when we believe in our magnificence and take the step toward meaningful action. Miracles take place when compassion envelops our hearts and we see more clearly how to forgive and let go. Miracles follow us when we recognize the endless possibilities we have to create for ourselves. Miracles are everywhere when we truly believe that we're One and that healing the planet will begin with healing ourselves.

We are finally blessed by miracles when we make peace with the divine Presence in our lives.

Close your eyes for a moment. Imagine a bridge. What does it look like? Is it strong and steady or is it a rope and wood bridge that sways back and forth? Does it have a solid foundation or is it in need of repairs? What is it made of? Is it a covered bridge? Is the bridge in a forest or over water? Is it obscured by fog or overgrowth? When you look at your bridge, does it give you confidence? Would you cross it? Your bridge represents the quality of your faith – faith in your dreams, in yourself and in a divine Voice that whispers guidance to you and sustains you during periods of doubt.

In the Bible the Apostle Peter talks about having to step out of the boat and into the water. He's afraid and he can't muster the courage to take the step. Then, through the mist, he sees Jesus walking on the water toward him. Peter can face his fear and take the step only while he has his eyes locked firmly on the eyes of his Master. If he looks down for even a second, he loses his nerve. As long as he keeps looking at Jesus, he too can step into the sea and fear nothing. Like Peter, if we are to take that step into the abyss or over the bridge or into the sea of fear, we need to keep our gaze fixed on the vision – that which is sacred to us, that which nurtures us spiritually.

My hope is that the following pages will inspire you to cross the bridge to whatever future you desire. Once you're inspired, you'll have more confidence and courage to take bold steps. The answers are inside you; sometimes all you need to bring them forth are the right questions. May the reflections, personal stories, inspirational poems, quotations, suggestions and practical exercises I've included in this book trigger the right questions for your spiritual journey.

As you're reading, let your mind meander to your life. Pause to reflect and jot down ideas that speak to you. Ask yourself, "How does this apply to my life?"

Ideas are like seeds. They are the raw material on which our bridges are built. When we nurture the seeds of faith, we realize we can do anything – even climb smooth vertical walls. What would you like to do but feel is impossible? If I were to say to you, "Take the step – the bridge will be there," what would you think of first?

Faith and action are like two wings of an airplane that keep your life in flight. If only one wing works, your voyage may be turbulent. You will not get to your final destination. You may not even make a safe landing. If you want to move your life forward, you need to make the journey with both wings. "Take the step – the bridge will be there" could easily be "The bridge is there, so take the step." It doesn't matter which part of the equation you work on first. You need faith *plus* action if you are to actualize the best version of yourself.

I was concluding a number of seminars in Australia when a young woman from Melbourne hugged me hard and whispered in my ear, "Thank you, Grace. You've changed my life." A month later I received a postcard from her saying, "You know when I whispered in your ear that *you* had changed my life? Well, I want you to know that you inspired me, but *I* changed my life. I didn't know that then, but I know that now and I wanted to share it with you." She had figured out the secret to her own empowerment.

Books, people and resources can be rays of sunshine in your life, but remember, you are the sun. You are a unique work of art in progress. Every day your choices help create your masterpiece. Savor the journey. Belong to this world and shine.

GRACE CIROCCO

PART 1

Take the Step

One day the hero
sits down
afraid to take
another step
and the old interior angel
limps slowly in
with her no-nonsense
compassion
and her old secret
and goes ahead

"Namaste"
you say
and follow

David Whyte

1

Authenticity

Who Am I?

Truth is within ourselves, it takes no rise
from outward things, whatever you may believe . . .
— ROBERT BROWNING

I was riveted to the car radio, listening to Sister Eva Solomon, an Ojibway woman, tell her story. When she was fifteen, she was called to the bedside of her uncle, who had been hospitalized after being badly beaten by his friends. While sitting next to him, feeling both angry and sad, she asked God in desperation, "Why do Native people beat each other up?" And then, like a flash, came the insight that would change the course of her life. "It's not alcohol," she thought. "*It's because they don't know who they are.*"

When we feel alienated from the Self, we are disconnected from our Spirit. We've lost the key to our magnificence. We no longer feel like the unique miracles that we are. We are estranged from our core, authentic selves. Eva Solomon has spent her adult life helping Aboriginal people reconnect with who they are and deal with this problem of self-alienation.

"Who am I?" is the central question facing every human

being, and it is at the root of our spiritual quest. We must ask it again and again in order to begin our inner dialogue. This question will lead us on a conscious journey – the way out of self-alienation. This is how we can reconnect with our authentic selves. This is the way home.

STOPPING YOUR LIFE

**All of humanity's problems stem from man's inability
to sit quietly in a room alone.**
– BLAISE PASCAL

Who we are is not our jobs, our bodies, our families, our bank accounts, our cars or any other material object. Who we are is not even the roles we play for others – mother, father, teacher, wife, neighbor, business person, manager, friend. Who we are transcends this world. Who we are is Spirit, Light, Love. How do we connect to this part of us in our crazy, fast-paced world?

Have you ever wondered what would happen if suddenly one day you just stopped your life? You know, as if someone had hit the "stop" button on an assembly line and everything came to a screeching halt. Have you ever wanted to take your Spirit on a holiday – just you and your Spirit? Have you ever wanted to take time out to just *be*?

I love watching people in busy urban centers, in train stations, shopping malls or just on the street, walking briskly to their next destination. I've always wanted to pretend I am some sort of pollster, so that I could stop some of them and ask them where they are going. "Excuse me, sir, I'm from the ABC Company. We're doing a poll this evening. We want to know where people are going. Could you please tell us in your own words where you're off to at this precise moment?"

I'll bet I know what they would say: "I'm going home," or "I'm going to work" or "to see a movie" or "to meet a friend for dinner" or "to the gym" or "to the baby-sitter's" or "out for a walk." No one would look me in the eye strangely and say, "Gee, I don't know . . . I'm taking my Spirit on a holiday to just *be*."

We've all got such busy lives. We squeeze so much in. We're modern-day warriors pounding the pavement in the name of progress and economic growth. I marvel these days when I see people in airports linking themselves electronically to their offices via cellphone and e-mail. They're always trying to get in some last bit of business before boarding their planes. Most people are busy "going somewhere," their lives moving along at sometimes frightening speeds.

So what if you *could* stop your life? What if you had the luxury to step outside yourself and ask your authentic Self a few key questions – questions that would put your life into perspective? *Who am I? What do I really want? How do I want to belong in this world? Am I living an authentic life?*

Thousands of people asked themselves these questions during this past decade, when they were restructured out of jobs and pushed off the precipice, with no safety net below. When they landed, they had to pick up the pieces of their shattered worlds. Some, like Mark Albion, decided to catch up with their lives. In his book *Making a Life, Making a Living*, he says, "While my high-paying, high-prestige job made me the envy of neighbors, I felt the life being sucked out of me, leaving me homesick for some place I could not name. . . . I had broken one of my own guidelines – don't get really good at something you don't want to do – and I was paying the price – an inauthentic life."[1]

It is so important that we give the world our authentic gifts and talents, but how can we do this if we don't know who we are?

WAKING UP TO OUR AUTHENTICITY

There are no role models for waking up – waking up is not something that society regularly condones or endorses. Waking up involves challenging the status quo. It's for brave hearts.

– GRACE CIROCCO, *JOURNEY TO THE SELF*

Regardless of the catalyst, "waking up" can and does shake up the soul. There are sure to be thrills and chills along the way. Waking up can be a curse or a blessing, depending on your attitude. The journey can be messy, varied and long, but also beautiful, inspiring and adventurous. Waking up is the soul's destiny. It is your right, not a privilege. It's all part of the plan, the unfolding of the Mystery. But how does one go about it?

Seeking to live the authentic life is an ancient quest. We have been searching for the truth forever, it seems. When we pull out the dictionary, we learn that the word "authentic" means "genuine, not false or fictitious, original." Is that what you see when you look in the mirror?

It is unlikely that people will embark on a spiritual quest for their authentic Self without some prompting or an external "wake-up call." First of all, we don't have time. We haven't learned the secret of stopping our lives in order to examine them. So for some of us, wake-up calls are inevitable. These are events such as a personal tragedy, a brush with death, an illness, the loss of a job or friendship, divorce or betrayal. They can also come with the passing of time, when we've celebrated yet another birthday ending in zero.

After one of my seminars a man came up to me in tears to

share with me his wake-up call. He was responding to research I had shared with the class that showed how men and women react differently to stress. When women have too many demands on their time, they will make sure they do a good job at work, as well as take care of their family responsibilities at home. What gets put on the back burner are exercise and girlfriends, the very things women need in order to cope with stress. For men, it's different. When men feel the pressure, they will deliver the goods at work and still manage to make time for exercise, but the one thing that gets set aside is family.[2]

"I thought that if I kept bringing the paycheck home, I was okay," he told me, wiping the tears from his eyes. "I was worried about getting fired at work. What I didn't realize was that I could get fired at home."

"What happened?" I asked. As soon as I spoke, I wanted to take my words back, because his chin started to tremble.

"I came home one day to find that my wife and two young daughters had left. She later divorced me."

That had been a big wake-up call for him, and he obviously still needed to heal. He's not alone. So many of us don't know what's important until it's too late.

My friend Meranda, who is an aesthetician, runs her own business. She's worked extremely hard over the past two years to establish a solid clientele, so I haven't seen much of her. Recently, her aunt, whom she had been very close to, died suddenly. It was a shock to everyone, and it made Meranda feel sad, reflective and thoughtful about her life.

"It sure has made me realize a few things," she told me, "like who's important to me and how precious life is. I have been working way too hard."

Wake-up calls come in all shapes and sizes. They come unannounced and they can cause us immense grief. No one knows why bad things happen to us. Sometimes we want to scream, "Why me, God?" But if we face them square in the eye and work through the feelings – the fear, anxiety and turmoil they produce – they can act as purification for the Spirit, a way for us to grow our souls. "Each problem is an assignment designed by your soul," the author of *Why Me, Why This, Why Now?* teaches. Robin Norwood recommends the view that adversity is a path to our healing and that suffering has meaning and purpose and dignity.[3]

Wake-up calls, although painful, bring us closer to who we are. They can begin our journey – a spiritual journey – to discovering our authentic core. The spiritual journey is the voyage back home to our Self. We're going back to our roots. We're reconnecting with our Spirit.

"This journey is not easy," my client Tom would tell me when he came for his weekly coaching session. Tom's wake-up call came at fifty-two, when he was told by his company that he was no longer needed. He had known some cuts had to be made, but never thought his position would be affected. Although he was shocked at first, today – three years later – Tom feels renewed, invigorated. He's learned some pretty amazing things along the way. For one, he's found out that the computer industry in which he was working was corroding his soul. He had been ignoring his body's signals that his health was failing. He had also been ignoring what mattered most to him, his wife and children. During his two-year journey he also discovered that he has the heart of an artist. Today Tom paints, and he has managed to sell some of his paintings to friends and on the Internet. He says, "It makes me happy to know that I am giving the world what my authentic Self wants to give, rather than what my boss wanted me to give."

We are, in the end, like that beautiful phoenix that flames

and dies, to be reborn from the ashes into a magnificent new creation. We are all works in progress.

What wake-up calls have you had? What do you need to pay attention to? What teachers have arrived on your doorstep? What wisdom is your soul ready for? Every event in your life is a teacher, a messenger from the unconscious. The Buddha said that our only job is to wake up. Wake up your soul to this possibility, and you will look with new eyes at your life.

TAKING OFF OUR MASKS

**The soul would much rather fail in its own life
than succeed at someone else's.**
— DAVID WHYTE

How do we wake up from our sleep? How do we wake up to our magnificence, to our divinity, to the fact that we are living, breathing, walking, talking miracles? One way is to begin removing our masks.

We are conditioned by advertising and the popular media to feel skeptical about our appearances, our failures and our personality flaws. In order to feel good again, we assume various masks to try to please the people around us. Sometimes we put on these masks as children in order to cope with loss, loneliness or a dysfunctional family. Sometimes we assume the masks out of fear – fear of pain, fear that we won't be loved, fear that we'll fail, fear of abandonment. We take on the masks because we have somehow bought into the belief that our authentic Self is not okay. It requires honesty to recognize our various masks, and courage to peel them off and live authentically. To express who we are to the world, we must first become aware of who we are and who we are not.

9

If you can, seek solitude. The false Self tends to come out in the presence of others. The true Self is more likely to emerge when you're alone. Arrange a stretch of uninterrupted time; perhaps take a long walk alone or sit in a quiet comfortable place. I love going to the forest near my home, where I have a favorite log that I sit on. I go there to get in touch with *Grace*. When I was a child growing up on a fruit farm, I'd go to the canal behind our farm to write in my journal, "Sam." Perhaps when you were a child, you had such a place, too. What about now? Find a place where you can celebrate your solitude. Whether it's at home or out in nature, you need someplace where you can be alone.

Then turn to the following two questions (or write the questions in your journal now and think about them at the park tomorrow or when you're driving home from work or while you're soaking in the tub). Let these questions plant a seed in your mind and let the answers come forth when they're ready. When you have insights, though, it's important that you write them down.

- Who do I pretend to be, and with whom? For example, "I pretend to be strong with my kids" or "I pretend to know it all with my boss" or "I pretend to be in control with my customers."
- What do I risk by being me? For example, "I risk being judged harshly" or "I risk being hurt" or "I risk feeling out of control."

Then take a look at the masks listed below. Many are masks that we assume unconsciously. Over time, these masks become perceived as our identities; peeling them off is very difficult. This is part of the Self-discovery journey. We need to strip away this pretension to find our buried truth within.

not enough	self-sufficient
too much	super mom/dad
perfectionist	stoic
tough guy	busy bee
know-it-all	caretaker of the world
have-it-all	victim
done-it-all	martyr
nice guy/gal	saint
class clown	flirt
weaker sex	judge
party animal	rebel
dumb blonde	expert
workaholic	

- Which of these masks do you know that you wear?
- What would you lose if you took them off?
- How does wearing these masks alienate you from your authentic Self?
- Which ones are you ready to say goodbye to?

The first step in removing these assumed masks is to be aware of them. Be conscious of when the masks come on and with whom. Who pushes your buttons? Many of us have been socialized to sacrifice our authentic Self in order to meet society's expectations. In pleasing everyone else, we have lost our unique personhood. After we have assumed layers of masks, reconnecting with the authentic core can be an arduous task.

MASKS AND RELATIONSHIPS

**At breakfast a beloved asked her lover,
"Who do you love more, yourself or me?"**
– RUMI

The authentic Self comes out when we feel safe. What are you like with your best friend? Your parents? Your childhood friends? Your neighbors? Your colleagues at work? Your boss? Your lover? Your children? My experience is that we allow different parts of ourselves to come out at different times, depending on how safe we feel in the relationship. When we feel unconditionally loved and accepted, we are relaxed enough to leave the masks behind and bring out our authentic Self.

Think about masks and your relationships, and ask yourself:

- Whom do you allow to see the real you?
- Which relationships bring out your deepest and most authentic Self?
- With whom do you feel vulnerable?
- What masks do you wear with your employer?
- What masks do you wear with your parents or siblings?
- What masks, if any, do you wear with your significant other?

There are times when both parties in a relationship put on their masks. This is perfectly normal in situations where something is at stake. Take, for example, two people negotiating the sale of a house. The seller says the house is perfect. To hasten the purchase, she wants the buyer to know that there is plenty of interest in the home. The buyer, on the other hand, wants the seller to think that he too has other options, and he doesn't show much emotion, even if he loves the house. Both are protecting their own interests. Both have a hidden agenda.

But sometimes people do show their vulnerabilities, their fears, their hopes and dreams. They share both their pain and their joy. They are not afraid to be who they are because they know, regardless of the demons they take out of the closet, that they will not be judged or rejected. These relationships are the most sacred to us and make our lives worth living. We can take risks in such relationships, with the knowledge that, should conflict arise, it's okay. We have faith that all will be well and that love and acceptance will always be at the core. The people with whom I can share all of me and risk being truly authentic I call my soulmates. Soulmates are connected on a spiritual level. They've shared past lives together. There is deep understanding and comfort between them. Conflict becomes but a spoonful of water in the vast ocean of Love.

MASKS AND EMOTIONS

When you share your joy with me, you tell me what you belong to.
– ORIAH MOUNTAIN DREAMER

Sometimes we bring our authentic, vulnerable Self out into the world like an enthusiastic puppy – only to run up against the masks of others. When this happens, we feel not only foolish, but also deeply betrayed. I had such an experience about ten years ago. I was part of a women's healing group that met once a week. We were about to go on a weekend retreat, and before we went our leader wanted to take us through an exercise that would gauge how safe and comfortable we felt with each other. We were going to be doing some intensive "inner work" on the weekend, so it was important that we felt safe enough to bring out our authentic selves.

Our facilitator gave each of us a sheet of paper with the names of all the women in the group, and three sets of stickers. Red stickers were like red lights. They meant, "Stop! I'm not comfortable with you. I have an issue with you." (Basically they meant, "I don't like you.") Yellow stickers were like amber lights: Proceed, but only with caution. Getting a yellow sticker meant, "I don't really know you. I could feel comfortable, but I need to talk to you more." Green stickers were green lights. The message was, "I like you. I feel comfortable with you." After we had placed stickers beside all the names, we were told to meet each person individually to share how we felt about them.

Being who I am, I gave most people a green light. There were only a few ambers, but that was because I had missed a few sessions and hadn't got to know everyone in the group yet.

Then, after I told one woman – I'll call her "Sue" – all the reasons why I had given her a green light, she responded with all the reasons why she had given me a red one. I remember the horrendous confusion and hurt that swelled inside me. I was shocked, especially because I had been totally loving and generous in my praise of her.

She had a problem, she said, with the way I blurted things out in the group, the way I was always asking everybody questions. She also had a problem with my "bubbly personality" and my "sickening enthusiasm." In short, I was too intense, too loud and too much for her, and she didn't think she could feel comfortable around me. I couldn't believe my ears. If she felt this way about me, why hadn't I picked up on it sooner? How could I have been so naïve? Her words wounded me to the core. I spent the rest of the evening alone, too ashamed to face the others. It took a lot of courage and prompting from the leader and the rest of the group before she and I even considered going on the weekend, but eventually we both decided to go.

That weekend, during a psychodrama re-enactment of a dream, I learned things about Sue that opened my eyes and my heart to her. What came out was that, as a little girl, Sue had been very much like me – passionate, excitable, always bubbly, asking everyone lots of questions. Her mother didn't like her that way and one day in a fit of anger she poured boiling water over her arms to shut her up. From that day forward, Sue took on the mask of "reserved, quiet little girl" and buried the part of herself that her mother did not accept and love. The adult Sue had been unaware that her authentic Self was more like me. Instead, she hated anybody who reminded her of the person she wasn't allowed to be. That weekend experience was not only an eye-opener, but a soul-opener, too. It brought healing and forgiveness to our relationship and to the group as a whole. I became Sue's unofficial coach, encouraging her to put her "quiet" mask aside and let her authentic Self come out to play with me.

We put on our masks to protect ourselves, and while we were children, they worked. But now it's time to ask yourself some questions. Do your masks represent who you truly are? Are they betraying you? What are your emotional triggers? Could the "difficult" people in your life be aspects of your buried Self? Could these people provide the keys to unlock some of your unconscious masks? Are you projecting your masks onto the people in your life?

Masks keep us from uniting with our authentic Self. They prevent us from experiencing the joy, love and freedom that are our birthright. They also prevent us from crossing the bridge toward our dreams and the life we want. Wake up. Think. Be aware of anyone who causes you to put on a mask, and think about why you do so. The *why* may be a sign that it's time for you to set your masks aside and bring forth your authentic core, your authentic Voice. Go deep. Connect with your inner child. Do some soul work. Mourn for the person you were not allowed to be. Expose the unconscious masks and let go of them. Better yet, have a ceremony – bury them and say goodbye.

THE LAST OF THE MASKS

We are not meant to stay wounded. By staying stuck in the power of our wounds, we block our own transformation.

— CAROLINE MYSS

Don't be fooled by the tricky masks. Those are the ones that appear to give us feelings of self-worth, even an identity. They are the ones to come off last. Take, for example, Elaine, a dear neighbor of mine. She was always in pain. She had sustained a back injury in a car accident several years ago. Despite what her doctor and friends recommended – craniosacral massage, acupuncture, chiropractic, hydrotherapy – Elaine didn't seek any help. I couldn't understand this, until one day when I saw her with a group of people. It was summertime, and the neighbors were gardening or walking their dogs. I watched as she told people about her back-pain woes, skilfully evoking sympathy from each. "Poor Elaine," everyone would say. "How do you get through the day?"

I realized then and there that Elaine was married to her pain, and that as long as she got that reaction from people she was going to wear that mask of pain. She was getting the attention and sympathy she craved, but she was also stuck in her illness. A few months later, I read about this exact phenomenon (called *woundology*) in Caroline Myss's book *Why People Don't Heal and How They Can*. Here's what Myss says:

> I began to discern when a person was genuinely going through the specific stage of healing that requires a witness and when someone had discovered the "street" value or social currency of their wound – that is, the manipulative value of the wound.[4]

I will discuss wounds and healing in more detail in Chapter 7, but for now, ask yourself whether any of your masks are protecting your self-esteem. What would you lose if you took them off?

THE QUEST FOR AUTHENTICITY

**Seek not abroad; turn back into thyself,
for in the inner man dwells the truth.**
- ST. AUGUSTINE

My husband and I had been reading Anthony de Mello's book *Awareness*. One day, while visiting our friends Sandra and Mario, we found the same book on their shelves, except that it was a Spanish translation. I found it interesting that the title of the Spanish version was *Despierta!*, which means not exactly "awareness," but more like "wake up!" I began to think about the relationship between these two concepts. We need to be aware in order to wake up, but we need to wake up in order to be aware! So be aware of events that come disguised as problems in your life – your wake-up calls. And then be observant (or aware) of the people, places and events that you call into your life.

Let me take you back to a time when I was a student at Queen's University in Kingston, Ontario. Many universities and colleges sponsor writers-in-residence, who are invited to live on campus and interact with students. In my first year of university, I got to meet and become quite close to one such writer. His name is Giorgio Bassani, and he wrote the international bestseller *Il Giardino dei Finzi-Contini* (*The Garden of the Finzi-Continis*), on which a film was later based.

Most days after class, we'd go strolling – often arm in arm, Italian style – across the campus. It was autumn; I have beautiful memories of crunching through leaves beside the pale limestone buildings. This gentle man of letters shared with me his philosophy on life. "Be always observant, Graziella," he'd say in his native Italian. "A good writer observes even the tiniest of details. One must observe, or else life goes by, and you miss it."

Then we'd stand still and observe the wind on our faces, or the squirrels in the trees, or the crashing waves of Lake Ontario. Sometimes students would walk past and he would whisper, "What did you observe in that relationship? What did you see on her face? His face?" He told me that his job as a writer was to observe the world and then to report back his findings.

What if someone were commissioned to write a book about your life – your thoughts, your feelings, your friends, your choices, all that you are – with nothing to go on but what you had to say? The author would be totally dependent on you for all the material. Each day you would have to report a new observation about your life. Do you think you would start to pay more attention to your world? Do you think you might wake up to your life, to the magnificence that is you? Do you think you would become more aware of your feelings and of the conversations you have inside your head?

Recently I heard David Whyte speak at a conference. He's the author of *The Heart Aroused: Poetry and the Preservation of Soul in Corporate America*, as well as several collections of poetry. He kept stressing to the crowd the importance of "conversation." At work, if we don't maintain conversations with colleagues and customers, we lose them. At home, not maintaining a conversation with our mate and children means we lose those relationships. And if we don't maintain the internal conversation with ourselves, we end up losing the Self. The quest for Authenticity begins when we start to pay attention to that conversation.

PAY ATTENTION TO YOUR FEELINGS

For too long we have been blind to the cognitive riches of feeling!!
- JOHN O'DONAHUE

A very powerful way to get to know who you are is through your feelings. Feelings are sacred. They don't lie. They are a vehicle for the expression of your authentic Self. They will say who you are perhaps more than anything else. That's why we need to pay attention to them. We learn when we are young that to survive in the "real world" we must fake it, put aside our feelings, get rid of our vulnerabilities and not show people how much we are hurting. We have learned to hide our authentic feelings, especially if they are negative.

Anger is one of the most threatening of emotions and children learn from a young age that it is unacceptable to express it. Rather than retaliate or abandon children when they get angry, parents need to let them have access to all their feelings. Parents must survive the anger and the hatred and find a way to return unconditional love. The relationship between parent and child is bound to involve upsets and conflict. This is a normal part of any relationship. However, if parents are emotionally needy, insecure or depressed, they can't offer unconditional acceptance when their children display unhappy emotions. As a result, some of us learned as children to shut down our anger and turn off our passion and intensity. Without knowing it, we put our parents' needs ahead of our own, creating false impressions of who we were just to get the love and approval we craved.

The consequence is that we have both surface feelings and deep ones. If you're angry, what are you afraid of? If you're hurting, what makes you sad? Gently quiet any thoughts and focus on feelings. Some people are so out of tune with their feelings that when you ask them how they feel, they'll give you a judgment, a statement or a thought. Your feelings are waiting to give you so much wisdom, if only you would listen. More than anything else, they bubble up from your authentic core and can be the impetus for embarking on your spiritual journey. A lot of literature out there describes the benefits of becoming more "heart-centered"; I will discuss this concept in more detail in Chapter 9.

PAY ATTENTION TO YOUR DREAMS

Dreams begin to awaken us to the fact that we are spiritual or interdimensional beings . . . they are like a letter from the higher self to the conscious mind.

– BETTY BETHARDS

Dreams have been known to predict the future, save lives, solve mysteries and unlock the key to our authentic Self. They are the highway to the unconscious. Sleep research centers have found that we need to sleep because we need to dream. We need to visit the unconscious world – the world of dreams – and we need to do so on a daily basis.

I've always been fascinated by the dream state. Where exactly do we go when we dream? I used to love watching my babies sleeping because I could see them dreaming. Their eyes would move from side to side and their faces would break into bright smiles. My grandmother used to tell me that babies are very connected to the spirit world and that during their dreams they are able to communicate with God and the angels.

Many therapists work with dreams to loosen emotional

blockages and speed the healing process. We need to pay attention to our dreams because they can link us with what is truly authentic in ourselves. Sometimes a dream will come to us over and over again because we may be ignoring its message. This book started with a dream that I had many years ago, and the dream gave me its title.

Everyone dreams, but not everyone remembers their dreams. One way you can begin to remember them is by making a conscious decision to do so. Before you go to bed tonight, say to yourself, "I want to remember one dream. I will remember one dream." Repeat this three times, out loud if possible. Do this several nights in a row. Keep at it; don't give up too quickly.

You can also try keeping a glass of water near your bed. Just before going to bed, drink half the glass. Tell yourself out loud, "Tomorrow when I wake up, I will drink the other half and remember one dream." In the morning, as soon as you're awake and while still in bed, drink the other half and see what happens. Some of my clients say they haven't even begun to drink the water before they're aware of something.

Another technique for remembering dreams is to wake up softly. Alarm clocks that buzz you from unconsciousness scare dreams away. If you can, wake up on your own. If you can't, then do it with soft music. Some people are woken by their pets and others by their children – all preferable to loud mechanical noises. Then linger in bed for a minute or two, stretching your limbs and gently reaching for images from your dream world. This technique always works for me.

Make it easy to remember your dreams. Keep a journal or notepad at your bedside. When you wake up, write down what you remember before you get out of bed. Hang on to whatever images or phrases are in your mind. The act of writing them down will stimulate more dream memories. Later in the day, return to the journal. Is there anything else you remember? Write down any associations.

Pay attention to your dreams. They are whispers from the other side. If you have not paid attention to them for a long time, they may be in hiding. They need coaxing to come to the surface. Ask yourself what are they trying to tell you. According to Carl Jung, dreams are not to be taken literally; they are symbolic interpretations of the Self. So, for example, if you dream that your mother is seriously ill, think about what your mother means to you. It may be a part of yourself, perhaps your nurturing Self, that is sick.

All dream interpretation guides are just that – guides. There can be no universal dream interpretation bible because everyone is different. In the end you are the best judge of what your dreams may be trying to tell you. Ask yourself whether the dream situations or emotions remind you of anything that is going on in your waking life. What associations do you make with the people and events in your dreams? What themes can you see emerging over time? Making a mental note to remember your dreams, discussing them with those closest to you or with a professional, writing them down – all these things will tell your subconscious mind that you respect its wisdom. The more it is respected, the more information it will give you as to who you really are. Dreams are a vehicle to help you expose the unconscious masks you have assumed over the years. Pay attention to them.

PAY ATTENTION TO YOUR WORLD

**Nobody sees a flower – really – it is so small it takes time –
we haven't time – and to see takes time . . .**
– GEORGIA O'KEEFFE

My husband is short-sighted. He was eleven years old the day he got his first pair of glasses. He recalls the excitement he felt that first day looking through the lenses that would reveal what the world was really like. "It was amazing," he told me. "Everything was so crystal-clear. I could actually look at a tree and see the individual leaves on it. Leaves! Up until then, I didn't know leaves were something you could see except from very close up." He told me he spent hours that first week walking around his neighborhood observing everything that he had missed without glasses. "It was as if I was seeing everything for the first time."

What if you tried on a pair of glasses that allowed you to look at your life with more clarity, what would you see? What if you could look at life with awe and childlike wonder? How different might your life be? What if your magic glasses helped you see everyone with more compassion, more love? Would your life change at all? Look around you. Open the eyes of your soul. What do you see? Be observant of everything and you will discover things that will help you find your way – your unique place in the Universe.

Angeles Arrien, the American anthropologist and author of the *The Four-Fold Way*, shares her wisdom with her four rules for living. It's interesting that Rule number 2 is "Pay attention." That means "be aware, be observant, be conscious." Different words – one message.

TASHI DELEY

**The problem of the meaning of life
is solved by the mystery of love.**
- SAM KEEN

Sometimes we discover who we truly are through the eyes of another. When we feel loved to the core, we feel understood, blessed, liberated. I've discovered that one of the reasons why couples fall out of love is that they no longer feel "seen" by their partners. I don't mean seen with the physical eyes, but on a different, more spiritual level. When you see your beloved with the eyes of your heart and of your soul, you can penetrate to their very Essence, to that abundant Light that the Creator put in all of us.

I asked a good friend and long-time confidante when it was that she fell out of love with her ex-husband. She told me it happened while she was expecting her third child. Even though it was the third time around, she felt excited to be once more carrying God's miracle within her. But her husband wasn't awake to that miracle. "He barely noticed me," she recalled. "He made it seem like it was routine, not special at all." She felt so alone and sad throughout that pregnancy. Even though the decision to have a third child had been mutual, he could not allow himself to see it fresh, as if for the first time. He could not see his wife's beauty and radiance. He could not see the Spirit of their unborn child.

When we're not seen for who we are, we disconnect. We mourn. The Tibetan people have a traditional greeting. When they see each other, they put their hands together palm to palm, fingers pointing up, in front of their chest, bow and say the words *"Tashi deley."* The words mean, "I honor the magnificence in you." Isn't that beautiful? Imagine what a kinder, gentler world it would be if everyone greeted each other in such a holy way. Imagine saying hello to your boss, colleague or neighbor that way. Imagine saluting the magnificence in your friends. Imagine giving recognition to the Light in your children every day. *Tashi deley* expresses a deep reverence for one another. It is what our world needs today. It would help us realize who we are if the people around us would, at least on occasion, reflect our magnificence.

The Tibetans are a gentle people. I had an opportunity to meet some of them in a refugee camp in Darjeeling, India. Even though the political oppression in their country means they must live as transients, displaced from their families, they can still use their spiritual eyes to bless one another. When they thanked me for buying some of their handiwork – crafts and sweaters they sell in order to stay self-sufficient – their eyes were warm and moist. They *saw* me in a way that was far different from any other exchanges I've had. I left them feeling blessed. It's perhaps fitting that their spiritual leader, the Dalai Lama, says that his religion is compassion. The Tibetans know how to communicate compassion and kindness with their eyes. They see straight into your God Essence.

In the past it used to bother me when I noticed parents acting indifferent toward their children. I'm sure they loved them, but rarely did I see a parent who knew how to soak up their children with their eyes, who could *see* the miracles their children were. How sad this made me. I was puzzled as to why they behaved so casually around their precious offspring. I vowed to myself that I would never take my own kids for granted, never allow their presence to become commonplace, to be anything less than holy.

My children are ten and eight as I write this, and I'm sure I've broken that promise many times. No one is immune to bad days or stress. The clock ticks on, and there are days when we forget our own magnificence, let alone see it in others. I encourage you to see your children as much as possible with new eyes. Celebrate the perfect souls that they are. Recognize the Divine spark in each of them. Witness the miracle of their birth every time you lay eyes on them.

Next time you see your beloved, drink him in. Spend a few minutes staring into her eyes. What does the poet say? The eyes are the windows of the soul. What stories does the soul hide? What treasures lie buried and undiscovered? Who is this person? Before you make love, *see* your beloved! See the beauty and the abundance; salute the magnificence. Say hello to the God within.

A Few Helpful Exercises

1. Now that you've read this chapter, spend some time thinking about Authenticity. Take out your journal and make notes on any topic at all. If you get an idea for an action step – great! Write it down immediately and post it somewhere. Then tell someone about it, because when we declare our action steps, we're more likely to keep our commitments.

2. *"Peel the Onion"*
   Have a partner ask you the following questions over and over again while you try to go deeper and deeper into reflection. Make sure your partner pauses after asking the question and then asks it again. Each repetition will be an invitation to dig deeper into your authentic Self. It takes time to reflect and go deep, so give yourself time. For example, your answer to "Who are you?" might be a woman, a father, a manager, aunt, wife,

lover, piano teacher, student, etc. That is the top layer of the onion.

But when you go deeper you may find that different qualities begin to emerge. Who are you? "Sad." Who are you? "Lonely." Who are you? "Passionate about life." Who are you? "Frightened for my health." Who are you? "Someone who longs for intimacy."

Here are some useful questions for "peeling the onion":

- Who are you?
- Why are you here?
- What do you want?
- Who do you pretend to be?
- What makes you angry?
- What makes you sad?
- What are you afraid of?

3. Write down, draw or find symbols to represent some of the masks you know you wear. Think about why you wear them. Then ask yourself, "What will I lose if I let them go? How do they protect me? How do they rob me of my Authenticity?" Finally, ask yourself, "Which one am I prepared to let go?" Then have a funeral and bury it. Dig a hole in your backyard and say goodbye. It may take you several weeks or months to let go of one mask, and some masks you may not be ready to let go of at all. Just do what you can and honor where you are right now.

2

Truth

LIVE YOUR TRUTH

The truth is always simple,
but living it is not always easy.
— REV. ALFRED MILLER

Before we take the step, we must be honest about what it is that we want and where we want our journey to take us. Often the reason that people can't take action is uncertainty. They feel stuck. They can't cross the bridge. They've lost their compass. But truth will illuminate the journey, and living our truth allows us to nurture action and take the step.

One of my clients, a married woman, came to me one day because she was consumed with love for another man. Mary was in her mid-thirties, with two children and a decent, loving husband. She explained to me that she hadn't been looking for another relationship, but this love had taken her heart totally by surprise and wouldn't let go. The affair had been going on for about six months, but now she had decided to pull the plug. However, she was absolutely sickened by the thought of never seeing her lover again. I advised Mary to write a letter to him. Whether she gave it to him or not, at least it would help her clarify whether or not she should see him again. The following week, she brought me the letter.

Dear Love of my life:
I don't know why your angel eyes entered me so deeply last April. I was relatively happy in my own little world last spring when I first felt the burn of your penetrating gaze. Why me, I thought. Why is he looking at me? I remember how strange and awkward it was to tell you my name; me, a happily married woman. I knew then that that was the beginning of the end, that we were destined to be. We were drawn to each other from the very beginning, like some sort of weird cosmic destiny.

I know that we are both married, but essentially we belong to no one except perhaps to that Infinite Universe from where we came. We are who we are – and we're all here on borrowed time. Our stories unfolded so naturally, softly, gently, like leaves falling one by one in the autumn air. It feels like I've known you my whole life. It was destiny that brought us together so we could reconnect from the past and weave our present moments together.

People come and people go in our life and our hearts know who to trust and who to love. And sometimes our hearts feel things that the so-called rule-book says are wrong. Why is our loving each other wrong? Because we're married, because it's considered "betrayal." But I love both of you! You and my husband, just in different ways. Why is this so difficult for people to understand? Why is it that I can love more than one female friend, more than one child, and yet only one man? I've always admired the loons who mate for life, and yet, even though I know I've mated for life with my husband, I can't imagine a world where I can't love you, too. I heard that even though the loons mate for life, they always winter apart. Perhaps if couples adopted this practice, they might be able to keep passion alive.

You said to me once, "We're on a train that's going nowhere." I think it's time we got off the train. I don't want to lie anymore. Our families need us. We can't abandon them and I can't keep seeing you behind his back. The guilt is eating at me. I'm a mess. I can't cope with it any longer.

I want you to know that you've brought infinite joy to my life and for that I am eternally grateful. I feel I've been blessed. And I wasn't looking for this. You found the key to my heart and slipped in before I had the chance to realize what was happening.

I'll always keep your memory locked inside me like a tender secret, your beautiful eyes imprinted on my soul, your smile etched in my mind, your words printed on my heart. My life is and will always be richer because you were in it. Look for me in your next life. I will be there waiting for you. My love for you is eternal.

Mary could barely read it to me, she was crying so much. But it was important for her to read her words aloud to see if they still rang true.

"Are you sure this is what you want to do?" I asked her. "Are you sure this is your truth?"

"No, it's society's truth, not mine," she exclaimed angrily through her tears.

"What do you mean?"

"The moral ethics of the day don't approve of what I am doing."

"Do you approve of what you're doing?"

"Yes . . . no . . . I mean, why did God send this to me if it were such a bad thing?"

"Good question. Why did God send it to you?" I asked.

"To help me fall in love with myself and life again. To bring joy to my life. To make me realize that life is precious and I should not take one single minute of it for granted."

Then she began to cry again. "Why, Grace? Why can't I love both of them? Why do I have to make a choice?"

"Why do you feel you must make a choice?"

"Because I'm not supposed to have my cake and eat it too, I guess. I don't know."

"Well, what stops you from living your truth?" I asked.

"My guilt. I feel like I'm betraying my husband," Mary said.

"Are you?"

"Technically, according to the Ten Commandments, yes. But not really. In my heart I feel like I'm a better wife, a better mother, a better version of myself. But if my husband found out, he would never forgive me. He would be devastated. We'd probably break up."

SELF-BETRAYAL

This above all: to thine own self be true.
– WILLIAM SHAKESPEARE

There will be times in your life when you reach a fork in the road. Choose one path, and you betray yourself. Choose the other path, and you betray someone else. Either way, there will be suffering. Too many people avoid embracing their truth because they want to avoid pain. When faced with such life choices, they will take the path of least resistance, in the naïve belief that self-betrayal is the path of least pain!

If Mary betrays her husband, she will live with constant guilt and anxiety that he might find out. If he finds out, the marriage might end. Those are the consequences. But if she betrays herself, what then are the consequences? What happens to people when they betray their souls? There will be pain, unbearable pain. Will this lead to resentment? Bitterness? Illness?

I've had clients in similar situations who ended up resenting their spouses, and the resentment led to fault-finding, arguments and eventually separation. So what they were trying to prevent from happening happened anyway.

Too often we're trained to keep our promises and our agreements with others, but not those we make with ourselves. But what about our souls? The soul knows. How can we grow self-respect if we're betraying our own truth? How can we have integrity if we betray what is right for us? And yet we do it every day. We make a big deal when others betray us, but don't blink an eyelash when we do it to ourselves. How often we betray our souls because we think no one is looking! Sam Keen says that "human beings are the only animals capable of self-deception and therefore of self-betrayal."[1]

Those of us who approach life as martyrs – the ones who say, "What I want doesn't matter. It's what you want that is most important" – are usually liked and even celebrated compared to those empowered brave hearts who are true to themselves. If we sacrifice our truth for the sake of another, if we swallow our feelings and "do the right thing," then we're considered heroes. Since marriage is a pretty big commitment, considerable guilt and shame are associated with a breakup, regardless of how difficult the marriage has become. When my aunt left my uncle almost thirty years ago, she was completely shunned by her community. Even my mother, who is the most compassionate person I know, judged her harshly for leaving her family. Oriah Mountain Dreamer, in her poem *The Invitation*, wonders, "I want to know if you can disappoint another and be true to yourself; if you can bear the accusation of betrayal and not betray your own soul. . . ."[2] Being true to oneself today is not easy, but we must face this challenge if we are to lead authentic lives.

I tried to encourage Mary to listen to her truth, explore other possibilities, perhaps even discuss her infidelity with her husband. But she was adamant her husband would never understand. Besides, she said, she believed her destiny was the same as the heroine's in *The Bridges of Madison County*. Francesca didn't go off with her lover because she wouldn't turn her back on "a good man" and her two children. She would sooner sacrifice her happiness than destroy the happiness of her family.

Almost six months later, Mary started experiencing severe abdominal pain. She was devastated when she found out she had a malignant tumor in her uterus. After her surgery, she spent considerable time wondering why this had happened to her. When we talked about it, she told me she had figured out what the tumor was about.

"It's a punishment," she said. "Not because I committed adultery, but because I said goodbye to him before my heart was ready. Grace, I betrayed my heart."

After she had broken off the affair, Mary went through considerable agony. She was an emotional mess, grieving the love she had lost. Because her husband didn't know anything about it, she had to pretend that everything was okay. She told me that some days the pain got so bad, all she wanted was to crawl into a hole and die.

We're holistic creatures. When we betray our truth, we can call illness into our lives. Psychoneuroimmunologists like Herbert Benson, Joan Borysenko and Hans Selye, all pioneers in the mind-body connection, have found a link between disease and what we think and feel. Norman Shealy, founder of the American Holistic Medical Association and coauthor of *The Creation of Health*, wrote that seventy-five percent of his patients told him they wanted to die six to twenty-four months before they were diagnosed with cancer. When I shared this information with Mary, she was shocked.

"Do you think I'm going to die?" she asked me.

"I don't know, Mary. Do you want to die?"

"I don't want to anymore. But last year, when the pain was so bad, I wanted to disappear."

It's been a long road for Mary, but she is now determined to live life to the fullest. She eventually told her husband the truth and together they began to heal their marriage. She doesn't regret what happened and has decided that she will never betray her heart again.

When we betray ourselves, it may seem like the right thing in the short term, but in the long term nobody wins. In the past few years, many of my clients and friends have been at similar crossroads in their lives. No one knows why the miracle of Love comes to us. But every day, in cities and towns all around the world, people are falling in love. And then they must decide: "Do I betray myself or my promise to them? Do I break my heart or theirs?" I think it's one of the toughest choices we'll ever have to make. As I've learned, it's choices like these – especially if you don't shrink back, especially if you can live through them and embrace the highs and lows regardless of the outcome – that grow your soul.

FOLLOW YOUR JOURNEY

**Out beyond ideas of wrong doing and right doing there is a field.
I'll meet you there. When the soul lies down in that grass,
the world is too full to talk about.**

– RUMI

Nearly seven years ago, one of my best friends, "K," fell madly in love with a guy she met at a conference in California. K had been feeling disconnected and empty for a long time, but now she felt alive and pulsating with energy. Her body didn't need food or sleep. She was restless with energy. It never occurred to her to hide this new-found energy from her husband, Sam. As best friends, they had always told each other everything.

"Maybe you're in love with that Jesus guy," Sam suggested after K shared her symptoms with him on the phone. Throughout the week, she had told him about some of the people she had connected with at the conference. The "Jesus guy" was one of them.

"In love?" K was shocked that Sam was even suggesting such a thing. As soon as he said the words, she could feel panic gripping her heart. In love? Impossible. Happily married women with children don't fall in love. Her religious upbringing had taught her that good people don't have affairs. It was safer for her to deny her feelings. Besides, she told herself, the Jesus guy lived three time zones away. Nothing would ever come of it. "No, I don't think so," she replied.

But K was to learn that love has its own agenda and doesn't care about marital statuses. Sam, very sensitive to her turmoil, said to her one day, "God has sent you this experience for a reason. You need to follow your journey wherever it may lead you. Don't worry about betraying me. Just don't betray yourself."

Sam is truly one of the most gentle and wise people I know.

Some might think his reaction was foolish, but I truly believe he was able to respond this way because his love for K is unconditional. Unlike most people, he was able to put his ego on the shelf and think about what was best for her. Eventually, and not without difficulty, K and Sam both opened themselves up to what they were feeling and embarked on the emotional roller coaster of a lifetime.

What K learned was that by being true to herself she was able to be true to Sam. She instinctively knew that her marriage would survive if she embraced her feelings for the Jesus guy rather than deny them. By working through the feelings and going through the ups and downs, she and Sam both tapped into higher versions of themselves. They opened a dialogue of the heart and reconnected on a soul level. Somewhere in those ten years of marriage, they had fallen asleep to the beauty of being alive. It happens to many couples. They have children and suddenly get caught up in the banalities of everyday life—as Francesca in *The Bridges of Madison County* says, "the practical details of living." They don't make time to look their beloved in the eye and remind themselves why they fell in love in the first place. Passion dries up and they no longer see the beauty in themselves.

K's falling in love was a wake-up call in more ways than one. Had she denied what she was feeling and betrayed her heart, I'm pretty sure her marriage would have ended. And she would be less of an artist, less of a mother and less of a wife today; in short, a lesser version of herself. By feeling all of her emotions—the exhilaration and the guilt, the joy and the anguish—she was able to tap into an authentic version of herself. She finally ended the relationship with the Jesus guy. I always knew she would. She belonged with Sam. "I could never leave Sam," she used to tell me, "because I'm not sure any other man could love me the way he does. He is my best friend." Their courage to speak their truth and ride the often painful rollercoaster transformed their marriage into something more alive and real.

LOVE AND TRUTH

Where do love, and truth abide;
Like birds of a feather, side by side.
Only to find, that in the end
They are as one, an only friend.
And where are we, adrift in a mire
Consoled by life, and a longing desire
To rid our sins, of days, in the past
And hallo the future, with the truth at last.

– NICHOLAS OLENICK

Please do not think that I am recommending an affair as a way of rescuing a marriage. According to statistics, affairs bring a couple closer together only 40 percent of the time. If two people are disconnected, if there is emotional space between them, then there is vulnerability—someone else can come between them. Sometimes extra-marital love affairs can be opportunities to address what needs healing in the marriage, to kick-start more passion and commitment. But only if there is courage to speak and hear the truth. Only those who can stand in the fires of honesty and emotional nakedness can climb to a higher place. The point is not to run from the experiences your soul has called into your life, regardless of how messy they are. Life is messy. Please don't sacrifice your truth to avoid the mess.

For many people, the pressure to sacrifice their truth and thus betray themselves is too strong. The inner tyrant, that voice inside their head that grew out of years of social conditioning, says they must deny themselves. In Neil Walsch's

Conversations With God, Book II (pp. 95–97), God tells the author:

"Somewhere you've come across the idea that to deny yourself joy is Godly, that not to celebrate life is heavenly. Denial, you have told yourself, is goodness. You deny yourself this or that because you tell yourself you are supposed to, because society says it's wrong. Then you're satisfied it was the right thing, but you wonder why you don't feel good. Why your heart screams out in pain."

The conversation eventually leads to extra-marital affairs:

[God] Never, ever, ever fail to do something simply because it might violate someone else's standards of propriety, of what is right and wrong.

[Author] That means that others can hold you hostage. All they have to say is that such and such a thing would "hurt" them, and your actions are restricted.

[God] Only by your Self. Wouldn't you want to restrict your own actions to those which do not damage the ones you love?

[Author] But what if you feel damaged by not doing something?

[God] Then you must tell your loved one the truth—that you are feeling hurt, frustrated, reduced by not doing a certain thing; that you would like to do this thing; that you would like your loved one's agreement that you may do it. You must strive to seek such an agreement. Work to strike a compromise; see a course of action in which everybody can win.

[Author] And if such a course cannot be found?

[God] Then I'll repeat what I have said before: Betrayal of yourself in order not to betray another is betrayal nonetheless. It is the Highest Betrayal.

When was the last time you betrayed yourself? Was it years ago or just recently? To be aware of self-betrayal you must stay conscious and awake to your feelings. Some of us lie to ourselves in tiny, meaningless ways every day. It becomes habit. "This disgust with mendacity is disgust with yourself," Big Daddy tells Brick in Tennessee Williams' classic *Cat on a Hot Tin Roof.* "You dug the grave of your friend and kicked him in it—before you'd face truth with him." Mendacity is prevalent in our society. We lie, we wear masks, we betray ourselves, and eventually the truth that lives inside us is so submerged that we don't recognize it. Ask yourself, when and with whom do you swallow your truth? Are you a people pleaser? Do you feel obligated by others? Is guilt or truth your compass? Finding your authentic Self begins by living your truth.

Shakti Gawain reminds us that "every time you don't follow your own inner guidance, you feel a loss of energy, loss of power, a sense of spiritual deadness." One of my clients, a man in his forties, completely lost his enthusiasm for life and had to go on anti-depressants when he took a job just to pay the bills. He had been downsized by his company, so when his friend told his boss about him and put in a good word for him, he felt he couldn't refuse. He betrayed himself in order to stay loyal to his friend. His relationship with the friend who got him the job soured when he lost the company a huge contract. He realized that was not his type of work. He had ignored what his heart had been telling him.

What symptoms have you experienced as a result of not following your own inner guidance? We tend to discard our personal stories—what is true for us—for the truth of another. Why do we do this? Why do we sell out? We carry with us the truth of our ancestors, the truth of our convictions, the truth of our souls. Yet every day we close our ears to it so that we can hear other words, worlds away.

I know that for some of us the voice of fear speaks too loudly.

It prevents us from taking the step across the bridge. It is the reason why we betray ourselves. How do we overcome the fear? Ask yourself: What am I afraid of? What will I lose? At times, K was terrified that by following her truth she might lose Sam, that he might leave her. She was also afraid of what her family and friends would say. She lived with this fear every day, and yet she was courageous enough to embrace what she felt. She knew that if she tried to deny her feelings she would eventually end up hating everyone, including herself.

Don't let fear run your life! You must be willing to look your fears squarely in the eye if you want to take a stab at living authentically and experiencing the life your soul came here to live. Regardless of how others may judge you, in the end this is your life. If not now, then when?

Poet David Whyte reminds us, "The soul would rather fail at its own life than succeed at someone else's." Remember, nothing holy has ever been achieved through denial. Maybe you are willing to walk through the fire and see where your soul wants to take you. Do you need to wash away your shame? Come out of the closet. There is no shame in being true to yourself. There is no shame in telling yourself the truth. There will come a time, if you haven't already experienced it, when you find yourself at the crossroads. Turn left and you betray someone; turn right and you betray yourself. Tell me, what will you choose?

TELL THE TRUTH

The greatest of all true things
is a true heart.
Without truth no happiness,
though you try a million tricks.

— KABIR

At one point, not even the Jesus guy understood why my friend, K, told her husband the truth. "Is it for you?" he asked her one day. "Or is it for him?" He accused her of being cruel, suggesting that telling Sam was a way to assuage her guilt.

I think the Jesus guy was afraid that the truth would eventually build a bridge of intimacy between K and Sam, and that the Jesus guy would lose her. And that's exactly what happened. Truth is what saved K's marriage. And most of the time, it is truth told at the right time that saves relationships. I see it at my couples retreats. People arrive with secrets and shame, and those who have the courage to speak their truth, to cry their pain and to ask for forgiveness make it. Those who are too afraid, who keep their truth locked inside of them, don't. We are human. We make mistakes. We lose our way, but truth redeems and transforms us. It is quite miraculous.

But truth is risky. Many of us fear its consequences. Sometimes I think we don't give people enough credit. We think they can't handle the truth. Truth is difficult because it requires we have faith—faith in ourselves, faith in the other person and faith in the strength of our relationship. Relationships deepen when we communicate our feelings. Have you ever taken a risk with someone and told them how you really feel only to find out that they crossed you off their friendship list? Sometimes truth backfires. It depends on how you tell it, on what your intent is, whether you come from a place of revenge and hostility or from a place of love and understanding.

In most cases however, and if the relationship is worth keeping, truth told with compassion can deepen the bond. Truth allows us to climb to higher peaks of intimacy with each other. Truth helps us to heal old wounds. Without truth there is no trust, and without trust there is no foundation for a relationship.

An old neighbour of mine, Joe, works as an undercover cop on the drug squad in a large metropolitan city. He says that one of the reasons his job is so stressful is that he lies all day long. In order to gain drug dealers' trust, he must lie about who he is and what he wants. At the end of each day, he makes meticulous notes of all the lies he's told and to whom, so that he can study the list and continue the saga the next day until he has enough information to make the bust. Joe just celebrated his fortieth birthday, but he says there are days he feels like he's fifty! Everyone agrees that he looks older than he really is. I think the stress and burden of lying have taken their toll.

In 1945 in a cave at Nag Hamadi in Upper Egypt, a hidden library of early Christian writings was found. Included in these writings was the Gospel of Thomas. What's interesting is that when the disciples ask "the living Jesus" for direction on practical matters, he gives no specifics. He says only "Do not tell lies, and do not do what you hate: for all things are manifest in the sight of heaven." (NHC 11.33.18-21)

Do not tell lies and do not do what you hate. This is the only advice Jesus had for his disciples. In other words: Tell the truth (to others) and be true to yourself (i.e., do not do what you hate). It all comes down to this. Have the courage to tell the truth and then live it. Knowing your truth and then acting on it is what taking the step is all about.

PRACTICE INTEGRITY: WALK YOUR TALK

Today, millions are experiencing the pangs of hunger in passive helplessness. How can I speak to these millions or identify myself with them, without undertaking this fast and knowing myself what pangs of hunger mean?

– MAHATMA GANDHI

A woman who wanted her son to stop eating sugar visited the great Mahatma Gandhi in his village. "Come back in two weeks," the great master told her.

When she returned, Gandhi said to the boy, "Son, don't eat sugar. It's bad for you."

The woman looked puzzled and asked him, "Why couldn't you give my son that message two weeks ago?"

Gandhi smiled. "Two weeks ago, madam, *I* was eating sugar."

Integrity is not saying one thing and doing another. Integrity requires that your outer actions match your inner values. Imagine two pillars. One pillar represents everything that is sacred to you, everything that you value – your ethics and your principles. The second pillar represents how you think, behave and act every day. If both pillars match – if they are the same height and width – then your life reflects integrity. If the pillars don't match, there is a lack of integrity.

In order for you to practice integrity, your values must be congruent with your actions.

The more integrity you have, the more self-respect you gain. The greater your self-respect, the more you can nurture action. You'll have integrity when you keep your promises – including those you make to yourself. You'll have integrity when you live not according to someone else's desires, but according to your own version of what is true. You'll have integrity when your

44

principles are shaped by your inner knowing, not by your external circumstances. You'll have integrity when you can stay true to your principles and values even when it seems easier to compromise your ethics and give in. You tell yourself that no one will ever know. But your silent partner knows and hears all. That silent partner is your soul.

Without integrity, we cannot feel good about ourselves. Integrity allows us to approve of ourselves. And that approval is the foundation upon which self-love and self-acceptance are based. Every day there are opportunities, circumstances, situations where we must choose to either sacrifice our integrity or stay true to the inner compass that tells us what is right for us. Our society makes it easy for us to betray ourselves and lose integrity. You stick to the diet when people are around, but when you're alone – who will ever know? You don't yell at the kids in the grocery store, but as soon as you get in the car – you let them have it.

You may ask yourself, "Don't I have the right to do this?" Yes, but is it the right thing to do? How do you feel later on? Acting with integrity is easy when people are watching. When you are by yourself, with no audience, acting with integrity becomes more difficult. We wouldn't admit to cheating on our taxes or stealing from our company, yet we have to live with this knowledge every second. We may think it doesn't affect us. Consciously we put it out of our mind, but our subconscious mind knows. Our Spirit – the part of us that is divine – knows. When we lose our integrity, we corrode our souls.

If you pay lip service to principles and ethics but don't practise them, then you are not walking your talk. If you don't walk your talk, you don't have integrity. Two of my good friends smoke. Their daughter smokes. They would like her to stop; they're worried about her health. "But how can we tell her to stop when we're not prepared to stop ourselves?" they ask me. They may be weak, but they are wise. They are not hypocrites. I think we all admire people who practise what they preach, and those who don't preach what they themselves are not willing to practise.

I believe that more of us would like to stay true to our principles – if only we knew what those principles were. That's why self-knowledge is vital. It's foundational. You must know who your authentic Self is and what is important to you before you can practise integrity. You must be willing to peel off the masks. People who walk their talk, whose character is solid, have always been admired in our society. They are the ones who can walk with their heads held high. We believe in them. We admire them. At times we even put them on a pedestal.

Another way to build integrity is to speak up when you know it's the right thing to do. We don't for a variety of reasons, and fear is the largest of those. Every day around the world, people keep their mouths shut when they know in their hearts they should be speaking up and speaking out. When was the last time you lost self-respect because you didn't speak up?

We have to acknowledge the voice within and pay respect to our inner guidance. When we refuse to put on masks for others, when we speak up and tell our truth, when we listen to our heart, when our actions match our values, then we show our integrity. The two pillars match. Integrity nurtures self-respect. The more self-respect we have, the more action we take in our lives.

A Helpful Exercise

When was the last time you betrayed your soul? What, if anything, has been eating away at you lately? What conversations have you had that left you uneasy and unsettled? Pay attention to those feelings. You may have compromised your ethics, and those feelings are the residue.

In your journal, divide the page in half. On one side, write down all that is sacred to you, what you believe in, what is important to you, your principles and your moral laws. On the other side of the page, write down a corresponding action step or behavior from your life that has supported that value. As you do this, you'll begin to clarify what integrity looks like to you and, hopefully, diagnose those times when you haven't been completely true to yourself.

When in doubt, ask yourself, "Do I approve of this? Do I feel good about myself? Do I respect myself? What would my soul say if it could talk to me directly? What would the person I admire most in the world say? What would God say?"

3

Destiny

WHAT'S YOUR DESTINY?

There is a wick within you that is waiting to become the light
of your soul. When this inner flame burns brightly,
you will feel a magnificent awakening of your life.

– BRADFORD KEENEY

A few years ago, the members of Willow Creek Community
Church, located near Chicago, conducted a survey in the United
States. They wanted to know this: If people could ask God only
one question to which they were guaranteed an answer, what
would that question be? Topping the list was "Why is there
suffering?" Many of us seek the answer to that question.

However, the second concern people had was one of destiny.
Three questions tied for second place. They were

1 What is the purpose or meaning of life?
2 What is going to happen in my future?
3 What is going to happen when I die?

Those who asked question 1 want to know "What is my
destiny in life?" Those who asked question 2 are seeking the

answer to "What is my destiny in this world?" Those who asked question 3 are asking "What is my destiny in eternity?" All "destiny" questions. People today are on a spiritual quest. They long for clarity about who they are and where they're going. They want to know their destiny and the purpose of this life.

So, what is destiny? It's the root word of "destination," and comes from the Latin *destinatus* (fixed or decided). It is a question of direction: Where am I to take my life? What am I meant to do with my life? The word also conveys a sense of fate or purpose. Some people connect their fate to God's plan for them.

Your destiny contains your "mission" and the vision you hold of your life. If you understand your destiny, you will know what is waiting for you on the other side of the bridge – it motivates you to take action.

I'm convinced that people don't take the step because they're not connected to their destiny. They don't see the big picture. They feel powerless, not special. Everyone's life has purpose and meaning. It's up to each of us to figure out what it is.

Once I was teaching a workshop to some government employees and talking about destiny, when suddenly a woman in the audience yelled, "Oh, I get it!" The group seemed amused and intrigued, so I invited the woman to share her moment of illumination.

"I just realized now why I am so stressed out in my life," she said. "It's because I'm whatless."

"Whatless?" I inquired.

"Yeah, I have no *what*, no destiny, no purpose and no meaning." As she finished explaining, quiet descended on the group. She had touched a nerve. She had pinpointed a source of angst for many people.

It's very stressful to be without a destination. Imagine getting in your car but not knowing where you're going. Imagine boarding a plane, but the airline hasn't told you where the flight is headed. That's crazy. How will you know what to pack, how to plan for your trip? Yet that's how many of us live our lives.

Picture yourself adrift in a fast-flowing river (wearing a life preserver, of course). The river represents change. The river's current is constantly moving you, crashing you into rocks, rushing you past fallen trees and large boulders. You feel powerless. Every now and then you pass by a place that intrigues you. You would like to tell the river to stop, to let you off so that you can explore the place further and discover the gifts that might be waiting for you. But the river doesn't listen. It has its own agenda and you, after all, are only along for the ride.

So many of us believe in the glory of the afterlife, yet we have no clear vision of what we want in *this* life. We spend more time thinking about and planning a one-week vacation than we do our whole lives. It's great that we can, for the most part, take one day at a time. But it's sad that so many people have no idea of who they are or what their destiny is. We're drifters. We're not connected to what makes us truly great and truly unique. We don't set goals. We let our dreams die.

Your *what* – your mission, vision, vocation, calling, bliss, meaning, destiny – won't come from reading a book or taking a workshop. There's no such thing as a hand-me-down destiny. You must create it from scratch, like good bread. It comes from the well of passion deep within you. It takes time and work to get to your authentic Essence, your precious core. The journey to find your destiny is the journey to find your Self. To cross your bridge you must become something of a spiritual warrior.

Spiritual warriors want to connect with something greater than themselves. They thirst for meaning and clarity. They want to understand their purpose – why they're here.

Why are you here? What is your life about? What's important to you?

YOUR VALUES: WHAT WOULDN'T YOU SACRIFICE?

Often people attempt to live their lives backwards: they try to have more
things, or more money, in order to do more of what they want
so that they will be happier. The way it actually works is the reverse. You
must first be who you really are, then, do what you need to do,
in order to have what you want.

– MARGARET YOUNG

Nelson Mandela refused to sacrifice his freedom. He worked hard to bring an end to racial injustice in South Africa. His fight landed him in prison, where he spent twenty-seven years. He suffered unrelenting isolation and hard labor, but he did not break. Eventually, after his release from prison and following reconciliation with then-president F. W. de Klerk, a democratic election was held. During a historic four days in 1994, millions of blacks across South Africa exercised their right to vote – a right they had never had before, and for which Mandela had risked his life.

Freedom. That's what we think of when we hear the name Nelson Mandela. What wouldn't you sacrifice? In other words, what is sacred to you? What matters most? What values do you hold dear? What priorities do you live by?

Your values are a compass for your life. I love the symbol of the compass, because today most of us badly need one. We're not aligned with what is most important to us. We don't walk our talk. We say family is important, yet, day after day and week after week, we put the family on the back burner while our work takes priority. We make excuses. We compromise. We say that good health and exercise are important, but every day we eat junk food in front of the TV. We say we're committed to our faith, our spiritual journey, yet we haven't learned to really go within and listen to God. We say we want to keep learning and stay current, but we don't seem to have the time. We seek balance, but we falter. So we sacrifice our ideals and our values.

THE IMPORTANCE OF COMPASS

> Imagine life as a game in which you are juggling five balls . . .
> work, family, health, friends and spirit. Work is a rubber ball. If you
> drop it, it will bounce back. But the other four balls are made
> of glass. If you drop one of these, they will never be the same.
>
> – BRIAN DYSON

Knowing what your compass is and how to align your choices and actions with it are the key ingredients for living a happy and fulfilled life. So much of our frustrations and stress arise from incongruity – incongruity between what we think, feel or say is important and how we actually spend our time. For example, I'll ask people, "What's most important to you?" Most will list family as their highest priority, but when they look at how they spend their time, family is usually at the bottom. Our values don't match our actions. Perhaps what's needed is a values-clarification exercise, or learning to say no to the unimportant things. You must let your compass be your guide.

I first started teaching people the importance of compass

after reading the ideas of Stephen Covey. No one does a better job of showing us how we have been leading incongruent lives. It's not just individuals who are ignorant of their internal compass, but companies, governments and organizations as well. Leadership today is about giving a team a clear vision, mandate, purpose, destination – in short, a compass. Aligning effort with compass produces results: Everyone is on the same page and communication flows. The end is achieved.

Compass is also important for personal time management. For so many of us, time management remains the last frontier. We can do everything but manage our schedules and cope with the ever-increasing to-do list. After Stephen Covey published *The Seven Habits of Highly Effective People,* his organization did a survey to find out which habit people had the most difficulty with, which habit was toughest to live. The survey found that it was Habit 3: "Put first things first" – in other words, time management.

I think the reason people can't put first things first is that they don't know what their "first things" are. This idea has been reinforced by the many workshops and seminars I have delivered. When we look at the clock, we know that we must move our feet, but where will we go? Compass tells us where.

If we don't have a compass, we do what most people do – go in circles, become distracted, procrastinate or waste time on the unimportant. We ignore the priorities of our lives because they are not clearly defined, or we lack the motivation to be true to them. Compass tells us what these priorities are. I have found that when it comes to our individual life, most of us need to reacquaint ourselves with our compass. We knew what was important once, but the river of life has taken us downstream, far from our bliss, far from what's important to us. We need to make the journey back home. We need to realign our lives.

How to Align Your Life

*When we do what matters most,
we are not at the mercy of what matters least.*
— STEPHEN COVEY

STEP 1: CHOOSE YOUR CORE VALUES

The following is a list of values. Take out your journal and think about them. Which ones are most significant to you? Choose your Top Ten. If you have a value that is not on the list, add it.

Love	Loyalty	Meaning	Wisdom	Education
Family	Spirituality	Money	Service	Friendship
Security	Creativity	Health	Career	Pleasure
Joy	Honesty	Environment	Altruism	Learning
Faith	Beauty	Humility	Playfulness	Growth
Balance	Religion	Courage	Compassion	Adventure
Music	Freedom	Status	Solitude	Fun

STEP 2: PRIORITIZE YOUR VALUES

Now put your Top Ten in order from most important to least important. Number them by assigning your most important value a 1 and the least important a 10.

STEP 3: GIVE YOURSELF A SCORE

Look at your top five values. Now grade yourself according to how well you have lived out that value in the past month. For example, if you chose Family as one of your top five values, ask yourself, "In the past month, has my behavior reflected this value?" If not, how should you behave in order to live this value? To some people, quantity of time is important. To others, it's more the quality of fun, laughter and connection with a family member. Whatever it means for you to live that value, how well did you do in the past month? How true have you been to this value? Write this down: "In the past month I have been able to live this value _____% of the time." Now, do this for each of the top five values you chose.

STEP 4: EVALUATE YOUR VALUES

Look at your least important five values and perhaps even the ones that didn't make your list. Are you devoting time to these lesser values? If so, why? Do you need to say no? Do you need to stop procrastinating? Do you need a wake-up call? For example, let's say you listed Service as number 10, but you notice that in the past month much of your time has been spent sitting on committees, going to meetings and doing volunteer work – at the expense of your top values. Ask yourself, "Why am I being distracted from my top values?"

I find that this step allows for introspection. People ask themselves questions they've never asked before. For example, "Where did I get this value? Is it really my value or did I inherit it from my parents or my culture?" Alignment happens when your values match the convictions of your authentic Self.

STEP 5: IDENTIFY ACTION STEPS

Beside each value, identify one thing that you can do – one action step – that will help you align yourself with the priority that value has in your life. For example, if Health is number 2, identify one action step you can take that will take you closer to that value. You might say you will go for a walk at lunch, get more sleep or avoid deep-fried foods. If you can identify more than one action step that will bring you closer to your value, so much the better.

There are times when you have to say no so that you can give your energy and time to your top priorities (see Chapter 9 for learning to say no). There are only twenty-four hours in a day. I know that most of us need far more than that to get everything done. Our lives are busy most of the time. But life is about making choices. When we don't live according to our values, we're living according to someone else's values. We lose our integrity. When our actions are incongruent with our values, we're not in control of our destiny. We are adrift in the river. Our souls become polluted; our spirits sag; our lives are out of alignment. It's time for you to take out your compass and decide what's most important to you, right now. It's time for you to create your personal destiny mandala.

CREATE YOUR
PERSONAL DESTINY MANDALA

Our lives are works in progress.
— SUSAN L. TAYLOR

So how do we find out our destiny? How can we know what we were born to do? The answers are within you. When you connect deeply with each compass direction, you gain insight into your destiny, purpose or mission. Creating a destiny mandala is an opportunity for self-discovery and personal reflection.

The North represents your spiritual dimension. It's the North Star in the night sky that helps lost travelers to find their way. Your Spirit is like the North Star. When you feel overwhelmed by what life sends you, you need to connect to your Source, your Creator, and get spiritually nourished. You need to be reminded of what is sacred to you.

The South represents your intellectual faculties, the vast power of your mind. This is the area of knowledge, wisdom and information. Life is a school. What did you come here to learn?

I've chosen the East to represent the realm of the emotions – East, where the sun rises and where possibilities are born. Within us, possibilities are born in our hearts. We must feel them, become passionate and then move our mountains.

The West represents our physical body. The West is the final frontier. It's for brave hearts who keep pushing forward. You need endurance to go West. You need courage to push your body's physical threshold.

Each cardinal point poses questions that you need to answer to complete the destiny mandala. The destiny mandala is meant to be a visual guide, a map reminding you of who you are and what's important to you in every aspect of your life. You might have to dig deep and become vulnerable in order to answer some of the questions that will arise. I encourage you to draw your destiny mandala on a large sheet of paper and answer your questions on it. Each direction can be a different color – be creative.

Your answers can be one word or a paragraph long. There are no right or wrong answers.

Destiny Mandala

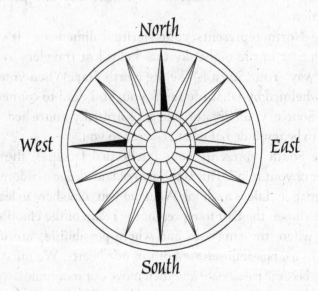

NORTH: SPIRITUAL COMPASS

1 Who am I?
2 What is sacred to me?
3 What did I come here to do?

4 How does God/the Universe/the Beloved speak to me?
5 How can I make the world a better place with my spiritual gifts?
6 What spiritual "undones" do I have?
7 What symbol expresses my true spiritual Self?

SOUTH: INTELLECTUAL COMPASS

1 What did I come here to learn?
2 What did I come here to unlearn?
3 What/whom did I come here to teach?
4 What are my intellectual gifts?
5 How can I make the world a better place with my intellectual gifts?
6 What intellectual "undones" do I have?
7 What symbol expresses my intellectual gifts?

EAST: EMOTIONAL COMPASS

1 Whom did I come here to love?
2 Whom did I come here to forgive?
3 What brings my heart joy?
4 What did I come here to heal?
5 How can I make the world a better place with my emotional gifts?
6 What emotional "undones" do I have?
7 What symbol best represents my emotional gifts?

WEST: PHYSICAL COMPASS

1 What part of my body needs healing?
2 What part of my body needs acceptance/nurturing/care?

3 How can I be kinder to my body?

4 How does my body want to express itself?

5 How can I make the world a better place with my physical gifts?

6 What physical "undones" do I have?

7 What symbol represents my body and my physical gifts?

EXAMPLES

John's North compass (spiritual):

1 *Who am I?* Sacred, funny, loving, magnificent.

2 *What is sacred to me?* Love, connection, meaning, synchronicities, God.

3 *What did I come here to do?* To help others heal.

4 *How does God/the Universe/the Beloved speak to me?* Through my feelings.

5 *How can I make the world a better place with my spiritual gifts?* Teach people about love and faith.

6 *What spiritual "undones" do I have?* Learn to meditate. Develop my psychic abilities.

7 *What symbol expresses my true spiritual self?* A kaleidoscope.

Kate's East compass (emotional):

1 *Whom did I come here to love?* Everyone.

2 *Whom did I come here to forgive?* Those in the dark.

3 *What brings my heart joy?* Love, flowers, springtime, little children.

4 *What did I come here to heal?* Myself, my past.

5 *How can I make the world a better place with my emotional gifts?* Teach people to wake up and be passionate.

6 *What emotional "undones" do I have?* Forgiving those I know I must forgive.

7 *What symbol best represents my emotional gifts?* An angel.

After you have finished creating your destiny mandala, study it. Observe patterns. What words or ideas come up more than once? Your destiny mandala is a way for you to reaffirm what is most important to you and what you came here to do. It's a tool for self-celebration and self-actualization. The more aligned you are with what is sacred to you, the more likely you are to take action toward that end. Preparing a destiny mandala lays the groundwork for your life's mission statement.

A MISSION STATEMENT EXERCISE

You are either living your mission, or you are living someone else's.
- LAURIE BETH JONES

The word "mission" comes from the Latin *missio*, which means "sending." It can also mean "special vocation or calling" – as in "Medicine was her mission" – which can be associated with your career or life's work. The question here is: Where are you "sending" your life? To what destination?

Companies post mission statements or corporate values in their lobbies or boardrooms. These tell customers and remind employees what the company stands for. But mission statements are not only for companies and organizations. They're for individuals and families, too. A personal mission statement tells the world what you stand for, what your gifts are and how you want to make a difference. It describes your unique purpose and how you want to be living your life. Because you are unique, your personal mission statement will be unlike anyone else's.

Stephen Covey says that a personal mission statement "becomes a personal constitution, the basis for making major, life-directing decisions, the basis for making daily decisions in the midst of the circumstances and emotions that affect our lives."[1]

Your mission is what helps you take the step every day. It's the destination on the other side of the bridge. If you have a mission, then you are not "whatless"; you know where your life is to go. Your mission will cure psychic absence (see Chapter 4). That's because it represents a vision, a destination, a purpose. And when you wake up with a vision, destination and purpose every morning, you can't help but bring your soul to work. You will cure the spiritual malaise that is prevalent in so many lives today.

The faster the river of change, the easier it is to get distracted. Why do we do the things we do every day? Why do we chase the wrong things? Have we lost perspective? Have we sold out our moral principles? A mission statement brings you back on course. It's the compass when you're lost at sea.

There are different schools of thought as to how to write a mission statement and how long it should be. After all, why is it called a statement if some people need to use several paragraphs? There are no hard and fast rules. If your mission statement is a song lyric, so be it, as long as it speaks to you and gives you a sense of calling. I heard of a man whose mission statement was "I want to be the kind of person my dog already thinks I am." That's short and to the point. A client of mine once told me her mission was Love. That's it – one word.

Richard Bolles says in *How to Find Your Mission in Life* that we all have three missions. They are

1 to know God;
2 to make this world a better place;
3 to exercise the talent that is uniquely yours.

He says the first two missions are shared with others. The last one is unique to you.

You can cull information and inspiration from all kinds of sources, including your destiny mandala and the passion exercises you will do in Chapter 4, to come up with something that is uniquely yours. Most people's mission statements talk about what they are going to do according to what's important to them.

Philosopher Victor Frankl says we detect rather than invent our missions in life. If we have a special vocation or purpose, then we must stay alert to the calls our soul send us. We must pay attention.

There are many ways in which you can write a mission statement. Here is one way:

Step 1: The first part of the mission statement is information about you. Who are you? Say a journalist from another galaxy has arrived to interview you. What adjectives best describe your unique qualities, talents and gifts? Here are some examples:

- I am a beautiful, kind, articulate, passionate and sensitive person.
- I am an intelligent, original, inspirational, compassionate and powerful person.
- I am a gutsy, raw, artistic, creative, reflective and soulful person.

Step 2: What do you want to contribute? Talk about what you want to do for the world. How do you want to make a difference? Look at your destiny mandala. What brings you joy? What are you passionate about? What did you learn about yourself when you answered the mandala questions? Here are some examples:

- My mission is to acknowledge the sacred in all people and all things.
- My mission is to inspire, love and empower people so they can create the highest vision of who they are.
- My mission is to educate the world about conservation and protection of our planet.
- My mission is to help people in the Third World.

Step 3: Combine Steps 1 and 2 together. For example:

- I am a beautiful, kind, passionate, sensitive and soulful person whose mission is to acknowledge the sacred in all people and all things.
- I am an enthusiastic, courageous, intelligent and adventurous person whose mission is to teach children how to take care of our planet.

You can spend hours – even days – on your mission statement trying to get the words to flow. Don't become frustrated. Focus on the ideas. Don't worry about poetry or eloquence. The right words will evolve as you revisit it.

If your mission statement still won't come, just sit and reflect for a while. You may need to let the wisdom of your unconscious mind percolate to the surface. When you have a statement that rings true, say it to yourself often. Try it out loud. Post it where you're likely to see it daily. Some great places are on a bulletin board in front of your workspace, on the first page of your agenda or on your refrigerator.

Your mission statement becomes your overall compass. It is the direction you want to move your life in. Your compass represents all that is meaningful and sacred to you. Living your life "on purpose" means you're living in accordance with your mission statement.

CONTEMPLATING OUR MORTALITY

The midlife crisis . . . probably reflects the fact that at midlife one's own death becomes less theoretical and more probable.

- ARTHUR J. DEIKMAN

In his bestseller *Tuesdays with Morrie*, Mitch Albom writes about his visits to his old college professor, Morrie Schwartz, who is dying of Lou Gehrig's disease, a brutal neurological disorder. As Morrie gets progressively worse, Mitch visits him every Tuesday and they have wonderful conversations about life. One week, when Mitch asks him about death, Morrie recommends that we imitate the Buddhists and be prepared for death at any time. The reason? So we can be more involved in our lives while we're living them.

"The truth is, Mitch," he tells his student, "once you learn how to die, you learn how to live."[2] Morrie's words are wise. It's only when we contemplate our mortality that we know how we want to live. It's only by contemplating our death that we feel the need to squeeze every last bit of joy out of our life. Morrie says that the reason we don't focus on our death more often is because we're all sleepwalking, living our lives by habit, not by intention. If you were told you had only one year to live, would you see things differently? Would you stop postponing your life and start taking action? How do you want to make a difference? How do you want to be remembered?

WHAT WILL THEY SAY AFTER YOU'RE GONE?

All that is real in our past is the love we gave and the love we received. Everything else is an illusion.
- MARIANNE WILLIAMSON

One of the most poignant exercises I've ever done was to write down what I wanted people to say at my funeral. These are the sentiments you would want people to express about you after you're gone. While our children were visiting their grandparents, my husband and I both sat down to visit with our destiny. It was New Year's Eve, 1999, the close of one millennium and the dawn of a new one. It was time to realign my life.

I focused on what I wanted my friends and family to say about me after my death. What celebration statements would they offer? How would they evaluate my life?

When I got to my children, I was overcome with emotion. I found myself asking, "What kind of mother do I want to be? How do I want to influence their lives?" With tears in my eyes, I wrote, "She showed me kindness, compassion and unconditional love. She inspired me to reach for the stars. I am the person I am today because of my mother's love."

What did I want my friends to say? "Grace was a true friend. She believed in me and loved me, and always inspired me to look for the best in myself and others. She was an angel of compassion – that's why God sent her to us."

What did I want my clients to say? "Grace Cirocco inspired me to *just do it!* She taught me how to live life to the fullest and go for my dreams. Her passion for life and her love for all people means we are all richer just to have known her."

The underlying question in the exercise is this: If that's what I want each person to say about me, then what do I have to do every day to get there? In other words, what actions, what steps must I take to get those results?

Admitting to myself that this was the legacy I wanted to leave behind was a powerful exercise for me. I now had a clear path ahead. I revisited my mission statement and wrote down my goals. I needed to know where I was going to "send" my life in the new millennium. When it comes to the most important relationships in your life, doing an exercise like this will help you decide what is on the other side of your bridge – what you're working toward. Once you figure out your *what* in each relationship, it's easier to take action.

Sometimes you need to contemplate your death so you can reprioritize your life. Do you have a birthday coming up? Are summer holidays around the corner? Perhaps New Year's Eve? If not, any day will do. Make yourself a pot of tea, put on your most comfortable clothes, sit in your favorite chair, and open your journal. Decide what you want people to say about you when you're gone.

LISTENING TO THE CALL OF YOUR SOUL

The heroic life is living the individual adventure.
To refuse the call means stagnation.
– JOSEPH CAMPBELL

Another way to gain clarity about your destiny is to listen to the call of your soul. When your soul speaks, it is felt in the heart. So what is this "call of the soul" and how do you know whether you've experienced it? A calling is similar to a mission or purpose, but it is more general. For example, you may feel a calling to do community work; when you investigate the contributions you can make, you realize that what you really want is to help the disabled become more self-sufficient. This becomes your mission, or destiny, but you wouldn't have found it had you not listened to that original feeling, the "call."

When you actively listen to your soul's calling, you are also listening to God. Your calling is the voice of intuition that gently urges you to see what possibilities you can manifest in your life. When you pay attention to that inner hunch that says "follow this passion" or "talk to that person" or "read that book," then you are honoring your soul – you are surrendering your life to a higher power. The soul calls us to express our creativity and our unique gifts. It is a tug from the future, pulling you toward limitless possibilities and endless potential.

In his book *The Call*, David Spangler remarks that a call is different than a summons – a summons offers location, place, destination – a compass. A call is merely a lighthouse – calling our attention to the light – pay attention.[3] I think we can feel this call about many things in a lifetime. Sometimes it is a whisper, a subtle tug at the heart that says "I want to know more" or "I like this." Sometimes it's very loud. It hits us over the head with a hammer and doesn't let us sleep, eat or function until we pay attention.

No one really knows the origin of this call. It comes from your soul, yes, but why this call and not another one? Why was I called to inspire and empower people on how to live more meaningful lives and not, for example, how to maximize their investments? Because the former mission is part of my destiny and the latter is not. The soul knows its destiny and wants us to live it out. And so it helps us. It gives us messages, yearnings, warnings and feelings that will eventually lead us to that destiny. Some people are good at hearing the call; others are not. The more conscious you are, the more connected you feel to your Creator and to your authentic Self, the greater your ability to recognize the call when it comes.

Sometimes we get the call when we are children. One of my clients got the call to be a marine biologist and dolphin trainer when as a child he saw his first dolphins on a trip to Florida. He was smitten, he says. He knew right then and there that he wanted to learn everything he could about these magnificent creatures.

In one lifetime we may have several callings that point us in the direction our soul needs to go. We can experience callings about our work, our careers, our education, our surroundings (where we need to live or travel to), our relationships and our spiritual mission. The call from the soul doesn't have to be a final destination. In many cases it is only leading us toward our mission or destiny. Sometimes several calls are components of one mission. Sometimes a call may be a stepping stone, something you need to learn before you can fulfill your life's work.

I was once invited to be on a television program where people could phone in with their questions. One person asked me, How could he distinguish between a calling and a fantasy? A good question. He said that his fantasy was to live by the ocean.

"So what's stopping you?" I asked him.

"It's not realistic," he said. "We both have jobs here, plus we just bought a house."

I told him that this yearning was like a call from his soul. He might call it a fantasy, but the fantasy was calling his name. Sometimes the call from the soul may have nothing to do with your vocation, but everything to do with your happiness. If you're happy with your surroundings, you'll be happier with your life, and the happiness will spill over into other areas of life as well. Wanting to live by the ocean may not be a vocation, but it can certainly be a call from the soul. Sometimes a fantasy is an image built up of what we think it will be or what we want it to be. Perhaps we call it a fantasy because we do not truly believe we can achieve it.

A calling, on the other hand, is felt in the heart. Sometimes callings are not logical. Just when we think we have our life in order, our soul grows restless and begins to grumble. It hands us something right out of the clear blue sky. We think, "This can't possibly be real. Look at my life. I'm organized. Everything is set. I'm happy. Aren't I?"

THE CALL THAT COMES WITH ENTHUSIASM

Years wrinkle the skin, but to give up enthusiasm wrinkles the soul.
– SAMUEL ULLMAN

There were two hundred women in the large hotel conference room. Our seminar leader was talking about how we all have our own communication style. It was a professional seminar – my first – and suddenly I got "the call." Actually, it was more like a lightning bolt. That whole day I kept thinking, "This is it! This is what I want to do when I grow up." I could barely contain my enthusiasm.

I went home and told my husband. Three months later I was competing with more than five hundred other hopefuls in a hotel ballroom. We were there because of an ad in the newspaper: "International seminar company looking for seminar leaders to expand its business." There was no telephone number, just the location, time and date.

I had recently given birth to my daughter, Kajsa, and was still breast-feeding her, so I could not leave her alone for more than a couple of hours. The meeting was at least an hour away. How was I going to do this? How was I going to balance the call of my soul with motherhood? (There are women who face this challenge on a daily basis!) My husband, always prepared to support my call (bless his heart), came through with a solution. "Let's all go together. I'll wait in the lobby with the kids. That way, if Kajsa gets hungry, you're close by."

Everything I heard during the presentation made me even more excited. "Yup, yup, yup," my soul was saying, "this is for you, Grace." When the meeting was over, we were invited to come back the next morning and audition on videotape. "Speak about what you know," the interviewer said. Those were the only instructions we got. I was a broadcast journalist, so I knew about writing for the ear, and that's what I talked about.

It took the company several months to go through all the tapes and make a decision, but eventually they shortlisted six candidates to undergo train-the-trainer training. I was one of those six. Although we had been selected to be trained, we were told not to assume that we would get the job. It was just another part of the selection process.

After the training, I got the phone call that invited me to join their team. I was one of two candidates to be hired. I was thrilled. I had been true to my calling and now the Universe was rewarding me. My life and career took a dramatic shift. I was getting closer to my mission.

A friend once told me that a piano has eighty-eight keys. It occurs to me that before we die our job is to play our song on all eighty-eight keys. Earlier in my life I had received the call to be a broadcast journalist. I wrote, edited and produced newscasts and current affairs programming. I was good at it. I liked it. But I wasn't playing my song with all eighty-eight keys; on good days I used maybe sixty. As a seminar leader, speaker, coach and now writer, I feel I am finally playing my song with eighty-eight keys – perhaps not every single day, but I know I have used them all. I consider that a privilege.

When your work is in line with your calling, it doesn't seem like work. Everything flows. You feel exhilarated, excited by the next possibility. You're empowered and things happen as if by magic. Some of us get the call for meaningful work (using all eighty-eight keys) as a child, like my client who knew he'd be working with dolphins. For others, like me, it's a cumulative process. Each call that we pay attention to and act on lays a foundation for recognizing the call that will have us playing on the whole keyboard. When was the last time you heard your song played with all eighty-eight keys?

One way to know that you're getting close to the eighty-eight keys is to gauge how enthusiastic you are about something. The root of enthusiasm, *entheos*, is Greek and means "filled with God." When we're filled with God, we're also filled with soul. Enthusiasm is, therefore, the language of our soul. When it speaks to us, we need to listen – our soul's calling may be close by. This enthusiasm can be for anything. If you're enthusiastic about a career, a branch of knowledge, an idea, a place, a book, a song or a person, pay attention to it. It's your soul's way of telling you that your eighty-eight keys may be on the next page of the music book.

THE CALL THAT COMES
IN DIFFERENT GUISES

Sure the mind can postpone the call, suppress, and sell out.
You will not therefore necessarily be punished and damned.

– JAMES HILLMAN

My friend Wally is almost forty years old, yet he has been receiving calls for what he says will be his life's most important work. He works at a manufacturing plant, but he's also a drummer who has toured the world with his band. He loves his music and has always felt that it is his true calling. Yet now, as he approaches middle age, he feels pulled to do something different with his life, something he says God wants him to do, something that will bring him more meaning and satisfaction.

The call first came to him after helping a motorist in a car accident. While he was driving on the highway one day, the car in front of him lost control, hit a guardrail and flipped over onto its side in the ditch. Wally stopped his car, grabbed a blanket from his trunk and took it to the driver, who was trembling from shock. As soon as Wally handed him the blanket and comforted him, his face relaxed. Wally waited with him until the emergency vehicles arrived. When they parted, there was something in the other driver's eyes that Wally will never forget. He says, "Helping him made me feel so good. It gave me such a high." He began to consider becoming a rescue worker or maybe a firefighter. All he knew was that he wanted to help people in trouble.

The call came again a few months later when Wally's aging father was taken to the hospital. He was in the final stages of Alzheimer's and most days was unable to recognize his children or even his wife. Wally took time off work to spend with his father and his mother, who never left her husband's bedside. He showed up every day to hold his father's hand, give him a shave, help bathe him and wheel him around the hospital. "I feel called to be there. I love doing this for him," he told me.

When he was younger, Wally saved his brother's life by giving him one of his kidneys. Even though there were eight other siblings, Wally was the only one who offered to undergo the painful surgery. I think the decision to save his brother came from a similar call in a different disguise. The fact is, he's been getting the same call his entire life. He's a helper, a healer. He cares about people and is always the first to offer help. As he gets older, I predict this call will get louder. In the meantime, he continues to be in the right place at the right time in order to be there for people.

THE CALL THAT WON'T LEAVE US ALONE

*Is that what they call a vacation, what you do with joy
as if you had fire in your heart, the devil in your body?*
— JOSEPHINE BAKER

His name is Brother John, my husband tells me, and he performs miracles. He heals people. Santo heard about the healing miracles of Brother John through a friend who had been cured of a back problem that had kept him in bed for ten years. Brother John had spent time in prison for crimes related to drug and alcohol abuse. He was not your typical miracle worker, but he finally had to listen to the unusual call he kept getting. He was seeing visions of Mother Mary, who would come to him while he was sleeping. Sometimes he'd open his eyes and there she was in his bedroom, telling him that he was to heal people, that he had special powers to help the sick. He was terrified that he was going crazy and for two years completely denied the visions. He kept insisting that she had the wrong guy, but the call from the Virgin Mother was persistent.

Eventually John gave in. Today there are people who feel they owe their lives to this man. He is playing his song with all eighty-eight keys. His compass and his mission have made him a modern-day healer empowered to perform miracles. I don't understand how it works. I do know that amazing things can happen if you have faith. Whether the healing miracles happen because of Brother John or because of people's faith in his powers, it's not important. What is important is that he eventually had the courage to heed the call that wouldn't go away. He has done a lot of good in the world by visiting and healing the sick. Because he listened to his special call, Brother John lives his unique mission every day.

Sometimes people will ignore the call. Rita, a client of mine who is in her fifties, is sad that she didn't have the courage to listen to her heart when she was younger. When she was in her early teens, she knew she wanted to become a Roman Catholic nun. From the beginning she had been a missionary, wanting to bring people to Christ. When Rita mentioned this career choice to her parents, they flipped out, she says. Too afraid of losing their love and acceptance, she sold out her soul's longing for something her parents approved of, eventually enrolling in secretarial college.

For most of her life, Rita felt lost. She had denied who she was in order to make her parents happy, and for many years she drifted in and out of jobs and relationships. Today she feels more in control of her life because she met and married a man who's something of a missionary himself. They volunteer at their church and in the community, speaking of Jesus to whoever will listen. Even though she didn't become a nun, she says she's happy now. There are many ways to manifest our calling. And it's never too late.

WORKING ON YOUR GOALS

A journey of a thousand leagues begins with a single step.
– LAO-TZU

Many of us don't take action because our path is not clearly laid out. The secret is this: Make a plan. Write down the baby-steps you must take to listen to the call from your soul or accomplish a goal. Brainstorm. The best way to do that is to draw a goal map (see the next page). Write your calling or goal in a circle and then draw spokes radiating from the circle. Write your ideas on the spokes. Once you have your ideas written down, prioritize each step. Ask yourself, "What do I need to do first?" Make a list of the necessary steps and assign yourself a deadline.

Each week, schedule one or two things in your agenda that will move you toward your goal. This is effective goal-setting. Life is just like this – a series of small steps. Sometimes we are paralyzed with fear because the thing we want to do over-whelms us. Break this fear down, tackle one element at a time and soon you'll be across the bridge.

Goal-setting is a habit of highly effective people. They don't get discouraged. Rather, they plug away at their dreams every day while balancing their job and family obligations. Rome wasn't built overnight, and neither will be your dreams. It's consistent action taken over time that will give you the results you want.

Creating a Goal Map

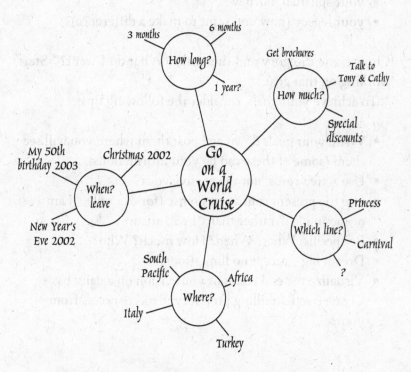

Prioritize the steps: what do you need to do first?

After doing the exercises in this chapter, if you still don't have a clear idea of what is waiting for you on the other side of the bridge, consider goals in the following categories:

- personal growth and development
- career/work
- adventure/travel/fun
- family/friends
- your spiritual journey
- your legacy (how you want to make a difference)

Choose one category and then ask, "What do I want?" Start working on that goal.

To achieve your goals, consider the following tips:

- Write your goals down and post them where you will see them (some of these can be your affirmations).
- Use active verbs, not the passive voice.
- Use the present continuous tense (for example, "I am attracting . . ." rather than "I will attract . . .").
- Be specific: What? When? How much? Who?
- Dream big – accept no limitations.
- Visualize the end result of your vision on a daily basis.
- Create a self-fulfilling prophecy: Expect success from yourself.

4

Passion

A PASSION FOR LIFE

*One has to abandon altogether the search for security
and reach out to the risk of living with both arms.
We need to embrace the world like a lover.*

— MORRIS L. WEST

What makes your heart beat quickly? What makes your eyes
shine and every cell in your body feel electrified? When was
the last time you embraced the world like a lover? Passion is
the stuff of dreams. It can be hot, intense, colorful. It brings
texture and meaning to life. It is the antidote to depression. It
keeps you alive and in the joy of the moment. Passion is a
pulsating energy that keeps you connected to your own life
force, to your purpose and to the universal Intelligence present in nature. Passion is the fuel of artists, poets and those
who thirst for a more meaningful journey. Passion ignites the
soul. Passion is courage that propels us forward across the
bridge. Without passion for life, getting out of bed in the
morning would be a meaningless experience.

Passion is much more than the sexual feelings we have for a
lover. Remembering the life and death of Diana, Princess of

Wales, Sarah Ban Breathnach explained passion's broader meaning: "Passion is color; most of us live in black and white. For me Diana's great gift was that she was willing to embrace her passion, to attempt to live authentically. . . . If Diana's death imparts only one lesson, it is that passion is holy, to be embraced, even if we tremble with fear."[1]

Passionate people are committed. They follow through. You cannot be both passionate and self-contained. Passion wants to burst forth, to fly up and be noticed. It wants to express itself in creative ways.

The enemy of passion is fear. Why don't we take the step toward our heart's longing? Because we're afraid. If we could connect to our passion, find its source deep within us, we could also learn to start taking small steps toward what is meaning-ful and sacred to us. Passion is the solution for so much of the malaise we feel – and yet we ignore it. Why?

WHY DO WE PUT OUT THE FLAME OF PASSION?

Passion lops off the bough of weariness. Passion is the elixir that renews. . . . Oh, don't sigh heavily from fatigue: seek passion, seek passion, seek passion!
– RUMI

I think we have been trying to put out the flame of passion for hundreds of years. A genre of books and films that has always fascinated me explores the sanity/insanity issue. The main characters in the films *One Flew over the Cuckoo's Nest*, *Mr. Jones* and *Man Facing Southeast*, for example, are deemed crazy by the outside world; but to me they personify passion in its highest form. These are heroes who take risks and live on the edge. They can't be classified as "normal" because they get too excited about life and wear their passions on their sleeves. They live life at full throttle.

In both *Mr. Jones* and *Man Facing Southeast* there is a scene where the main character loses control while listening to Beethoven's Ninth Symphony. He is so filled with music that he stands up and starts conducting from his seat (obviously, this distracts the other patrons). Eventually, unable to contain his joy, he walks on stage and tries to lead the orchestra, much to the shock of the conductor, who is only trying to do his job. "Normal" people don't do this. Both characters break the rules. The verdict? They must be crazy, so in both films the police arrive and take them away.

It seems there is a fine line between being passionate and being crazy, between insanity and being high on life.

When we can't tame passion, we amputate it. It starts in childhood. So many of us were raised by controlling parents who wanted to choose our clothes, our music and our friends. If you flew too high, or even imagined you had wings, you'd soon find them clipped, maimed or worse, plucked out. I think I was too much for my poor mother. She didn't know what to do with such an intense child, her daughter who was so outrageously passionate about life. She tried her best to stamp out my "craziness" and make me conform to her idea of what a nice girl should be – but I had my own ideas. There were adventures I wanted to experience, places I wanted to see and things I wanted to do. I refused to follow anyone's path, especially not the path prescribed for girls by my Italian heritage. That made me "different" and "difficult."

I think my mother was frightened that my passion would one day get me in trouble. She was worried about me, but by the time I reached adulthood she had become resigned to my iconoclastic ways. I think she finally grew to understand me because she could remember a time when she too had the passion stamped out of her.

I sometimes use a personality profile called True Colors, which was developed by Don Lowry. Based on the Myers-Briggs personality type indicator, it is designed to help people understand themselves and others in a simple way. The four personality colors are Orange, Gold, Blue and Green.

Oranges are spontaneous, adventurous, fast and nonconforming. They love expressing themselves in creative ways and they're not afraid to live life to its fullest. Oranges are the wild ones, the ones who really know how to party. Everyone has all the colors in them, but one tends to be brighter than the others. It is fascinating to note that people with dominant Orange make up only fourteen percent of the adult population, but among children they represent fifty percent. I think that collectively we do a good job of beating the Orange out of kids. The question is "Why?" I believe it's because passion is threatening.

Marianne Williamson, in her book *A Woman's Worth*, remembers how fond she was of "Betty Lynn," the glamorous woman who lived across the street when she was a child. Betty Lynn was outrageous and drove a champagne-colored Cadillac. She always had a drink in her hand, and it was alcohol that eventually killed her. Williamson writes, "Why do people who have the most ardour, the most enchantment, the most power so often feel the need for drugs and alcohol? They do not drink just to dull their pain; they drink to dull their ecstasy. . . . Betty Lynn crucified herself before anyone else had a chance to."[2]

It's true. Sometimes it seems like the world is not ready for our passion, our "Orangeness," our high-octane Spirit. So we apologize for it, hide it or kill it. People may be jealous or scared that our passion will take something away from them. They're afraid of where passion might lead. It might break the rules and lead to change, and change is not always easy to embrace. Yes, there is still a lot of fear surrounding passion. This is the fault of a world that is still somewhat unenlightened, but the tide is turning. We're entering a new millennium, one that promises to embrace Spirit and, hopefully, celebrate passion. In the meantime, let's look at why passion is so difficult for some people to feel and show.

CHOOSING BETWEEN THE TWO PATHS

I found out that I can do it, if I choose to – I can stay awake and let the sorrows of the world tear me apart and then allow the joys to put me back together, different from before but whole again.

– ORIAH MOUNTAIN DREAMER

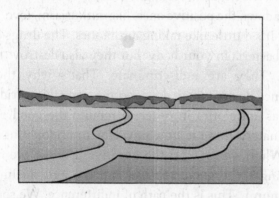

I believe we have a choice in life to take one of two paths – the path of consciousness or the path of indifference. The path of consciousness is for spiritual warriors, for those committed to feeling passionate about life. They know that joy and sorrow are two sides of one coin and they're not afraid to feel their feelings. The truth is that this path of consciousness was the starting point for all of us. We entered the world able to feel everything, experience everything and respond to everything in the present moment. Some of us are still like that, childlike in our approach to the world. Trusting and loving, we put our hearts out there every day.

But for other people, the sorrows and betrayals of life have been too much to bear. Little by little they shut down their emotions in an attempt to stop the pain. Others opt for complete anesthesia; they turn off their pain with drugs and alcohol. I like what author Toni Morrison said recently in an interview with Oprah Winfrey: ". . . everything is designed to encourage spiritual and mental sleep. You shut down and start buying stuff."[3] Shopping is another way to "numb out." Buying stuff tricks us into thinking we have filled the void.

Here's the unfortunate truth about this scenario: When you shut down the negative feelings – when you stop feeling – you also shut down the positive ones, like enthusiasm, love, joy and passion. It's a little like taking antibiotics. The drugs destroy the bad bacteria in your body, but they also destroy the good bacteria. They are indiscriminate. That's why the more enlightened doctors these days recommend taking acidophilus as well as antibiotics in order to rebuild the good bacteria. Unfortunately there is no equivalent to acidophilus for the Spirit. When we turn off the negative feelings, we turn off everything – the good, the bad and the ugly feelings. We become numb. This is the path of indifference. We spend our days "putting in time," "surviving" and "getting by."

One of my favorite stories is told by author and motivational speaker Og Mandino in his book *The Greatest Miracle in the World*. His inspirational message is given via the hero of the story, Simon Potter, the wise ragpicker who comes out of nowhere, like some prophet or mystic, into the author's life. Simon reminds us that most people die at forty but are buried at eighty, and that the greatest miracle in the world is when people wake themselves up from a living death. "Pour the wine. You have been reborn. Like a butterfly from its chrysalis you will fly . . . and neither the wasps nor dragonflies nor mantids of mankind shall obstruct your mission."[4]

The cure for indifference is passion. Ask yourself, "Have I stopped caring? Feeling? Have I been taking the love, friendship and kindness in my life for granted? Am I hiding behind a mask of indifference? Who am I running away from? Can I show my ecstasy?" Look at yourself and then look around you. Do you notice others who have opted for the path of indifference?

Barbara De Angelis, in her book *Passion*, says that some people try to excuse their indifference by masking it as spirituality, saying that they're practising a form of detachment. De Angelis calls this "a kindergarten understanding of spiritual achievement."[5] In fact, she says, history reveals to us countless examples of saints, teachers and holy beings who are the embodiment of passion and caring. The truth is that the holier we become, the more we feel for our fellow human beings. The more we feel, the more connected we are to our passion.

"Why should we grieve that we've been sleeping?" asks Rumi, the Sufi poet. "It doesn't matter how long we've been unconscious. We're groggy, but let the guilt go."[6]

Rumi is right. Let the guilt go. Focus on the future. Focus on waking up. Let's each take responsibility for choosing the conscious path, for being true to our passion, our authentic Self. How? By being aware of how we feel, by asking questions, by speaking the truth that is inside our hearts, by beating our own drum. Be interested in people when they talk to you – they have a gift for you. Be interested in the blade of grass, the sound of the wind and the perfect blue of a robin's egg. They have gifts for you, too. The truth is that the Universe wants you to belong to it. It wants you to feel deeply the passion that beats in its core. Open your heart. Only then will your Spirit decide to get out of bed and join the human race. Only then will you be able to embrace the passion that is your birthright.

PSYCHIC ABSENCE

My isolation was acute. . . . I wasn't dead. I wasn't alive.
I was suspended in a near-life experience.

– SARA BAN BREATHNACH

The woman cutting my daughter's hair was lifeless. There was a heaviness, an indescribable sadness about her. She dragged her feet. She didn't want to be there. I thought, "Perhaps it's her job. Perhaps she's suffered one too many rude and ungracious customers." My daughter squealed with delight as her new, layered look came to life. As we left, we made a fuss over the stylist, letting everyone in the shop know how pleased we were. A faint smile flickered across her lips, but then it retreated. Driving home, I thought about her. I wondered whether she was grieving someone she loved or whether her indifference was a symptom that she was tired of her job, or perhaps tired of life. I wondered whether there was anything that brought her joy. My heart went out to her. I wanted to tell her she's beautiful, magnificent and one hell of a hairdresser. I wanted to tell her that life is precious and she has the power to create her life anew, regardless of what setbacks she may have suffered. Instead, I sent her a prayer that she might heal her heavy heart.

There are many reasons why we turn off. Some of us are grieving the death of a loved one, some of us can't cope with the challenges of life, some have lost the connection to their Source, some have unhealed wounds from the past, others are lonely and depressed and some are just tired of everything. So we shut down. We opt for the path of indifference. We become psychically absent. We show up but keep our souls in hiding. We do what we need to do, but we've lost the joy, the meaning of what life is all about.

Nowhere have I seen this lack of passion, this psychic absence, more than in the world of work, especially in the last ten years. One of the biggest problems today is a disengaged workforce. People get up in the morning and go to work, but they leave the best parts of themselves, their passion, their enthusiasm and their creativity – in short, their Spirit – at home.

"My work is not about healing people any more," a friend told me with sad resignation when we met for coffee the other day. "It's about dollars and cents." She sipped her latte and then stared off into the distance. "You know, Grace, I started working in the health profession because I cared. But those bastards have slowly sucked the blood out of me. I'm afraid I don't care any more."

I've just heard that the husband of one of my clients, an engineer who for twenty years devoted himself to his organization, a multinational aeronautics company, has been fired. There was no warning and no compassion. Six senior people were called into the general manager's office and told that their services were no longer required. They were to empty their desks, collect their belongings and leave with the security officer waiting to escort them off the premises.

These organizational brutalities happen all over the world.

I've heard similar stories from seminar participants in Australia, New Zealand and the United Kingdom. The sentiment expressed to me is always the same: "It's not what they did, but how they did it." Outplacement firms, career counselors, therapists and coaches are still helping to pick up the pieces of those shattered lives.

A few years ago, I talked to hospital administrators who refused stress-management training for nurses during a difficult period of "re-engineering" because, according to them, "They're nurses – they should already know how to manage their stress!" While it's true that most of us know what to do, the problem is that many of us have been pushed to the limit in our workplaces, and our threshold for stress has been compromised. We're no longer resilient. We don't have the resources or the energy to bounce back. The result – no psychic energy.

Some experts believe that this psychically absent or disengaged workforce is largely the result of a top-down management approach. This management style *tells* people what to do. It belittles rather than engages the human Spirit. Top-down management is based on certain patriarchal beliefs that include (1) managers are smarter than everyone else, which is why most information flows downward, (2) people have to be controlled because, after all, they are a commodity, (3) business is a game and (4) profit is how you keep score. These attitudes have not made it easy for the soul to come to work.

Another reason for psychic absence at work may be the lack of trust that we feel in our professional relationships. "No one is really close any more," clients complain to me in coaching sessions. "Ever since the restructuring, trust is out the window." When there is no trust, there is no relationship. Betrayal is rampant. People grow apart; they stop talking. This alienation has been compounded by technology. Why go down the hall to speak to your boss or colleague when there's e-mail? Information flows from one person to another, but usually via a machine, not an organic being. If you don't feel connected to anyone at work, passion stays home.

THE UBIQUITOUS MORALE PROBLEM

In the end, indifference robs you of your greatest strength, your greatest protection and your greatest blessing – the abundant love and passion that lives in your heart.
- BARBARA DE ANGELIS

In the work I do with organizations, employee motivation is a big issue. The most common request I get from organizational leaders is "Can you do something about the morale problem?" When people feel like commodities, unvalued and unappreciated, the human Spirit shuts down. Passion stays home. Our Light grows dim. We become numb. We produce mediocre results. Work is just a job, a means for paying bills.

If there is apathy in one part of our lives, it tends to spill over into other parts. Life is one indivisible whole. Many of us bring our troubles from work home with us whether we realize it or not, letting the stressors and negativity affect our personal lives. This psychic absence pervades every area of life. Some of us slip into depression and we don't even know it. Depression is a disease that affects millions of people, and more every day. Twenty-four million people take the antidepressant drug Prozac. We are dulling our senses in order to cope with a passionless world.

Listen to how people talk about their work. "I can't believe it's Monday already!" "This job is killing me." "I can't wait until Friday." "I can't wait to get out of this place." "I've got five more years to go before retirement." Results from an annual

Gallup poll showed that eighty percent of employees dread returning to work on Monday morning. The largest incidence of heart attacks and strokes is between 8 and 9 o'clock on Monday mornings. If it's time for your body to check out, why do it on a Friday when you have the weekend ahead?

The root of the word "employment" is the Latin word *implicare*, which means "to be involved." And being involved today means much more than security and a paycheck. Contrary to popular opinion, people go to work to feed their souls – to feel connected, to enhance self-worth, to learn, to have fun and to contribute to something larger than themselves.

We need to change the focus and think about work as a contribution of our authentic gifts, as a vehicle for self-expression, as a way to align with our passion and purpose and, finally, as a vehicle for spiritual evolution and the healing of our planet. Some things need to change.

The good news is that things *are* changing. A spiritual awakening is happening – yes, even in the corporate world. Many organizational leaders I've worked with, in both the private and the public sectors, not only believe in the physical, emotional, psychological and even spiritual health of their staff, but are also willing to invest in it. I'm always impressed by these brave hearts, as I call them, and their attitude gives me much to hope for. Robert Fritz, in his book *The Path of Least Resistance*, says, "The historic period in which we live is a period of reawakening to a commitment to higher values, a reawakening of individual purpose, and a reawakening of the longing to fulfill that purpose in life."[7] This reawakening of purpose is being spearheaded by spiritual warriors who are tuned into a higher frequency of consciousness. They are facilitating the path for Spirit in the workplace. They are committed to bringing more meaning and more passion to everyday life.

A HELPFUL EXERCISE:
WHY DO YOU GO TO WORK?

When we work without passion, we quickly get burned out.
- BARBARA DE ANGELIS

Why do you go to work? Ask yourself that question. Make a list of all the reasons you go to work and then evaluate each reason. Is it an External Motivator (EM) or an Internal Motivator (IM)? External motivators are things like *pay my mortgage; send my kids to a private school; a nice office; a bigger home.* Internal motivators are such things as *to contribute my talents; build friendships; help people; because it's my calling.*

Your reasons for doing the work you do are personal and unique to you. Your evaluations will depend on your filters and your interpretation. Don't get too hung up on whether you're interpreting a reason correctly. If you're having difficulty deciding whether it's an internal or external motivator, it's probably both. And that's okay.

To experience job/life satisfaction, we need to cultivate a balance between the external and internal motivators. If you're getting too many EMs, it could be that there is no joy keeping you in this job. It's just a means to an end. You may be psychically absent, taking only your body to work. If it's a temporary job situation, that's okay, but if not, think about making a change. You may have to do some soul-searching first. The exercises in Chapter 3 and in this chapter will help you define and refine who you are and what gifts you have for the world. In the meantime, scan the horizon for additional opportunities. Make a plan.

If all you have are IMs, perhaps the job is running your life. You're out of balance. You get all your emotional needs met at work, so why have a personal life? People with only IMs eventually burn themselves out. I know all about this on a personal level.

As a producer for a radio current affairs program, I worked twelve- to fourteen-hour days. But I didn't mind. I loved it and generated a lot of self-worth from my work. Then one night my husband came to the studio to bring me some food, and I couldn't get out of my chair. It was as if every single muscle in my body had locked. I spent two weeks in bed recovering from severe muscle spasms and had to take another month off work. I was physically burned out. When we love what we do, we're more likely to let the job take over our lives. Let the EMs and IMs open your eyes. To stay healthy, keep thinking *balance*.

TAKING OUR PASSION TO WORK

Passion doesn't come from business or books or even a connection with another person. It is a connection to your own life force, the world around you, and the spirit that connects us all. You are the source.

– JENNIFER JAMES

When Wayne Gretzky retired from playing hockey, he thanked God for giving him talent. Then he paused, thought about it and said that it probably wasn't so much talent as it was the passion to play hockey. Without passion for our work, we lack the means for discovering our purpose. And without purpose, our life has no meaning.

Since so much of our identity comes from our work, it's important for our emotional, psychological and spiritual well-being that we become more passionate about and engaged in what we do. Unfortunately, a common misconception has it that one can feel passionate only about certain careers and that the others are just "jobs" to pay the bills.

"It's easy for you to be passionate," a workshop participant once told me. "You have glamorous work. You get to travel all over the world teaching seminars and workshops. Some of us have to do the crummy jobs."

I have met people who are passionate about jobs that I would never want, like the plumber who came to help us with a flooded basement several summers ago. My husband had found him in the Yellow Pages. Then before he went off to teach his night school class, he told me someone would be coming around 7 p.m. When I went to the door, I found myself facing a man over six feet tall, with long, greasy hair and an unkempt beard. He was wearing a dirty white T-shirt with a pack of cigarettes rolled up in one sleeve, just like Jimmy Dean. His jeans were old, dirty and tattered. His arms were covered with tattoos. He smiled and said, "Hi, I'm Jack. I understand you've got a problem with yer pipes." And that's when I noticed some of his teeth were missing. "Is this guy for real?" I thought. But there was something genuine about him.

"Follow me," I said. As soon as I got him to the flooded basement, his mastery began to show. He tried several things, all the while trying to isolate the problem. He seemed driven, working like a demon. I watched, impressed. My kids watched, fascinated.

Finally he stood up. "I've got to get my snake out of the truck. If that thing won't do it, ma'am, you probably have a bigger problem than I can solve. But my snake usually gets them all." With that he rushed up the stairs.

I followed him, and that's when I noticed he had a woman passenger in his pickup. He brought the tool into the house,

Grace Cirocco

and when I asked him about his companion, he replied, "Oh, that's my girlfriend. I just picked her up from work." Apparently, coming over to fix our drain was more pressing than taking her home first.

Back downstairs we went, Jack, the snake, both my toddlers and I. Once more we watched with fascination. After the steel snake had been fed into the drain and retrieved, the drain was still plugged. Then the plumber did something that made me want to throw up. He stuck his arm – right up to his armpit – into the drain and started feeling around. Then he pulled out a massive clump of stuff and looked up at me with satisfaction. "Ma'am, your problem is roots!" he announced with glee. His voice sounded like I had just won a million dollars.

To this day I remain impressed by Jack's enthusiasm, his energy, his drive and expertise. In short, the man was passionate about clogged pipes. Now, I wouldn't want to be sticking my arms into people's drains, but you could tell that Jack was born for this type of work. He took pride in it. He loved his work. The point is, you can be passionate about anything. Whether or not others think it's disgusting or mundane or tedious doesn't matter. What matters is the attitude you bring to your work.

My father is retired now, but he's passionate about motors. His eyes widen when someone brings him a sick motor to be fixed. He loves the challenge of taking it apart and finding the problem. He can work on his tractor or truck for hours, often forgetting to eat or go home.

My mother's passion is her fruit farm and garden. The last time she was in Italy, when she buried her father, she brought back a tiny walnut seedling from her parents' garden. That seedling grew to over seventy feet high and produced forty bushels of walnuts a year. For her, that tree was sacred. It carried the Spirit of her father, and every time she discovers a new walnut seedling, she says it's one of the babies of the original tree.

This is *passion* as a verb. This is the passion you bring with you to work, to your relationships, to everyday life. Being passionate is having an attitude and an energy inside you. It's a filter through which you look at the world. It's like permanent sunshine for the soul. This kind of passion is in the eye of the beholder. It's not some magical ingredient intrinsic to the work itself. There are no passionate jobs, only passionate people. The source of passion is *you*. It's the attitude you bring to your work that brings passion to your experience.

Perhaps you're thinking there's no way you can become passionate about your current job. Maybe you're in the right field but working the wrong hours. Perhaps you love some parts of your job but not others. Maybe you love the people but hate the structure; maybe you love your boss but hate the ethics of the company you work for. You may have some fine-tuning to do, and that's okay. We each deserve to hear our song played on all eighty-eight keys. If you're playing your song on fewer keys right now, maybe it's time to reconnect to your purpose. Passion can take you there.

YOUR PASSION IS LINKED
TO YOUR PURPOSE

I want to be used up when I die. . . . Life is no brief candle to me.
It is a sort of splendid torch which I have got hold of for a moment,
and I want to make it burn as brightly as possible
before handing it on to future generations.

– GEORGE BERNARD SHAW

Passion as a noun means your connection with a *what*, a thing, a person, place or activity that brings out the best in you. It is a sacred link to your innermost Self, your own life force. It is a connection to Spirit, God, or the Universal Energy. Your passions are what you love, and your loves define you. Your passions, not your bank account, tell the world who you are. By connecting to your passion, you stay authentic and true to yourself. Passion teaches us how to live.

For Barbara Braham, author of *Finding Your Purpose*, the words "passion" and "purpose" are synonymous. In fact, she says, when we dissect *passion* we find three words: *pass, I* and *on*.[8] Passion, therefore, is about passing something of yourself on to the world. It's your legacy. It's your way of making a difference, your unique calling, your opportunity to bless the world with your gifts.

We are more than what we do to earn a living. The truth is that for some of us, what we do at our job doesn't come close to describing who we are. For some of us, it's only part of the story. Say you study the movement of planets or the mating habits of gorillas, or you spend most of your day changing wheels on trucks, cooking hamburgers, writing reports, making sales calls, building roads or fixing pipes. Is that all you are? It may be your job, but it's not your purpose. Or it may be both your job and your purpose. How do you know?

Purpose has to do with meaning, and meaning is connected to passion. One of my favorite stories is about three bricklayers who are looking for work. During a job interview, the prospective employer asks them to describe what they did in their last job. The first bricklayer pipes up and says that he laid bricks. "That's what I did all day. I took bricks and mortar and put them together." Then the interviewer turns to the second bricklayer and asks him the same question. He says, "I built walls. I traveled to wherever they needed me to build walls." Finally, the interviewer turns to bricklayer number three. "Tell me, what did you do in your last job?" This bricklayer smiles as he pauses a moment to reflect. Then he leans in, eyes aglow, and says, "I built a cathedral."

If your work is your calling, if it's really what you were meant to do – your purpose – then you are building cathedrals every day, regardless of what type of work it is. Your ability to connect to the big picture is what nurtures not only meaning but also pride in what you do. Can you see the cathedral you're building, or do you feel at the end of the day that all you've done is laid bricks or built walls? Some leaders are helping their staff connect to the big picture by sharing the values and mission statement of the company. Still, finding meaning and purpose at work is your responsibility.

For those of you who may not know the differences between purpose, mission and destiny, suffice it to say that passion is an ingredient of all of them. Our passions define us and point to our destiny. They also give us a reason to move our feet. A passionate embrace of your passions will fuel action. Passion doesn't come from the head; it comes from your heart. You feel it when you're not in the right job. You feel it when you're with the wrong person. You feel it when you've betrayed your soul. It's time we paid attention to those feelings.

GETTING IN TOUCH WITH YOUR PASSIONS

**I say follow your bliss and don't be afraid,
and doors will open where you didn't know they were going to be.**

— JOSEPH CAMPBELL

Okay, so you're convinced you want to live life with more passion. But how can you take off the mask of indifference? You might ask, "I want to connect to my passions, but how do I do it?" Many people ask me that in my workshops. Here are five questions that will help you access your passions:

1. WHAT ARE YOUR LOVES?

Exploring what you are passionate about will help clarify who you are. In the nineteenth century, the German philosopher Friedrich Nietzsche said, "Your true being does not lie hidden deep inside you, but incalculably high above you. The question to ask yourself, looking back on your life, is 'What have I really loved?'"

Well, what do *you* love? What makes your heart sing? Follow your bliss, says Joseph Campbell. What is *your* bliss? When are you truly happy? Try different things until you discover what you love – and then go for it with all your heart. Don't hold back. What activity makes you feel excited and passionate, and makes the time fly when you're doing it?

Take out your journal and draw a heart in the center of the page. Inside the heart, write "My Passions." Then draw lines emanating from the heart like bicycle spokes. On these lines write your passions, your loves. Ask yourself, "What makes me happy? What makes me excited? Enthusiastic? What makes my Spirit soar?"

Your choices may be tangible things like Italian food, palm trees, chocolate, your kids or your cat, or non-tangibles like rainy days, justice, beautiful sunsets, ideas, Sunday mornings. As you write, keep asking yourself, "What do I love? What do I care about? What's my bliss?" You'll have begun the journey to your passions. The truth is, once you commit to your passions, doors will open. It's one of those laws of life: Do what you love and the money will follow. Follow your bliss and the doors will open. Take the step and the bridge will be there.

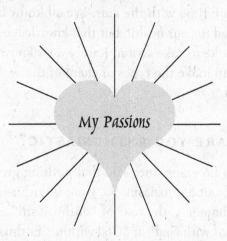

My Passions

2. WHAT ARE YOUR GUT FEELINGS?

Gut feelings have saved lives, discovered cures and made people rich. They might come as a hunch, a flash, a deep knowing. The problem is that so many of us tune out our intuition in favor of something more logical or rational. But feelings are sacred. They are your barometer for what's really important.

Go inwards and listen. Keep a journal. Make friends with your feelings. Gut feelings are tugs on your heartstrings. They may arrive as an intuition, a hunch, a feeling that you know something, but you don't know how you know. Gut feelings come from the deepest part of you. You must learn to listen to them, pay attention to them and learn from them.

It's not enough for people to know what to do to take the step – they must *feel* it in their gut. Feelings compel us to make fools of ourselves in love. Feelings are the inspiration that gives us the power to take risks, all kinds of risks. Feelings force us to take action. Knowledge is weak in comparison. Think about all the things that you already know you should be doing, like eating less junk food, exercising more, getting more sleep, spending more time with the kids. We all know by now that smoking is bad for our health, but that knowledge alone is not enough to make us take action. Rarely does knowledge alone motivate us to make the types of changes that will move our lives forward.

3. WHEN ARE YOU ENTHUSIASTIC?

Ralph Waldo Emerson once said that nothing great was ever achieved without enthusiasm. So, what is enthusiasm? As we learned in Chapter 3, the root of "enthusiasm" is the Greek *entheos*, "filled with God" or "God within." Enthusiasm comes from your well of passion deep inside. It is holy. When you feel this way, your soul is speaking; you feel endless energy and exhilaration. Studies show that enthusiastic people have stronger immune systems because they're high on life. When you find yourself enthusing about something, pay attention! Your purpose is close by.

Bill Gates, the cofounder of Microsoft, is famous for saying

"What I do best is share my enthusiasm." If you're enthusiastic about something, chances are your energy is contagious. You get people on board. You motivate a team, a community, a company. Management schools are trying to teach enthusiasm to our future leaders. The world needs more enthusiasm, because where enthusiasm lives, passion does, too.

4. WHAT INSPIRES YOU?

We have been trained to death. We have enough skills to solve all the world's problems, but what we lack is inspiration. When we're inspired, we take action. To get to our passions, we need to plug into our inspiration. The word "inspiration" is derived from the Latin verb *inspirare*, which means "to breathe into." The *Oxford English Dictionary* says that inspiration is "divine influence, especially that which is thought to prompt poets and that under which books of Scripture are held to have been written."

Sometimes when I'm in front of an audience I'll amaze myself by saying things that I never planned or that I didn't think I even knew. Then later someone will tell me how significant that story or example or metaphor was for them. When we're doing our life's work, it takes little effort, because we're visited by the muse of inspiration. God is within us. Canadian singer/songwriter Loreena McKennit called one of her recordings *The Visit* because, as she explains in the album notes, "the creative impulse is a visit . . . a thing of grace, mysterious. You don't know when it'll drop in."

When you are visited by this muse, you are blessed with creative genius.

Creativity fertilizes the soul. Work is too often repetitive, boring and meaningless, whereas humans are born to create.

When our creative Spirit is restrained, it rebels. The individual Spirit yearns to be awakened and released. By its very nature, inspiration is transforming – its gifts are Spirit, "aliveness" and passion.

Like passion, inspiration can ignite action. I know this from personal experience. I can accomplish more in one hour when I'm inspired than in two weeks when I'm not. Simply put, when we're inspired, we take action. When we're not, we procrastinate.

Inspiration will also fuel your desire. So many people want to change their lives for the better. They know what to do – they even have the skills to do it – but they lack the desire. That's why inspiration is so powerful. Inspiration is empowering and motivating.

In your journal, make a list of what inspires you. Then ask yourself, "What can I do today to inspire my heart and take one step toward my bridge?" For example, I knew I wanted to write this book, but attempting it all at once seemed overwhelming, especially when I was working and balancing my family responsibilities. But each time I felt my heart overflowing with inspiration, I would take out my journal and write down what I was feeling, perhaps just one or two ideas. Inspiration would come after seeing a great movie or reading stories of courage and faith; after greeting the sunrise on a beach or hearing a beautiful piece of music; after a rich conversation with friends or after delivering a really great seminar. I never waste inspiration. You might think that single ideas don't amount to much in themselves, but for me those single ideas eventually turned into the book you're now reading.

5. WHAT SYNCHRONICITIES HAVE YOU EXPERIENCED?

The term "synchronicity" was coined by psychologist Carl Jung to connote not just any coincidence, but meaningful coincidence. I first became aware of the magic of synchronicity after reading Milan Kundera's beautiful novel *The Unbearable Lightness of Being*. Kundera spends considerable time describing the meaningful coincidences that bring the two main characters, Tomas and Teresa, together. Kundera has his own word for these synchronistic events – he calls them *fortuities*.

I believe that synchronicities can point you toward your passions or your higher purpose, like the book that you heard about but neglect to read only to have it pop up everywhere you go. At the library, it falls off the shelf in front of you. You stop to have lunch with a friend, and the person next to you is reading it. You arrive home, and it's on your desk. Perhaps the Universe is sending you a message?

Synchronicities mark significant points of transition in our lives and point us in the direction of our purpose. We need to trust the hidden messages in synchronicities and pay attention to them when they happen. As Robert Hopcke writes in his book *There Are No Accidents: Synchronicity and the Stories of Our Lives*, "Those events which are synchronistic make us aware, again and again, of the beauty, order and connectedness of the tales we are living."[9]

We tend to meet the "right" person, read the right book, hear the right song or go to the right workshop when we're open to our spiritual journey and authentic calling. These synchronicities happen all the time to people tuned in to that higher frequency. Sometimes at my workshops people will say to me, "You know, I wasn't registered for this workshop. But then my friend got sick and I took her place. But now I realize that *I* was supposed to be here today, not my friend." For some people, it's the timing that is synchronistic. Spirit is always leading us by the hand.

Synchronicities also happen when you've listened to your heart and acted on an intuition. I was writing about the emperor penguins of Antarctica in order to illustrate to some clients the importance of teamwork and getting along. My memory of the details was vague, but I had been touched deeply by their story, which I had seen on educational TV years before. I was writing the story from the bits and pieces that I could remember. On one particular day I spoke to many people on the telephone, but only when I was talking to my friend John McCormick did a voice inside say, "Tell him about your penguin story." So I did. I shared with him how frustrated I was at not having time to track down more information on these amazing creatures.

That night when John went home he checked his mailbox and found that his *National Geographic* magazine had arrived that day. On the cover was a picture of emperor penguins – that month's feature story! He was stunned and so was I, but that's the power of the divine Mystery working in our lives.

The most amazing synchronicity that I've ever experienced has to do with my daughter's name. The summer after my first year of university, I took a job at the Calgary Stampede. I met many celebrities and media people that summer, and one of them was a journalist from Scandinavia. She was beautiful and smart and I felt an immediate connection with her. Her name was Kajsa – pronounced kah-EE-suh. I had never heard the name before, but I loved it. I made a mental note that should I ever have a daughter, that's what I would name her.

Later that fall, I met the man I was to marry. He was a mathematics major and an avid chess player. He was the only person I knew who owned a chess library, with hundreds of books on the subject. Chess was his passion and he traveled all over to participate in tournaments. Needless to say, he took the game very seriously.

Several years into our relationship – actually, while we were making wedding plans – I brought up the subject of kids' names. "I don't have a boy's name picked out," I said, "but should we ever have a girl, I already have a name that I like."

"Oh?" he inquired. "What name is that?"

"Kajsa," I said.

I'll never forget the surprised look on his face. "Grace, Kajsa is the goddess of chess!"

That was in May 1982. Exactly ten years later we were blessed with a little girl. Of course we named her Kajsa. And like her dad, she loves chess. She's participated in a few tournaments already, and she likes to intimidate her mostly male opponents by letting them know that she was named after the goddess of chess.

Synchronicities – sacred coincidences – sometimes come to us like Delphic oracles telling us what to do next. They are messengers. They stand up and hit us on the head. Synchronicities are part of the language of people in love. Lovers yearn to be together all the time, but when they can't be, synchronicities are there to fill the void. For example, you meet a stranger at the bank and quite by accident find out her birthday. It's the same day as your beloved's. You're out driving and the numbers on the license plate of the car in front of you add up to his age. The restaurant you choose for lunch that day is featuring his favorite wine, and so on. Psychiatrist and past-life expert Brian Weiss says, "It is extremely important to pay attention to the coincidences, the synchronicities, and the déjà vu experiences in our lives because they often represent the convergence of our spiritual plan and the actual path we are traveling during our lifetime."[10]

Synchronicities bring meaning to our lives. They remind us that there is a Mystery at work that we may not always understand, but if we pay attention, it can lead us to greater purpose. "Synchronicities, magical openings, omens, personalized revelations, oracles delivered by passing strangers . . . what do they prove?" asks Sam Keen in *The Passionate Life*. "That the world is more like a love affair than a battlefield," he answers.[11]

Yes, indeed.

KEEPING PASSION ALIVE IN YOUR EVERYDAY LIFE

We need to live each moment wholeheartedly, with all our senses – finding pleasure in the fragrance of a backyard garden, the crayoned picture of a six-year-old, the enchanting beauty of a rainbow.

– BARBARA BARTOCCI

The next time you go to a party, wait until you're asked the inevitable question, "What do you do?" Then break the mold and reply, "I'll tell you what I'm passionate about instead." Don't ask people what they do, because that may not define who they are. Ask them instead, "What are your passions? What do you love? What turns you on?" It's a risk, I know. But go for it – there is genius in boldness. If they give you weird looks, blame it on me.

At my workshops I have a soft, squeezable heart that I toss around to people. Whoever catches the heart has to stand up and share one of their passions. I'm amazed at the diversity of passions and how much people love to talk about them. There's something else I notice. When people talk about their passions, their whole demeanor shifts. They soften; they start to glow as they remember who they are and what brings them joy.

Sarah Ban Breathnach, in her book *Something More*, talks a great deal about passion. She says that asking to be delivered to our passion is the only thing worth praying for. In fact, passion is so important to her that she had stenciled on her white bedroom walls – in gold letters, no less – the following definition, which she found on the back of a Passion Tazo tea bag: "True passion is intoxicating and invigorating, soothing and sensuous, magical and mystical. I just thought you should know what you're in for."[12]

Imagine yourself waking up to those words every morning. Do you think they would set the tone for your day? What is your definition of passion? How can you keep passion alive in your everyday life?

Decorate Your Passions

When we moved into our current house five years ago, I did something I had never done before. I went crazy with the paintbrush. One night – actually, in the wee hours of the morning, while everyone was sleeping except Michelangelo wannabes like me – I painted several palm trees on the walls of my bathroom. I have always loved the shape of palm trees; as a child I sketched them endlessly. When I was done, I painted a huge heart with the infinity symbol above it to greet my husband in the morning. To this day those palm trees and that heart still give me a thrill every time I walk into my bathroom. They are a testament to my passion.

In my office, instead of using a traditional fabric for the valance over my window, I opted for mauve wisteria flowers made of silk. They hang like clumps of ripe grapes, and they're delightful. Who says I can't use them as a valance? I'm sure some feng shui expert would say I've done it all wrong, but I don't care. When you walk into my bathroom or my office, you can get a sense of the person I am. More importantly, when I'm there, I know who I am. Decorate your passions! Look around you. What have you secretly wanted to do, but feared was not kosher decorating practice? Do it!

My friend Owen has motivational quotations all over his bathroom walls. They are written in a variety of fonts, weights and colors, and each quotation is set at a different angle. The effect is a stunning inspirational menu for his bathroom guests. To decorate her basement, one of my clients had her children dip their hands into different colors of paint and make imprints on the whitewashed walls. The result is a border of handprints that will forever remind her of her precious ones after they have grown up and moved away. The point is that there are countless ways to express yourself and to decorate your passion. Be creative.

Create a Sanctuary

I have always loved the colors of tropical beaches. That is where I feel my "bliss." Maybe it's because I was born near the Mediterranean, or maybe it's because I lived on a tropical island in a past life; I don't know. Throughout my travels, I've always been searching for the perfect beach. I found it – in Australia – and now I can see it on the walls of my office every day. I have a huge mural of the Whitsunday Islands near the Great Barrier Reef, the place I was visiting and, incidentally, where my first-born son was conceived. (Another connection to passion!) Turquoise shades of water, palm trees, mountains and white sand beaches greet me every morning as I walk into my home office. More than any other room in the house, my office is my sanctuary.

As I look around, I see that it contains so much of what I am passionate about: stacks and stacks of books and magazines – ideas captured on the white page; unique picture frames that hold photographs of the people I love most; lavender-scented candles; rocks and shells from the different places I've visited; angels; a bubbling fountain; my music; mementos and gifts from clients and friends; plants; a vase of yellow tulips (my favorite flowers) that are doing their own passionate dance; and of course the many paintings, pictures and cards my children have lovingly made for me. My filing cabinet is covered with beautiful cards I've received from my husband and friends over the years. When I look at them, I am reminded of how much I'm loved. I also have a huge solid-oak desk that I picked up second-hand nearly twenty years ago and that has followed me everywhere. I love the grain of the wood and the connection to trees that I feel when I'm working on it.

Which room in your home or office is your sanctuary? Which room could become one? If you don't have a sanctuary, how can you go about creating one? Use colors that speak to you. Let your passion soar. Give in to that creative impulse that comes from your deepest core. Choose a room in your home to remind you of your passions. Cover the beige walls with passion – your passion! Be outrageous. Let your authentic Self come out. Create a sanctuary.

Let Your Senses Take In the World

Give your senses a feast. Treat them to a sunset, an elaborate meal, a symphony, silk sheets or a fragrant garden. There is so much to see, hear, taste, smell and experience. Our senses are a vehicle that allows us to experience our world with more passion and joy.

When was the last time you caught a sunset? Sunsets are the sun's opportunity to make love to the earth. A sunset is the promise of another day, but it's also the sun's way of making a splashy exit. It paints extravagant mauves and pinks across the sky and it leaves an imprint on our soul. Do you remember your most beautiful sunset? In her book *A Natural History of the Senses*, Diane Ackerman tells us how, no matter what is going on at the office, she honors her ritual of watching the sunset from the picture window in her living room. She writes, "Each night the sunset surged with purple pampas-grass plumes and shot fuchsia rockets into the pink sky, then deepened through folded layers of peacock green to all the blues of India and a black across which clouds sometimes churned like alabaster dolls. The visual opium of the sunset was what I craved for."[13] That is one passionate sunset and one passionate woman!

My friend Catherine and I are moon goddesses – we love the moon. In 1999 Earth experienced two blue moons, one in January and one in March. A blue moon is the second full moon in less than a month. They are not really that rare, since they happen every couple of years, but two blue moons in one year *is* rare (the last one happened in 1961).

We weren't going to let the opportunity pass without a celebration. My fellow moon goddess and I got permission to eat outside on the balcony of a beautiful restaurant overlooking Lake Ontario so we could see the blue moon rising over the lake. It was March and not all that warm, but there we were, bundled up in our coats, enjoying our meal, our wine and a perfect view of the full moon rising over the moonlit water. It was simply breathtaking.

My friend Addie loves to cook. She doesn't just cook, she makes love to food. Addie is to food as Juliette Binoche was to chocolate in the movie *Chocolat*. She said to me the other night, "Don't you hate it when you go to lunch with someone and they say, 'Oh, I'll just have a salad'? God, when there are so many wonderful things to eat!" Addie loves to feed her friends. When we go over, the divine smells from her kitchen beckon us from the driveway. She's always got some new recipe for us to try. Visiting her kitchen is like taking your taste buds on an adventure. Can you cook with abandon or do you cook within the lines? Can you take your taste buds on an adventure? Do you experiment? Be passionate – spice up your life! Choose a new vegetable, one you've never cooked before. Try an exotic fruit. Share a decadent dessert. Let the different tastes and textures make love to your palate.

As soon as I step into my friend Sandra's car, I'm engulfed in the high-octane vibrations of Latino music. She's bouncy and excited. "*Ciao, hermanita!* You're not going to believe the music I found in Mexico! You've got to listen to this!" Then she cranks it up – loud enough, I'm convinced, to wake the dead in Argentina – and we cruise down the road to a pounding beat. Outside, it's cold, gray and windy, but in the car we might as well be on a tropical beach in Mexico. Sandra is from Central America and she appreciates music in a way that most people don't. At her house parties, she turns her living room into a dynamic disco, complete with lights, lasers and smoke. She's always the DJ and she always manages to get even the shy ones up and dancing. What music are you passionate about? How often do you treat yourself?

The point is, there is so much to be passionate about. Feast your senses on the passionate universe. Experience the colors, tastes, sounds and textures around you. Get intimate with life.

Practise Gratitude

The more gratitude you teach your heart, the more it will fill with passion.

I was in Florida and really wanted to see dolphins in the wild. After several dolphin-watching expeditions, I was disappointed that none had showed up.

We were staying right on the beach near Fort Myers. Early each morning, while my family was still sleeping, I would take my music and my running shoes and go for a long walk along the beach. On the last morning, to my delight, three dolphins showed up to say hello. They accompanied me on my walk for nearly two miles, swimming close to shore beside me. Every now and then, they'd jump out of the water and do somersaults, squealing with delight like three little children. I couldn't believe my luck! Had they perhaps heard the calling of my heart? I stopped to soak it all in. The beautiful beach, inspirational music in my ears and the happy dolphins beside me – it was almost too much for my heart to take. It was a blessed moment. Gratitude began spilling out of me, and I looked up at the sky and shouted, "Thank you, thank you, thank you!"

We were meant to be grateful for the privilege of being alive. The reward for our gratitude is a greater passion for life. Wake up every morning exhilarated and ready to take on the day.

When you feel blessed by perfect moments, secretly look up and say thank you. What are your perfect moments? Do you give thanks for them?

EMBRACE YOUR PASSION

You can have anything you want if you want it passionately enough. You must want it with an inner exuberance that erupts through the skin and joins the energy that created the world.

– SHEILA GRAHAM

Those who live their lives from passion are filled with light – they are leading authentic lives. They're living the life they want, not one that has been handed down to them. They live their truth. Passionate people savor life. They teach us how to love. They teach us how to live.

Relationship expert Barbara De Angelis tells us that passion is "your saving grace, for it will keep you going after your dreams when everyone advises you to give up, keep you searching for the right partner even when you're afraid he or she isn't out there, keep you traveling on the path of self-discovery even when you aren't sure where the road is taking you."[14]

Passion is far more than the white-hot obsession felt between two people, although it is that, too. It is the fire we feel in our hearts when perfect moments come together and we are free to express who we are. Keeping passion alive is about courage, the courage to be who you are, regardless of the consequences. Living with passion is about living on the edge – it's about pushing yourself to grow outside your comfort zone. By being true to your passion, you live authentically, truthfully, joyfully. Passion drives action. It will thrust you across your bridge toward that which is waiting to move your life forward. Squeeze the juice out of your life. Passion is your soul's duty. Don't apologize for your passion, and don't extinguish your fire for anyone.

5

Courage

BRAVE HEARTS

Life is either a daring adventure or it is nothing.
– HELEN KELLER

The tallest mountain in the world stands about 29,000 feet above sea level. The air is so thin at the top that helicopter rotors cannot keep the craft in the air. If you flew from either Katmandu or the base camp straight to the summit, your lungs would explode. That's why the climb must be made gradually; climbers must spend several weeks, even months, at each camp. I learned these things when watching *Everest*, a documentary about three people who attempted the climb. They are an American man, a Spanish woman and a Tibetan man whose father, Tenzing Norgay, was the first Tibetan to scale Mount Everest, with Edmund Hillary in 1953.

The most treacherous and challenging part of the journey is the last leg. Just before our three heroes set out on it, they get word that a violent storm the day before killed three other climbers who were attempting the summit. The news comes as a shock. One of the men who died had been one of the most experienced climbers in the world and a good friend of theirs.

Will the storm still be raging when they get close to the summit? Should they attempt it or go home satisfied that they had almost made it? It is an agonizing decision, but they choose to be brave hearts. At midnight they set out on the twelve-hour journey to the top of the world, in total darkness and sub-zero temperatures.

As they get closer and closer to the top, their bodies weaken. Hunched over, faces almost brushing the snow, they find each step forward a painful ordeal. Their cumbersome arctic snow suits, the heavy equipment on their backs and the thin air that makes breathing a grueling experience are all making these three adventurers move in slow motion. Watching them, I am stunned by the sheer strength of their will and the power of their desire. When physical exhaustion has almost swallowed them whole, something stronger keeps pushing them forward. When every cell in their bodies wants to scream, "Stop!" something else inside them screams even louder, "Keep moving!" "This is risk-taking, this is raw courage," I say to myself. The climbers stay true to their vision and are rewarded with a view of the world from the summit of the tallest peak on earth. They have conquered Everest.

Before you can take the step toward your dreams, before you cross your bridge, you must have a clear vision of what it is you want – your *desire*. To figure out what you want, you need to dig for your truth and uncover your authentic Self as we did in Chapters 1 and 2. In Chapter 3 we worked on creating a destiny mandala and a mission statement for yourself so you would have a better idea of where you want to take your life. In Chapter 4 we looked at the role passion plays in our lives and in helping us to move forward. Now in this chapter we will work on the final frontier – conquering fear.

When all is said and done and we have all the tools necessary to change our lives, why do we still not take the step? Why are we paralyzed? Why do we shrink back from what our soul came here to do? Fear – conscious fear, unconscious fear, mind-numbing fear, middle-of-the-road fear – it's fear all the same. Fear freezes us and makes us unable to move our lives forward. The antidote for fear is courage. Courage will take us across the bridge, but it will also help us stay authentic and not betray our hearts. It is courage that allows us to express all the colors of our passion and it is courage that will help us choose our destiny. The fact is that we need courage to stay optimistic when the rest of the world wants to drown itself in self-pity. That's why conquering fear is the last frontier.

Courage is the ability to face fear and take the step. Courage is feeling terrified but moving your feet anyway. Think of those times in your life when you were afraid, unsure or anxious, yet you managed to find the courage to do what you had to do. "I want to know if you can get up, after the night of grief and despair, weary and bruised to the bone, and do what needs to be done to feed the children," writes Oriah Mountain Dreamer in her poem *The Invitation*.[1] Sometimes our fear seems all-pervasive, tyrannical and overwhelming, yet something stronger pushes us across the bridge. You might be thinking, "No, not me. When I'm afraid, I just freeze."

In order to conquer fear, you grow courage. Courage is the art of feeling comfortable about feeling uncomfortable. Let's begin by defining courage.

DEFINING COURAGE

*To one who waits all things reveal themselves, so long as you have the
courage not to deny in the darkness what you have seen in the light.*

– COVENTRY PATMORE

The *Oxford English Dictionary* defines "courage" in two ways:
(1) "a readiness to face and capacity to endure danger" and (2)
"an inherent freedom from fear."

Let's look at the first definition and break it into two parts.
First, "a readiness to face," which acknowledges that an undertaking is scary and risky but you're ready to do it regardless.
Most people would agree that the thought of climbing Everest
is a scary idea. What's a scary idea for you? What have you
wanted to do but were afraid to? For some people, contradicting
their boss is a scary idea; for others, it's changing their
wardrobe, committing to a relationship, going to a Third
World country or dealing with conflict. The willingness to face
your scary idea is the beginning of courage.

The second part, "capacity to endure danger," is what you
call upon within yourself to help you go through with the
action that makes you fearful. In other words, enduring the
uncomfortable feelings associated with doing something you
fear. This is what our three heroes had to do on the last leg of
their journey. The capacity to endure danger means that
although some things in life are going to be risks, you understand that risks are part of life. You take risks because you have
courage, because you want to live life fully. "The credit belongs
to the man who is actually in the arena," said Theodore
Roosevelt, the twenty-sixth president of the United States, in a
speech delivered in Paris in 1910, "whose face is marred by

dust and sweat and blood, who strives valiantly, who errs and comes up short again and again . . . because there is no effort without error and . . . if he fails while daring greatly, knows his place shall never be with those timid and cold souls who know neither victory nor defeat."[2]

Part 2 of the definition is "an inherent freedom from fear." Once upon a time there were knights and warriors who fought battles and whose courage was honored in lands all over the world. Every battle took hundreds of lives, yet each young soldier knew that fighting was part of his lot in life. They were fearless and stoic. Who has this kind of courage today? I find that most young children are fearless. They don't just walk across their bridge, they do somersaults across it. But for adults fear remains a common denominator.

If we feel fearful, does it mean we can't be brave hearts, can't be courageous?

Not at all. I believe that courage comes when we face the fear and do it anyway. So many of us don't because we need to feel comfortable before taking action. Fear makes us feel uncomfortable. The objective is not to rinse your body and psyche clean of fear; the objective is to survive the fear while moving forward. That's courage. Make fear your ally. Make fear your friend and overcome your need to feel comfortable all the time.

"Facing it, always facing it, that's the way through. Face it," said one of Joseph Conrad's characters. Face the fear, but do what you have to do. Don't give up, don't run away, don't numb out. Stay in the arena and play. The Japanese have a similar philosophy. Their Morita therapy says, "Be scared to death, but still do what you have to do." We need to acknowledge the fear, smell it, taste it, feel it – but still take the step. That is courage. That is the person who Roosevelt says "is actually in the arena."

FACING FEAR AND TAKING ACTION

Stop to look fear in the face. . . .
You must do the thing you cannot do.
- ELEANOR ROOSEVELT

When were you most afraid and what did you do about it? Freeze? Run? Lie? I'm not talking about the kind of fear you feel when you have writer's block or when you're procrastinating about a decision you don't want to make or when you can't ask someone out for a date. I'm talking about the gut-wrenching, life-or-death, fight-or-flight kind of fear. Have you ever experienced this kind of fear, when your life or the life of someone you loved was in danger? How did you behave? Chances are you stared fear down in order to survive and not only that, you did what you had to do. You took action.

I was eighteen years old and living on my own in Paris, France, studying French at Sorbonne University. It was late evening and I was coming home from the library. While walking on Boulevard Saint-Michel, I sensed that I was being followed. I picked up my pace and finally arrived at my building, but it had one of those heavy steel doors that shuts slowly after it's been opened. I looked back down the circular staircase and saw three young men slip through the doorway just before it closed. My heart started pumping hard. "Oh, my God! They're after me," I thought. What did they want? And then I remembered the warning I received when I first arrived, from the lady who owned the *pâtisserie* down the street.

"Be careful, *chérie*. Young girls like you are raped and dumped into the Seine River. Every week they pull bodies out of the Seine. I see it on the news. And they're mostly foreign girls like you." Those words echoed in my head. Should I run? My room was at the very top; I still had eight flights of stairs to go. "Why doesn't the elevator work at night?" I thought angrily. "Maybe if I stand perfectly still they might think I went through one of the other doors on the main floor." While all these thoughts were rushing through my brain, my feet kept going, up, up, up, round and round and round, trying to be as quiet as I could. My heart was pounding heavily. My legs were about to give out. I was getting dizzy. But I kept moving. I made it to my door, but the men had caught up to me. We got a good look at each other as I hurriedly turned the key and dashed inside. I was so scared I was shaking, but I managed to lock my door and push the big dresser in front of it. Then I sat on my bed, trying to catch my breath and feel my legs again.

Just as I was thinking, "I'm safe. I made it. It's okay," the young men started banging on my door and yelling at me in French. When that didn't work, they tried to cajole me out with sweet talk. Then they got angry and threatened to break my door down. I had no phone and none of my neighbors was coming to my rescue. Eventually, after what seemed like hours, I couldn't hear them anymore; but I was still too terrified to open my door. I never saw those men again, but I know that fear had made my feet move faster than I would ever have thought possible. My fear had saved my life.

I have noticed that the times when I was most afraid were also the times I felt most compelled to act. When faced with situations that threaten our well-being, we activate our "action" button. That's why human beings can sometimes perform incredible acts of physical strength and endurance in life-or-death situations. In those situations we tune in to our warrior energy and do what we have to do. This reaction to fear is hard-wired into our nervous system as a survival mechanism. It's called the stress response – we get fired up with hormones so that we can take action. In extreme situations, we usually have two choices: Either we fight, or we take flight.

WHEN FEAR CLOUDS OUR THINKING

**And since the root of all error is fear,
only the undoing of fear will bring correction.**
– PAUL FERRINI

Sometimes when we experience extreme fear, we lose our ability to think straight. Have you made any bad decisions because you were fearful? This happened to me the time I thought my sixteen-month-old baby girl had been kidnapped. I had hired as a nanny a woman who spoke little English but who loved children and seemed to be very kind-hearted. After working with us for about a week, she said she wanted to take Kajsa for a walk in her stroller. It was a beautiful day and I agreed.

Expecting that the nanny would walk up and down our street a couple of times and then return, I was surprised when half an hour had passed and there was no sign of her. After one hour had passed I became alarmed. Where could she have gone? I went out to look, but there was no sign of them. With each passing minute, my fear grew more intense. Not only that, but my mind started putting together a case for why this woman would want to steal my baby and leave the country. I began to remember snippets of conversation – how she had tried to have a baby but couldn't, how she had always wanted a little girl and how Kajsa was the most beautiful baby girl she had ever seen and that she even resembled her.

I looked at the clock. More than an hour had passed. Where

were they? Suddenly I realized I didn't even have the spelling of her last name. "Of course, that way I can't trace her when she takes my baby out of the country!" I yelled to my husband. I grabbed the car keys and ran out of the house.

Every second that went by seemed like an eternity. I turned north onto the main road but didn't see them. My heart was pounding in my chest. What to do? What to do? Tears were cascading down my face. "This is what it must be like to go crazy," I thought. My hands were shaking on the steering wheel. This was bone-chilling fear. This was fear as I'd never experienced before. This was worse than any threat to my life – this was my precious baby. I stopped the car right in the middle of the road, got out and started screaming like a crazy person.

My angels must have been out in full force, because a police cruiser just happened to be driving by while I was having my lunatic moment. The officer escorted me home and tried to reassure me that they would do whatever they could to find my baby. Soon there were five cruisers in front of my house. A missing child is serious business.

The excitement brought my neighbors out to see what the commotion was all about. When they heard the news, they were alarmed. A few of them came over to me, but I was in no condition to talk to anyone. I was in my blackest hour, experiencing a terror that I had previously never even imagined. Meanwhile, I overheard a policewoman gently asking my husband for a recent picture of Kajsa to put on the six o'clock news and to give to airport security. Another officer was talking about organizing a search party. My brain was spinning. Six o'clock? Search party? By that time the nanny could be anywhere! Why weren't the police doing something *now*? "This is what parents of missing children go through," I thought. "This is the hellish nightmare they live through. And now it's happening to me. How will I survive this?" I walked onto the front porch in tears, and that's when I saw the nanny nonchalantly pushing along my daughter's stroller.

I went inside to tell my husband and the police. Immediately, tears of relief streamed down my face. And then, almost as immediately, feelings of guilt and shame washed over me. "Oh, my God, what will the nanny think?" When she walked in, she was stunned to see the house swarming with police officers. As soon as she saw my face, she understood why.

"Where were you?" my husband asked her.

"I went for a walk. I stopped to do some shopping," she said. I was too weak to say anything. I grabbed Kajsa from her stroller and pulled her close to me. I looked at the nanny. How could I tell her that her lack of judgment had taken years off my life? That her two hours of shopping were the blackest two hours I'd ever experienced?

It was wrong of her to do her shopping during working hours and wrong of her to take my baby along. Nevertheless, had I not been so gripped with fear, I might have saved myself two hours of anguish and terror. For example, I might have spent a bit more time looking for them before having my lunatic moment right in the middle of an intersection. Had I turned south, for example, I would have spotted them. Had my judgment not been clouded over, I might not have built up such a convincing case for baby theft. But my fear swallowed me whole that day. It was brutal. Sometimes when fear activates us, it pushes the wrong button.

WHEN FEAR DOESN'T MOVE US TO ACT

Only those who dare to fail greatly can ever achieve greatly.
- ROBERT F. KENNEDY

There is another type of fear that I call "everyday fear," the kind that doesn't automatically activate the action button. What are these everyday fears?

When you need to speak up or do the right thing but don't; when you should apply for a job, confront a friend, give a presentation, make a tough telephone call, go to work for yourself or tackle an "undone" that has been demanding your attention – and you don't, then you are experiencing an everyday fear. Wouldn't it be great if our action button could be activated by this kind of fear, too? In addition to the fear of getting hurt, there are also fear of failure, fear of the unknown and fear of success. If these everyday fears don't automatically activate the action button, how can we take action and conquer them? We do it with courage, love and faith.

Taking action on these things is not a matter of physical survival, but of spiritual and emotional survival. To ignore the call from your soul, from the dreams that may be beckoning you from the other side of the bridge or from a relationship that is important to you means that you never reach your potential, you never actualize your fullest being, you're never quite the empowered individual you were meant to be. What's at risk is your "aliveness." That's why the poet W. H. Auden says that all men die, but few really live. If your spirit withers away but your body is still walking around, are you really alive? That's a question that many people today are asking themselves. Do you opt for the path of least resistance? Do you coast? Do you run away from your everyday fears?

You might be reading this and thinking, "Gee, is that what happened to me? Is that why I turned off my passion for life?" Maybe. And then again, maybe not. As I described in Chapters 1 and 4, there are many reasons why we turn off. Letting fear rule our lives and ignoring the call from our soul may be part of the reason. Especially at mid-life, many people seem to experience a sort of existential crisis when they come face to face with their mortality and the fact that time is running out. They look at their list of undones and are overwhelmed with regret and sadness. Fear can be an absence of courage, an absence of love or an absence of faith, or a combination of the three. When we can't or don't love ourselves enough or believe in our abilities, then we are incapable of taking action. Lack of action leads to feelings of failure and regret. Depression may set in, which can cause us to lose even more faith, more love and more courage. And that's how the self-defeating cycle works. We don't activate our action button because we're stuck in this negative cycle.

THE SELF-DEFEATING CYCLE

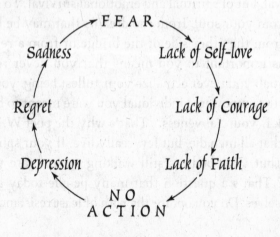

FEAR

Sadness   Lack of Self-love

Regret   Lack of Courage

Depression   Lack of Faith

NO
ACTION

BEFRIENDING FEAR

**Where the mind is without fear and the head is held high,
Where knowledge is free . . .
Where tireless striving stretches the arms towards perfection . . .**
– RABINDRANATH TAGORE

How can we take the step despite our fear? After all, feeling scared is not unnatural. Our tendency is to ignore the fear, hide it or deny it. But fear needs to be understood and befriended if you are going to activate your action button. Learn to recognize fear as soon as it appears. Name it and locate it. Where, for example, do you feel the fear? For some people, fear lives in the stomach. For others, it lives in the legs. For others, it's a pounding in the chest. Where does fear live in your body? You need to recognize it, acknowledge it and understand it before you can overcome it and activate your action button. Also ask yourself, "What is the worst thing that can happen?" Coming face to face with your worst fear is the first step in conquering its power over you.

Then, using all your senses, delve into your fear. Describe it. First, what does your fear look like? What color is it? What shape? If you could draw it, what would it look like? If your fear had a voice, what would it say to you? Write down all the things your fear would tell you. Next, what does your fear taste like? Be descriptive. Don't just say "awful" or "bad." Use expressive language. For example, "My fear tastes as putrid as a truckload of rotten eggs." Finally, how does your fear smell? Again, be descriptive. By getting to know your fear in such an intimate way, you can break out of it and take action despite the fear. It is no longer the monster you thought it was. By unmasking it, you will know what it is.

Once we've understood our fear, we can start to move through it. But for some people, understanding their fear is still not enough. They can't move forward because they are plagued by feelings of hopelessness and inadequacy. The cure for hopelessness is faith. The cure for inadequacy is Love. We must learn to have compassion for ourselves and to accept ourselves despite our weaknesses. The greater our self-acceptance and self-love, the more action we will take. For some people, this is all they need to start taking small steps, but it's a bit of a catch-22. You've got to believe in yourself to take risks, but you have to take risks in order to believe in yourself. You will learn techniques for increasing self-love and faith in Part Two.

Right now, let's activate the action button with courage. I'd like to help you start thinking like a brave heart. How can courage help us? The root of the word is the Latin *cor*, meaning "heart." So when we say "take heart," we really mean "have courage." "Courage" is also the root word of "encouragement." When we encourage someone, we are giving them reinforcement for their heart. Brave hearts are in contact with their fear every day, yet they walk through it. They take action.

JUST DO IT!

**It is not because things are difficult that we do not dare,
it is because we do not dare that they are difficult.**

– SENECA

Courage allows you to swallow your fear whole and step across that bridge. You're scared as hell, but somehow you face the fear and move through it. That's what it means to "just do it." Courage lets you activate the action button by employing your own sheer will to break the self-defeating cycle. Everyone admires those who can just do it. That's why the Nike ads were so successful – they resonated with people. We want to do it, but we feel impotent. We often make it so difficult for ourselves. We procrastinate. We're scared. We blame it on perfectionism. We blame our circumstances on the weather, our parents and our kids. We say we're not ready; we need to do more research or get another degree or additional credentials. We complain about all those things we still haven't done, yet we postpone taking action. When will we be ready to *just do it*?

When I lived in San Diego, California, I produced an afternoon radio program that went to air live from 3 to 6 p.m. I used to arrive early and start digging for good stories to feature. I'd hunt down articulate and lively speakers who could discuss the top stories of the day. I was always searching for what we called in the business "good radio" – people and stories that would touch the heart and add value to daily life. My search for the perfect show could have been endless. There was always one more telephone call I needed to make or one more lead to chase down. But every day at 3 p.m. I had to go to air with a show. There could be no more preparing or postponing. It was showtime. I was forced to *just do it*.

Wouldn't it be great if our lives worked like that – if at a certain time every day or week, our "producer" walked in and said, "Okay, enough procrastination. It's showtime. *Just do it!*" If you were forced to do it, how would your life be different today? What have you been postponing? If you could do one thing that would move your personal life forward, what would that be? If you could do one thing that would move your professional life forward, what would that be? If every day you took a step forward, even if it were a tiny baby-step, eventually you'd be on the other side, eventually you'd accomplish your goals. Baby-steps accumulate like compound interest. The critical first step is to face your fear – recognize it, feel it and endure it. Fear is uncomfortable but it doesn't have to stop you from crossing your bridge. Take action, even if it's just a tiny step. This will grow your self-confidence which will create courage in your heart. Once you feel courageous, you will be able to face more of your fears and take more risks and so on and so on. That's how brave hearts do it.

BRAVE HEART CYCLE

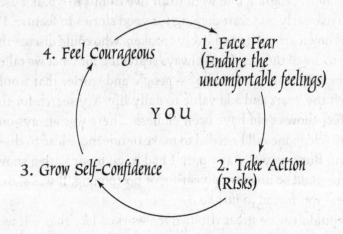

4. *Feel Courageous*

1. *Face Fear*
(*Endure the uncomfortable feelings*)

Y O U

3. *Grow Self-Confidence*

2. *Take Action*
(*Risks*)

Eventually you will have made it all the way across the bridge and accomplished what you set out to do. That will give you the confidence and courage to tackle more projects and cross more bridges. Imagine how different your life might be if you took consistent steps toward completing your undones instead of complaining about all the roadblocks in your way. In most cases, *you* are your biggest roadblock! It's your attitude. A colleague of mine is fond of saying, "The only problem in your life is *you*."

SOMETIMES WE NEED A PUSH

"Come to the edge," he said.
They said, "We are afraid."
"Come to the edge," he said.
They came.
He pushed them . . . and they flew.

– GUILLAUME APOLLINAIRE

Sometimes we can't *do it* until we get a sign, a nod or a push from someone. In a workshop I was teaching a few years ago, I asked people to think about what they really wanted. A woman stood up, walked over to the microphone and said, "I want to be the Grace Cirocco for French Canada. I want to give workshops and empower people just like you do." I looked at her and said enthusiastically, "Well, just do it!" Everyone broke into applause and the woman sat down. When she got home, she wrote me to say how significant my words had been for her. Hearing me say "just do it" right then had been a magical moment for her. It was the push she needed to move toward her destiny. Today she designs and conducts personal development workshops for women.

Recently this woman "Anne" sent me a long, reflective e-mail to tell me how happy she is to be doing her life's work and about the great response she is getting from her workshop participants. To my surprise, Anne still focused on that moment when she heard me say "just do it" in front of two hundred people. That was the moment she decided to be a brave heart and take the step. Sometimes we make crossing our bridge so difficult for ourselves. We think there is some complicated magical code that would make things a lot easier, if only we could crack it. The truth is that the magic is in you. All you need is a little push.

Make a list of what you want to do. Then ask yourself, "How can I break it down into small steps so I can begin taking action?" Action will empower you. It will grow your self-esteem. It will grow your faith. Action breeds courage and courage helps you take more action. What small step can you take? Keep your eyes, ears and heart open. I *en-courage* you to keep planting seeds – read, listen and learn. Stay alert to synchronicities. They are the language of your Spirit guides and your higher Self. Don't let anyone tell you there is only one path to your calling. Even if your calling is the same as a friend's, your path to it will be different. Honor your unique-ness. Do not get hung up on having the right skills, credentials, degrees or diplomas. If your soul is calling you to something, then you already have a natural talent for it. "Follow your heart and do not be afraid," advises Brian Weiss in *Messages from the Masters*.[3] Believe in your cause, but most impor-tantly, *just do it!* The rest will take care of itself.

CARPE DIEM

You are so afraid to live – so afraid of life itself –
that you've given up the very nature of your being in trade for security.
– NEALE DONALD WALSCH

One of the most time-honored expressions is *carpe diem*, which is Latin for "seize the day!" This is another way of saying "just do it." Seize the day, the hour, the moment. Do it now! Activate your warrior energy, the fire within your heart – and do it today. Don't wait until tomorrow because tomorrow might never come. Life has a way of accelerating as we get older. The days get shorter and the list of promises to ourselves gets longer. Stop postponing your life. Put the excuses aside.

Pause. Now take a deep breath. Close your eyes. Ask your higher Self, "What do you want to do this very moment, right now?" What is your first thought? Do you want to nap on a blanket under a tree? Do you want to call your friend who lives three time zones away? Do you want to go for a bike ride? Do you want to walk into your boss's office and tell him what you really think? Do you want to sip on a glass of cool lemonade and swing in a hammock?

What is enticing your Spirit? Your higher Self is offering you ideas all the time. But if you don't listen or never act on them, the ideas stop coming. Say no to the "hurry disease." Take a pause and live right now. What must you do to seize the day?

COMPLETE YOUR UNDONES

We each have a finite number of heartbeats, a finite amount of time. But we have enough heartbeats and enough time to do what is important to our lives.

– SUSAN L. TAYLOR

Undones are signals from your higher Self that you have unfinished business begging for completion. You know it's an undone because when you think of it, it saps your energy. Undones are mental nags. They remind you that you have broken agreements with yourself. They rob you of your self-respect. They deplete you of creativity. They drain you of joy.

Completing them brings internal peace and personal effective-ness.

Undones can be unresolved conflict, withheld forgiveness, unspoken love, ungiven appreciation, dreams never carried through, goals not met, promises not kept and tasks not finished. Do you have any of those? Undones come in all shapes and sizes and in every area of life. Some people have a whole basement full of undones. What are yours?

Relationship Undones

This is the biggest category of undones for most people. Do you have an unresolved conflict with anyone? Almost every-one I know has unfinished business with someone else: an argument that never got settled, a rumor that was never quashed, a conversation that we were too scared to have. Time passes. Life moves on, but the blocked energy remains. I once heard that if the end of the world were suddenly announced and we all had five minutes left, everyone everywhere would get on the telephone to say three important words to someone. Have you guessed what they might be? " I love you"; "I am sorry"; "I forgive you." Does anyone in your life need to hear those words? Do you need to write someone a thank-you note, show appreciation, celebrate someone's birthday? Do it now, while it's fresh in your mind.

Make a list of the people with whom you have some unre-solved issue. They can be living or dead. Then for each of them ask yourself what it would take for you to have a clean slate with that person. What healing do you need in order to cleanse yourself of the negative emotion surrounding that person? Maybe you need to have a conversation. Maybe you need to apologize. Maybe you need to let them know you've forgiven them. Maybe you just need to let go. (See Chapter 7 for additional help with this.)

When you think of your family, what's missing? What robs you of energy? A parent's death? A child's illness? A messy divorce? A love affair that had to end? What are your regrets? Have you lost touch with family? Are there family members in different countries that you would like to meet? Is your undone a family reunion that you keep talking about but never organize? Is there something you've always wanted to do with your family but haven't yet done? Perhaps it's the trip to Europe or the visit to Florida to see Mickey Mouse. Do you have practical undones, such as no will or life insurance?

Career Undones

Ask yourself whether you like your work or pine for a more rewarding career. Do you have some dream or goal that you have been too scared to think about? What did you want to be when you grew up? What was your fantasy career? Did it come true? It's never too late. I know people who started new careers in their forties and fifties and who are very happy. The average person today will experience at least seven career changes. Are you ready for a change? Perhaps you don't have the necessary skills or experience. Are you developing your talents? Are you learning new things? Perhaps you like your work but feel burned out. Maybe you need a sabbatical. Perhaps you like your work but you want to break out on your own so you can have greater flexibility and control. Our work is more than our livelihood. It's a way to connect to purpose. It's a way to share our gifts so we can make a difference. It's important that we feel good about it.

Financial Undones

When it comes to investments and finances, what are your undones? Do you save? Do you pay your debts on time? Are you planning for your retirement or your children's education fund? Are you saving for your dream house, a trip around the world, a sports car, a summer home? What financial undones do you have?

Physical Undones

We could all be taking better care of our health. When it comes to your physical health, what do you need to do? Quit smoking, start exercising, stop drinking, avoid fats, slow down, sleep more, take vitamins, run a marathon? What sports or activities would you like to try? Recently, I learned to downhill ski again after being away from the sport for many years. It is an exhilarating feeling to come down the hill at fast speeds. Taking up skiing has given me a renewed appreciation for the winter season as well as helped me stay active. What sport or leisure activity would you like to revisit?

Spiritual Undones

Do you tell the truth? Do your actions match your ethics? Do you keep your agreements and promises? Can others trust you? Do you pass on important information? Are you connected to your Creator and do you give thanks? Do you spend some time alone each day to reflect and pause? Do you meditate or pray? Did you always want to visit the Holy Land or some important religious shrine? Ask your soul, "What do you need?" To paint, to write poetry, to learn to sing? Spiritual undones are subtle, but they come from our deepest longings.

LEARNING TO LET GO

Realize that not all undones have solutions. Sometimes we need to accept what we cannot control, let go and move on. It may be a relationship or a career or a dream. A woman in one of my workshops told me how hard she had tried to nurture a relationship with her alcoholic brother. Every time she visited him, his behavior was erratic, violent and unpredictable.

"I never knew when he was drinking," she said. "I learned that it was almost all the time." When he wouldn't get help, everyone else in the family gave up on him, but not her. She kept visiting him and trying to convince him to get help. One night during an argument he punched her in the face, breaking her nose and glasses. "That's when I decided," she said. "I had to let go. He was one undone that had to be left alone!"

So many of us have trouble letting go. Monkeys in India are free to roam around in urban areas. In New Delhi I witnessed an interesting method for capturing monkeys in public places. Trappers would put bamboo cages filled with tiny bananas in a public square, then back off and wait. The monkeys would see the bright yellow bananas and eventually get close to the cage. One or two would stick their hands between the bamboo slats and grab hold of a banana. I learned that once a monkey has a banana in his hand, it won't let go for anything. So imagine this monkey holding on to his banana, but it seems to be attached to this cumbersome cage. He gets upset. He wants his banana, not the cage! He starts jumping up and down, all the while making a huge ruckus because he can't free himself of the cage. All he has to do is let go of the banana and he'll be free. But he doesn't – won't – can't. And so the trapper comes back and takes him away, banana, cage and all.

What are you holding on to so tightly that if you could only let go of it, you would free yourself? While most undones have solutions, there are some that we need to walk away from. What do you need to walk away from? What is robbing you of happiness and peace of mind? When I used to counsel couples who were at loggerheads over an issue, I'd tell them, "You can be right or you can be happy. You choose." What about you? You can hold on or set yourself free. You choose.

EXCUSES WE USE

When we talk of undones, excuses immediately come to mind. Think about your excuses. Here are some of the most common ones:

I don't have time.

Let's say you will live to be eighty. That means you've got 960 months, 4,160 weeks, 29,200 days or 700,800 hours. If you're forty, you've got 480 months, 2,080 weeks, 14,600 days or 350,400 hours left – that is, if you don't get hit by a truck. What you do with this time is your choice. Be proactive. You decide; don't let others decide for you. Do what matters most to you. Make every day count.

It's not my fault.

Or "I had no choice" or "It's not my responsibility." When we blame others, we give away our power. We are victims. Studies show that only three percent of prison inmates admit accountability for the choices they made that landed them in jail. Some of them, when asked why they are in jail, will answer, "Because my buddy screwed up and I got caught."

I keep forgetting.

A variation of this excuse is "I'll put it off and maybe it'll go away." People who use these excuses are the procrastinators. They need to learn how to activate their action buttons. They need to put the excuses aside and just do it.

No one told me.

Or "I didn't have any information" or "I wasn't aware." This is the immature response. When you're a child, you can legitimately use this excuse, but for an adult it won't wash. Get informed. Find out what you need to know and then do it. Take responsibility for your life.

That's the way I am.

In other words, "I'll never change." These people are choosing to remain closed and ignorant. They are suggesting that they are already complete and that if anyone needs to change, it's the other party. This is Ego speaking, and when your Ego speaks, your undones will stay undone. There is no resolution, no healing. Stay open. Entertain the possibility of another way. As a workshop participant once said to me, "Either you're green and growing or ripe and rotten."

Examine these excuses and be honest with yourself. Which ones do you use, and why? You can start tackling some of your undones right now if you're willing to let go of your excuses. We take our lives for granted. We postpone and postpone, thinking we have all the time in the world.

A police officer in my parents' hometown was out doing his job on the last day before his retirement. He had been on the force for thirty years, and he and his wife were now going to take it easy. They were going to do so many things, like take that trip to Fiji that he had always dreamed of. He had pulled over a vehicle with an expired license plate and was standing at the side of the road waiting for the driver to get out his papers, when a passing tractor-trailer struck him down. He died in the hospital three hours later. We never know when our time will be up.

TAKING RISKS: BEYOND THE COMFORT ZONE

Why are you afraid to take reasonable risks? Are you afraid of your reputation, afraid of what others think? Ask yourself these questions: What's to lose? What is the worst that can happen? Am I content to live the rest of my life this way? Against a background of death, is this so risky?

— BRIAN WEISS

In October 1994, the Scandinavian ferry *Estonia* sank off the coast of Sweden. A violent storm had created an imbalance in its load. The vehicles that had been lined up in neat rows were thrown to one side, making the ship lopsided. It didn't take long for water to pour in and start pulling the vessel down. The crew knew they were in trouble. They told the passengers that each of them had a choice to make and they had to do it fast. The choice was to jump into a tiny boat and hope to be rescued or to stay on board and risk sinking. There were a thousand people on board. Most of them looked at the choices and opted for the comfortable, dry surroundings they were in. A hundred people had the courage to jump into the unknown, into the raging storm. The ride was rough, but they held on and were eventually rescued. They took the risk and pushed beyond their fear and their comfort zone, and those hundred brave hearts are alive today. The rest of them – the nine hundred who stayed on board – went down with the ship.

You have a choice to make: Do you stretch yourself beyond your comfort zone or do you stay comfortable but stuck? Do you take risks and grow or settle for less? You have probably been told that even leaving your house is a risk these days. So is getting on a plane or behind the wheel, and yet we do it. What are some other risks? Speaking your mind even if it means contradicting someone else, leaving an abusive relationship, saying no, changing jobs or moving away. Risk is relative. What is risky for you may not be for me, and vice versa. Think about what risk means to you and what risks you would consider taking.

I have noticed that, for some people, all they have to do is take a risk and their bridge magically appears. Taking risks gives them the faith they need to believe in themselves and to go after whatever it is they want.

Risks must be taken if we want to live fully and participate in this miracle called life. I have been sharing the following poem with audiences for a long time. It paints a disturbing picture of a person who won't take any risks.

To laugh is to risk appearing the fool.

To weep is to risk appearing sentimental.

To reach out for another is to risk involvement.

To expose feelings is to risk exposing our true selves.

To place your ideas, your dreams before the crowd is to risk
   loss.

To love is to risk not being loved in return.

To live is to risk dying.

To hope is to risk despair.

But risks must be taken because the greatest hazard
   in life is to risk nothing.

The person who risks nothing, does nothing, has nothing, is
   nothing.

He may avoid suffering and sorrow, but he simply cannot
learn, change, feel, grow, love, live.

Chained by his attitude, he is a slave. He has forfeited
   freedom.

Only the person who risks is free.

– Anonymous

The paradox is this: All change is uncomfortable, but all growth requires change. In order to grow, therefore, you must get outside your comfort zone. You must do something different, try something new, activate your action button with courage. Gandhi said, "Be the change you want to see in the world." In other words, lead! Go first. Be an example. Take action. But how can we do this when so many of us are plagued by our past failures?

STUMBLE FORWARD

It is by going down into the abyss that we recover the treasures of life. Where you stumble, there lies your treasure. The very cave you are afraid to enter turns out to be the source of what you are looking for.

- JOSEPH CAMPBELL

The older I get, the more I realize that life is a series of steps – two steps forward, one step back – and that's okay. When we're young we're impatient for success and unrealistically think that our progress will be one line going straight up. When we experience setbacks, we become upset and give up. Brave hearts know that failure is part of life, that failure is our ally. Brave hearts learn from failure.

I remember how devastated I was when I learned that I got fifty percent on a calculus exam back in university. It was a pass, but for me it might as well have been zero percent. How could I have failed so miserably? I remember the shame and humiliation I felt. I went to the lake, sat on my favorite rock and cried my eyes out.

I had stumbled, but it wasn't forward. It took me a long time to see the value of my failure because it shook my confidence. Stumbling forward would have meant realizing that I had other academic strengths and that I didn't need calculus to fulfill my purpose on earth.

There will be times in your life when you will stumble, experience a setback, lose your job or fail miserably at a relationship. Instead of feeling bad and becoming depressed, stumble forward. Use the failure as information. Let it grow your soul. Don't let it rob you of confidence and stop you from taking risks. Let it guide you to define and refine who you are and what your mission is. Since birth we have been programmed for success. We see failure as a bad thing, something to be ashamed of. (Maybe that explains why some students would rather jump off a ten-story building than go home with their mid-term marks.) Yet failure is part of life. It's not the failure that holds you back, it's your attitude to the failure. How do you react when you stumble? If you learn from it, then you are still moving forward. If you don't learn from it, then it robs you of confidence and energy and you stay stuck.

I like the message in Paul Ferrini's *Love Without Conditions*: "This world is a school and you have come here to learn. Learning means making mistakes and correcting them. Learning does not mean being right all the time."[4] Mistakes are opportunities to redirect the ship of your life. When you stumble and things don't go your way, think of it as receiving a correction from the divine Mind. "The perception that you are being attacked or punished when things do not go your way is entirely guilt driven," says Ferrini. "Without that guilt, the correction would be received with gratitude. . . ."[5]

In Chapter 7 I talk about the "dark nights of the soul," periods in our lives when we find ourselves in the valley of darkness feeling alone and depressed. Failure can take you there. But this period of trial can be a sort of chicken pox for the soul. Just as childhood diseases like chicken pox are necessary to strengthen the immune system, so experiencing failure and the dark nights of the soul are necessary to strengthen your character, commitment and drive.

SPEAK UP

... the Nazis first came for the communists, and I did not speak up ... then
they came for the Jews, and I did not speak up ... then they came for the
trade unionists, and I did not speak up ... then they came for the Catholics,
and I did not speak up ... then they came for me ...
and by that time, there was no one left to say anything.

– MARTIN NIEMOELLER

So many of us have been taught to mind our own business, to not rock the boat, to say nothing. That's one of the reasons why six million Jews lost their lives. We walk past injustice, closing our eyes to cruelty, to homelessness, to despair. It's not that we don't care. It's just that our fear prevents us from doing what's right. Doing the right thing starts with speaking up!

A client I'll call "Wayne" was depressed. Six months ago, he had an emotional breakdown at work. He started crying and just couldn't stop. His sadness was overwhelming. Since then he's been on antidepressants and is slowly crawling out of his hole.

One morning he called me; he'd had a setback. Wayne is the youngest of five children. His mother had suffered a stroke and he and his siblings rushed to the hospital. The family prayed together in the chapel. Wayne said it felt good to have all of them together, talking about childhood memories. "I was really strong for everyone, especially for my sisters." But as the days wore on and he was spending his days and nights at his mother's bedside, the stress began to get to him. He couldn't sleep. He could feel himself slipping away.

"I feel like I'm going to lose it again," he said to me. After calming him down, I found out that, besides the lack of sleep and anxiety about his mother, two key events had robbed him of his self-respect.

145

One had happened at the hospital when his sister's know-it-all boyfriend criticized Wayne's family for not having put their mother in a nursing home. Wayne was terribly disturbed by this attack and the effect it had on everybody. He said nothing, but when he left the hospital, he was angry and shaking.

The second event happened the next morning when he told his wife he didn't feel like going to work. Expecting her understanding and support, he was shocked to hear her say, "Well, I hope you're not going to take any more time off." Again, he went silent.

Wayne hates conflict, and he's not alone. Many of us have been brought up to think of conflict as a bad thing. We try to avoid it if possible and then pay big bucks to intermediaries to solve the conflict for us. When I ask audiences in workshops to write down three undones, unresolved conflicts are always number one on the list. We're programmed from an early age: "Don't make a scene"; "Be nice"; "Don't say anything." All this programming has collectively muzzled us. We shut up, put up, keep quiet, give in and swallow our truth – and slowly, slowly we say goodbye to our self-respect.

It takes courage to speak up. Depending on how much self-confidence we have at any one time, many of us are not prepared to take the risk. "If I tell my boss what I truly think, I may be out of a job." "If I speak up at this family gathering, then everybody will be upset." "If I tell my friend what I think, maybe she won't like me anymore or she'll judge me unfairly." Sometimes, when there are intense emotions, it's okay to take a time-out and say nothing. It's okay to postpone speaking up, but not for long! The rule is seven days – if you don't address the conflict by then, chances are you never will. Sure, there are times we let things slide or turn a blind eye, and that's okay. But if it becomes a habit and you're consistently silent while inside you're screaming, then you need to pay attention.

Using our voices and speaking up is our birthright, but it is risky. If we don't risk it, though, we stay victimized. I don't have a large build, but I have always been able to use my voice to protect myself and those I love. When I was a kid, I used my voice to rescue my younger brother from bullies. John, who is three years younger than me, had a lisp, wore thick glasses and walked pigeon-toed. He was an easy target for abuse. I was smaller than the bullies and some of them were older than me, but the fury in my voice scared them away. They knew better than to mess with big sister.

Many people in my workshops tell me they're too afraid to speak up at work. You've probably seen this scenario. No one speaks up at general meetings, but afterwards in the halls, the bathrooms and the cafeteria, everyone has an opinion. You don't have to scream and shout. Be assertive, not aggressive. Assertive people are tough on issues but soft on people. They're not belligerent or rude, but they do ask to be heard.

Words can be powerful, but it's how you use them that's important. It's your tone of voice and your mannerisms. If you open your mouth but sound tentative, people will not listen to you. Act confident. Practise speaking up with a friend or in front of a mirror if you have to. Is there someone in your life you need to exchange words with? When we don't speak up, we lose self-respect and we also lose our nerve. It happens little by little, like a drip on a rock, eventually eroding who we are and what we stand for. Inevitably we end up paying a price. Depending on your chemistry, your unspoken truth will go to either your reservoir of anger or your reservoir of sadness. If it goes to your reservoir of anger, then eventually it will get full, and you'll explode. If it goes to your reservoir of sadness, you will shut down and eventually become depressed.

That's what happened with Wayne. We are complex, inter-connected, spiritual beings. When we swallow our truth and keep our thoughts and feelings to ourselves, we are denying a part of who we are. We push our authentic Self further and further away until we no longer know who we are. It's no wonder that so many adults in mid-life have an identity crisis. Remember Eleanor Roosevelt's empowering message: "No one can make you feel inferior without your consent." Speak up. Try it once and notice the difference. That will give you the confidence to do it again. Exercise your voice. Feel the fear, but open your mouth anyway.

PLAY THE GAME OFFENSIVELY

I've missed more than 9,000 shots in my career. I've lost almost 300 games. Twenty-six times I've been trusted to take the game winning shot and missed. I've failed over and over and over again in my life. And that is why I succeed.

– MICHAEL JORDAN

My son Jasper plays soccer. I asked his coach one season if he could try playing forward. He had scored a goal and talked about wanting to try a different position besides defense. His coach wasn't very receptive to the idea because, he told me, "I need Jasper mid-field. He doesn't let anything get by." While that was a nice compliment, I thought it odd that the coach's primary concern was protecting the net rather than scoring goals.

It occurred to me that there are people who play the game of life that way. If you play defensively, you're motivated by fear – fear that someone else might get the job, someone else might beat you to the punch, someone else might be better than you – so you're constantly on the alert and worried that someone might take something away. Consequently you pour all your resources into defending your net and waiting for the action to come to you. People like that never take risks because they're too focused on protecting their net. They never get past mid-field.

If, on the other hand, you play the game of life offensively, you go for the ball. You lead, you take risks. You're a brave heart. You're not afraid to take the ball and run with it. That doesn't mean that you never act defensively and it doesn't mean that you win all the time, it just means that you pour more energy into taking shots on goal than defending your net. The Brazilian soccer team plays that way. They're passionate and fearless. They go for the net. They don't always win, but they play the most exciting, entertaining soccer, and to me that's what it's all about. All of us need to be playing an exciting game of life. How about you? Do you play life offensively or defensively? Are you passionate about scoring goals or intent on protecting your net? Every day you have a choice as to how you will play in the arena of life. You can play it safe or you can take a risk.

CHALLENGE YOUR MENTAL MAPS

Each of us tends to think we see things as they are, that we are objective. But this is not the case. We see the world, not as it is, but as we are – or as we are conditioned to see it.

– STEPHEN COVEY

I had just boarded an airplane when I noticed a man in first class who had pinned his silk tie to his shirt with those huge safety pins you use for diapers. The tie was all bunched up and it looked ridiculous. Confused, I scanned his face. "Is he one of those idiot savant types who can multiply ten-digit numbers in his head but not dress himself?" I wondered. "Why didn't anyone check him out before he left the house this morning? Here he is traveling out of town in first class, looking like that. Poor man." I looked around to see if anyone else had noticed him, but people seemed indifferent. "Too polite, or too stressed out," I thought, and then as I moved up a few paces, I experienced a paradigm shift. The man's tie was holding up his arm, which was in a cast. I hadn't been able to see the full picture from where I had been standing before. I felt silly, but the incident made me think about how often we argue for our point of view when we don't have all the facts. Sometimes all we have to do is move up and look a little closer and a different truth will be revealed to us.

Our core beliefs or thoughts form a screen through which we experience the world. These are our mental maps, our filters or paradigms. We don't usually allow information that is inconsistent with our beliefs to seep through our filters. Thomas Kuhn found this to be the case even with scientists. In his book *The Structure of Scientific Revolutions*, Kuhn argued that only data that agree with the scientist's paradigms – that is, his world view – are allowed to filter through. In order for us to grow, we must be open to seeing the world differently. We must try on a different pair of glasses. When we do this, we experience an *aha!* – a moment of illumination or a paradigm shift.

Moments of illumination will not come if we are arrogant or too certain about our beliefs. Certainty keeps us locked into old paradigms. Where would we be today without discoveries and inventions such as electricity, the theory of relativity, airplanes, radio and the microchip? It takes courage to challenge our mental maps, to see the world from a different angle, to take off our blinders. Creativity happens when we can step beyond the norm and ask a different question. But to do this we need to be brave hearts. Perhaps we need to step outside our heads and see with the eyes of the heart. What area of your life needs a shake?

A few years ago I hired a young woman to help me with administration. Lori was also working at another part-time job, as well as taking evening courses. Her days were full, yet every time she met one of her relatives, she'd walk away feeling "less than" because she did not have that much sought after full-time permanent job. "What if you told them you're a consultant?" I suggested to her one day. "And that you already have two major clients!" Her eyes lit up. "I'll try it," she said. Her relatives were impressed and Lori walked away feeling empowered and in charge of her destiny. And all she had done was challenge her own mental map of how she earned a living, by reinterpreting her work experience.

To be able to challenge our mental maps, we need to become aware of the way we perceive the world. What perspective do we come from? My grandmother, whom I called "Nonna," lived in a small town in southern Italy for most of her life. She didn't do much traveling because she never left the side of her handicapped daughter, Barbarella. You can imagine the excitement when her son, my Uncle Jimmy, who was visiting from Australia, proposed that they go to Foggia to visit the shrine of the Madonna. In the car on the way home, Nonna gazed at the beautiful sunset and became pensive. Foggia was less than two hours by car from her home, but she turned to Uncle Jimmy and said, "*Mamma mia, come e grande questo mondo*," which means, "Oh my gosh, this world is so big!" It was an innocent remark from a woman who had led a simple life, but it charged up my uncle. "What would you think of the world if you had spent thirty-five hours on a plane?" he asked her. How is it that two people can share an experience yet feel such different things? It's because, as the Talmud says, "We do not see the world as it is; we see the world as we are."

In *Everyday Soul: Awakening the Spirit in Daily Life*, Bradford Keeney talks about an experiment carried out by the biologist John Lilly. Lilly recorded the word "cogitate" on a tape over and over again. Later, when people listened to the tape, they heard over two thousand different words and word combinations, for example, agitate, arbitrate, candidate, computate, stop the tape, can't you stay, conscious state, count to ten, cut a steak, got a date, got to take, gurgitate, marmalade, etc., etc. What you hear depends on who you are and what mental maps you have. Keeney writes, "Life itself is like an endless tape that repeats the same sound. What we hear, see, and feel are therefore statements about our participation in life rather than any objective representation of what is really happening to us."[6]

There's a story I love about a young man driving down a country road. He's got the top down on his convertible, the sun is shining and he's enjoying all the wonderful twists and turns in the road. Suddenly another car comes careening around the bend and nearly hits him. As it passes him, the driver sticks her head out the window and yells, "Pig!" Indignant, the young man thinks, "How dare she call me a pig? She's the one who can't drive." He accelerates around the bend and runs straight into the pig.

Sometimes we think the world is one way when it's not. Then the truth slaps us in the face and we must relinquish old paradigms. But that's how we grow; that's how we shed our old skin and make way for the new. What area of your life needs to be perceived differently? Who has been yelling "pig" at you? What possibilities and opportunities have been wait-ing for you to see them? Which mental maps have been preventing you from crossing your bridge?

ACT AS IF YOU KNOW

Act as if you are and you will draw it to you.
What you act as if you are you become.
– NEALE DONALD WALSCH

At a workshop I once attended, the instructor used the princi-ple of "act as if you know" when people got stuck and asked him for answers. He was teaching a visualization technique that involved imagining your future. A few people felt they couldn't do that and so, frustrated, they asked the instructor for the right answer. He very calmly asked them one by one, "Well, what do you think?"

The reply would come, "I don't know. That's why I'm asking you."

And he'd say, "Well, I know you don't know, but if you *did* know, what would the answer be?"

Instantly, they'd have an answer.

"Well, that's your answer then," he'd say, and then he'd move on to the next person.

As soon as each person experienced this amazing shift, they would sit back and grin. "Hey," they seemed to be saying, "I did have the answer."

When the light bulb went on for others, their faces would flush with embarrassment, as if to say, "That's it? It's that simple?"

It was absolutely magical to watch. We all have the answers deep inside us, but sometimes we need someone skilled to pull them out. Throughout the weekend, any time someone got stuck, he'd use the same technique:

"I know you don't know, but if you *did* know, what would the answer be?"

Brilliant. It got so that as soon as a question was asked, the rest of us would start to recite, "I know you don't know, but. . . . " By the end of the weekend, we realized that there was no such thing as not knowing who we were. If we had forgotten, we just had to be reminded. The truth is always there inside of us.

The Greek philosopher Plato wrote about this nearly two thousand years ago. His theory was that all knowledge is remembered – that knowledge precedes experience and that everything we seek to know is already within us. Modern-day philosophers are saying the same thing. Go within, find your authentic Self, tap into your inner wisdom, listen to your higher Self.

The next time you're faced with a difficult decision or uncertainty, act as if you already know. This is another way to activate your action button or give yourself the courage you need to take action. Ask yourself,

> I know I don't know what to do in this situation, but if I did know, what would I do?
> I know I don't know what to say, but if I did know, what would I say?
> I know I don't have an answer, but if I did have the answer, what would it be?

This is a very powerful technique for getting in touch with your intuition, your sacred Self and your higher wisdom.

Another way to take action, even when you feel afraid and

unsure of yourself, is to act as if you belong. I was fresh out of school and looking for work, and I knew that no one at the Canadian Broadcasting Corporation was hiring because of a recent, much publicized hiring freeze. I knew that if I was going to get into the celebrated CBC, I would need to make an impression. So I turned up in my best suit, straightened my back and walked in past the parking attendants and the security guards, up the elevator, past the receptionist and right into the office of the executive producer of CBC TV News. No one challenged me. No one asked for my ID. I just walked in. The executive producer was awestruck. Several times he asked me how I had managed to get into his office.

"I don't know, I just walked in," I replied.

He shook his head in disbelief. "But you don't have any ID. How did you get past security?"

I shrugged. "I just walked in," I said.

He told me that without any broadcasting experience I would find television too difficult a medium. "Learn radio first. In a few years you can try TV." He was so impressed by my nerve that he sent me to his colleague at CBC Radio News. I got an entry-level position and stayed with CBC for five years, working as a reporter, editor and producer. I know that my foot in the door there was due to the fact that I had acted as if I already belonged.

To take that first step over your bridge you may need to act as if you know, act as if you belong or act as if you have already succeeded in crossing the bridge, even if you're scared to death on the inside. Remember to ask yourself, "What's the worst thing that could happen to me?" Naming your worst fear is often the first step in relinquishing its power over you. Whether it's starting your own business, quitting your job, going back to school or declaring your love, you must start taking action – whether the fear is in your knees, your chest or your stomach. If your faith is weak and you don't believe you can do it, *act* as if you can do it, and watch your faith grow. You might just surprise yourself.

DON'T BE ATTACHED TO OUTCOME

Instead of worrying about specific outcomes and results, just do the right thing.
- BRIAN WEISS

Anthropologist Angeles Arrien, in her *Four-Fold Way*, cites four principles for living: (1) show up, (2) pay attention, (3) tell the truth and (4) don't be attached to outcome.[7] Although all four principles are challenging, I have discovered that most people find the fourth principle the most difficult.

As humans, one of our greatest faults is our overwhelming need to know the outcome. We are preoccupied with end results and this preoccupation creates much of our malaise. Consequently many of us lead conditional lives. "I'll love you if you love me"; "I'll give you this if you give me that"; "I'll be happy if everything goes my way." So we stop loving, stop risking and stop living because we're too attached to the results. We have come to care more about the score than the game, more about the destination than the journey, more about the marks than the learning, more about the answer than the question. We need to take action because it's the right thing to do. We need to show our love to the world, give away our gifts, try new things, take risks and not worry about what others will think or say. Our actions can have both good and bad results, positive or negative outcomes. Attachment to the results can make us fearful, and fear prevents us from taking action, from walking across the bridge.

Imagine yourself vulnerable, soft and loving – and pouring out that love to someone who's ungrateful and callous. Perhaps you remember a time when you made a fuss over a friend's birthday and then they forgot yours. We've all suffered disappointments. Those disappointments fuel our inability to live Rule number 4. "Hope is fine," says Brian Weiss in his *Messages from the Masters.* "Expectation is not, because when expectation is present, disappointment is always lurking by."[8]

"Don't be attached to outcome" means "do it anyway." Show your love, try out for the team, apply for the job, start that business, change careers, travel to Africa, dream big – *live.*

In the previous section, I told you to act as if you are, to expect success and it will come to you. Now I'm telling you not to have any expectations. Let me explain. I think it's natural to have expectations, but too often we expect great things from others but not from ourselves. Expecting the bridge to be there when you cross it is an act of faith – faith in *your* abilities. Whether others give you something in return for what you've given them is out of your control. Don't set yourself up for disappointment. You can't control others, just yourself.

MAKE DECISIONS

Move in the wind. Your life is a dance.
Your choice is a simple one. You can dance or not.
– PAUL FERRINI

Are you one of those people who can't make decisions? The ones who sit on the fence and wait for someone to push them off? Making a decision is a courageous move. That's because you must take responsibility for your decisions, and often we are too immature to accept the consequences. But your soul wants you to make decisions, because when you choose to move in the wind, you are expressing who you are. Making decisions tells the world who you are. Do I live in the country or in the city? Do I drive or take transit? Do I paint my apartment teal or orange? Do I rent or own? We make decisions every day. Do I eat chicken or pasta? Do I stop for this amber light or drive through? To live from your authentic place, you need to embrace decision-making.

It's better to follow your own path, make a mistake and learn from it than to make no decision at all and coast, or worse, wait for someone else to decide your destiny. When you make decisions, you come face to face with fear. Regardless of the outcome or whether it's a good or bad decision, when we make a decision, we grow. We can never know the result of an exam before we take it, just as we can never know if a choice is right before it is made. That's why decisions can be risks. Sometimes we make simple decisions like "It's time to go to bed." That is not a risk. I'm talking about life decisions: Do I marry him? Do I leave this job? Do I speak my mind? Do I move to where my heart is calling me? Do I step across the bridge?

If we don't make the decisions that need to be made, we end up postponing our lives forever. We're just buying time. Have you heard these? "I'll do it when I get a job." "I'll do it after we have kids." "I'll do it when we move to our new house." "I'll do it when the kids grow up." "I'll do it when the kids move away." Et cetera. Get the picture? What's life without courage, growth, choice, even if that choice includes error? The path of life will have potholes, but so what? It doesn't prevent you from jumping over them. You may fall and skin your knees or your pride, but that's how we learn. That's the way it's always been. We get up and try again. We stumble forward. We must take that risk in order to participate fully in the human experience. I en-*courage* you not to wait for someone else to make your decisions. Be a brave heart and decide! Take the step across the bridge today.

A Few Helpful Exercises

Carpe Diem Exercise

If I were to ask you to complete the following sentence, how would you finish it? "If there were no obstacles in my life, some day I would . . . ." If there were no obstacles in your life (for example, if you had enough money, time and courage), what would you do? Then make a list of reasons why you have not seized the day yet. Look at those reasons. Are they really obstacles, or does your perception need to change? Choose one thing you'd like to focus on and then write an action plan (see the exercise on setting goals at the end of Chapter 3). In other words, ask yourself what action steps you need to take in order to make this happen. These adventures and dreams are waiting for you on the other side of the bridge. They are all possible. All you need to do is to seize the day and just do it!

Meditation on Fear

To help clients move beyond their fear, I use this exercise to make them aware of how fear may show up in their bodies and be preventing them from taking the step.

Get relaxed.

Standing indoors or out, focus on your breath. With each inhalation and exhalation, feel your body relaxing. Concentrate on your breath for a few minutes and feel your shoulders – your whole body, in fact – sinking deeper toward the ground.

Focus on a desire.

Close your eyes and think of something you want, something that is waiting for you on the other side of the bridge – your heart's desire. It can be a tangible goal or something internal, like feeling more confident or more courageous. Imagine your life with this desire fulfilled. What does it look like and feel like to have this desire fulfilled? Use all of your senses. Make it vivid and colorful.

Start moving.

Now open your eyes and pick a spot right in front of you at least ten feet away. It may be the trunk of a tree in your backyard or the door to your bathroom or the fireplace or the fence. Focus on this place and imagine that it represents what you want, the desire you have been concentrating on. Begin moving toward it, taking note of how your body is feeling. If fear comes up, name it and identify its location and how it is affecting you. Don't try to ignore it or push it away or pretend it doesn't exist. Befriend it. But keep moving your feet toward your desire. If you have to pause, that's okay, but don't rush. Just stay with what you are feeling. Keep the vision of your desire alive in your mind. This will allow you to keep moving despite the uncomfortable feelings you may be experiencing.

Ask, "Did Anyone Die?"

I recently reconnected with someone I hadn't seen in twenty-five years. Ellen and I were best friends in elementary school. She showed up at one of my lectures, which had been advertised in her city's newspaper. It was great to see her again. In a letter she wrote to me afterwards she told me that she and her husband had lost their first baby because it had a heart defect. The experience had changed them and helped them to prioritize what was most important in their life. Now when there are upsets in the family or one of them is having a personal crisis, they'll ask, "Did anyone die?" It helps them focus on the essentials.

I think we could all ask this question more often when the world is crumbling under our feet and we are gripped by fear. It's similar to that other great question, "What's the worst that can happen?" For most people, the worst that can happen is death, and death is rarely the outcome of so much that we fear. It's not death that prevents us from walking across the bridge, it's fantasized events appearing real. Isn't that what the letters in f e a r represent? These questions – "Did anyone die?" and "What's the worst that can happen?" – express the sentiment that even though our fear appears to engulf us at times, it can be put into perspective. Fear may be the last frontier, but it doesn't have to run your life. To have courage is to have heart, to have hope and to move your life forward, despite the uncomfortable feelings.

PART 2

The Bridge Will Be There

The time will come
when, with elation,
you will greet yourself arriving
at your own door, in your own mirror,
and each will smile at the other's welcome,

and say, sit here. Eat.
You will love again the stranger who was your self.
Give wine. Give bread. Give back your heart
to itself, to the stranger who has loved you

all your life, whom you ignored
for another, who knows you by heart.
Take down the love letters from the bookshelf,

the photographs, the desperate notes,
peel your own image from the mirror.
Sit. Feast on your life.

Derek Walcott

6

Embrace Faith

THE WALNUT TREE

You don't find: diamonds in storerooms, sandal trees in rows,
lions in flocks, and holy men in herds.

— KABIR

"Why did you cut it down, Dad?" I asked my father the morning after he sawed down my mother's beloved walnut tree.

"Because it was dead," he replied, with a hint of anger.

"One branch was dead. Why would you cut the whole tree down? It was such a beautiful tree."

"Because in the Bible it says that a tree that produces no fruit should be cut down."

But the green branches he had secretly burned at the back of the farm had had walnuts on them.

"But Dad, Mom is so upset. She cried for hours last night. It was her father's tree. Her father's Spirit lives in that tree," I told him.

She had smuggled the seedling into Canada fifteen years earlier, on her last trip to Italy. It was the last thing she took from her parents' home, the place where she had been born, the site of so many sacred memories. Two days after burying her father, while the taxi was waiting to take her to the airport, she dug up the tiny seedling. Perhaps it was her way of taking one last memory, a tangible reminder of her father. The seedling not only survived a twelve-hour transatlantic journey, it thrived. It was my mother's pride and joy.

Over the years the tree produced bushels and bushels of walnuts and many seedlings of its own. During my many visits back home, Mom would always take me to the garden to show me more "walnut babies" hidden under foliage or vines. In fact, two other big trees — descendants of the original tree — were planted near the house. But the original tree was sacred to her. It came from Italian soil. It was the offspring of her father's tree, the tree she had climbed when she was a girl.

"Why would you kill something that is still alive?" I asked him, trying to understand. "You have twelve acres of land on this farm — why couldn't you just leave it alone? Besides, do you know what today is?"

He gave me a blank look.

"It's the fifteen-year anniversary of Nonno Emilio's death."

"I didn't know that," he responded sheepishly.

I thought, "Great, I'm finally getting through to him," but I was wrong.

His defenses went back up and once again he turned to the Bible.

"It says in the Bible that when people die, you've got to forget about them and focus on the living. Dust to dust, ashes to ashes."

"What about the Spirit?" I asked. "What about Mom's memories? The body is gone, but Nonno will be alive forever in her memories."

He paused and looked at me. I could detect no remorse, so I went in for the kill. "Is that how you want me to think of you when you're gone – forget about you completely? Have no memories of you?"

Dad had chainsawed Mom's tree while she was out visiting a neighbor. That night and the next morning we all tried to console her as she marked the anniversary of her father's death. My younger brother, Tony, went out to the back of the farm to rescue several living branches of the walnut tree before they were burned. "They can be rooted and planted," he told my mother optimistically in his attempt to comfort her. I loved him so much in that moment. We both understood her connection to her father.

RELIGIOUS FAITH VERSUS SPIRITUAL FAITH

> During these difficult times, the most revolutionary thing
> we can do is to have faith.
> – SUSAN L. TAYLOR

My father had never before been so rule-bound, so linear, so insensitive. His behavior seemed totally bizarre and out of character. He is a sweet man in many ways, with a generous heart. But he changed after he was baptized in his new faith a few years ago and programmed with *la verita* (the truth) – another example of how blind adherence to religious dogma shuts down compassion. Now he prays every day. He spends hours reading the Bible, morning and night. He knocks on people's doors on Saturday mornings and goes to prayer meetings three evenings a week and Sunday afternoons. He does all of this with the precision and commitment of a soldier. In many ways I admire his strong faith and commitment to his religion, but I can see the difference between the kind of faith my father espouses, which I call religious faith, and the spiritual faith that my mother has. One blindly adheres to the rules and regulations of organized religion, and the other comes from an authentic and individual relationship with God.

Religious faith teaches that there is only one path to God, but unfortunately every religion thinks it is the sole possessor of *la verita*. Spiritual faith, on the other hand, recognizes that there are many paths to God. Religious faith means that rules must be followed or entry to heaven will be denied. Spiritual faith teaches that once you have a relationship with the Divine within yourself, you promote the Divine in others; you show love, acceptance and goodwill to everyone you meet.

Religious faith is arrogant. Spiritual faith is humble. Religious faith doesn't accept other religions. Spiritual faith accepts other ways of knowing God. I believe that once you have God's love in your heart, your soul and your entire being, you will see everyone and everything with kindness and compassion.

My father's church elders have criticized my mother. Why won't she acknowledge *la verita*? Why won't she come out to meetings? My mother has always been a freethinker and she's not about to join "the sheep," as she calls them. Besides, she's got Barbarella to think about. For the past seventeen years, Mom has been taking care of her younger sister, who is mentally and physically disabled. Barbarella was two years old when she contracted spinal meningitis. Over the years her muscles have atrophied; today she lies in bed, a quadriplegic who is totally dependent on my mother. My mother practises what my father's friends only read about in the Bible.

Religious faith can be ardent, as it was for Abraham, who believed in God so much that he was prepared to sacrifice his only son. This is a burning love, a complete surrender to the Lord. It can also be fanatical, as it was for those hundreds of people who agreed to take poison because that's what their reli-

gious leader wanted. Religions can become dogmatic, intoler-
ant and ugly, and that's why they have turned off so many
people.

The problem with religion and the philosophy of "doing" is
that most people quit because they can never know when
they've done enough to please the Lord. Some feel guilty all
the time because they haven't measured up to the rules. Others
end up feeling not good enough to receive God's love.

Many in the West are attracted to Eastern religions because
they avoid the rule-making and dualistic thinking so funda-
mental to the Judeo-Christian tradition. Renowned world-reli-
gion scholar Huston Smith says his students are more
interested in spirituality than in religion, because religion is
institutionalized and authoritarian. Since 1970, the worldwide
population of Christians has grown by sixty percent, but
churches have lost twenty-five percent of their membership.[1]
In Britain and France less than ten percent of the population
goes to church at least once a month, and in Scandinavia, less
than three percent. In Amsterdam, beautiful, high-steepled
churches are being converted into luxury condos.[2] So the faithful have increased in number, but they're not going to church.
Where are they taking their faith?

Spirituality is the new religion. Spiritual faith is liberal. It
engages eclectic believers. People who are spiritual can take
what they want from Christianity, Jewish law, Buddhism and
New Age philosophy. I enjoy telling people that I belong to a
religion of one – my own.

I don't want to put all religions down. Some are more tolerant
than others. Some religions have been responsible for feeding
the poor, helping the sick and rebuilding shattered communities. Some religions contribute in positive ways. But in the past
twenty years many people have turned their back on organized

religions. A recent poll showed that while many people still believe in God and pray regularly, the majority of people do not belong to or practise a particular religion. That's because we have lost faith in institutionalized religion. We have become disillusioned.

A GENERATION OF WOUNDED BELIEVERS

I know many of my students are what I have come to think of as wounded
Christians or wounded Jews. What came through to them
was dogmatism and moralism, and it rubbed them the wrong way.

– HUSTON SMITH

I grew up as a wounded Christian. Sometimes I think of myself as religiously abused. Is there such a thing as religious abuse? My parents were born Roman Catholics, but from the time I was seven years old until I was twelve they were Jehovah's Witnesses. Since I was still going to a Catholic school, I was being indoctrinated with opposing "truths" about God, the devil, heaven and hell. My parents hired a Sunday school teacher, "Signora Maria," to tell me about Adam and Eve and the serpent and all the teachings of the Jehovah's Witnesses. I remember how disappointed I was when Signora Maria told me that only 144,000 people can go to heaven. I couldn't believe it. After all, my teacher at school had told me that we all go to heaven. But here it was in black and white in the Bible – only 144,000 spots, reserved for extra-special people. I figured that those spots would already be taken by the time it was my turn to die. I became fearful. Where would I go? Where would Mom and Dad and John and Tony go? Probably to hell, I thought.

During the week my schoolteacher taught us stories from

the Bible. When I detected inconsistencies, I brought them up with her. One day I heard her say that if we prayed and were good boys and girls, we would all go to heaven. I knew I had to set her straight.

"We're not going to heaven," I contradicted her. "There are only 144,000 spots in heaven, and they will all be gone by the time we die. I'm afraid we're all going to hell. You, too."

My teacher was so horrified that I thought she was going to send me straight to the principal's office. I had never seen her so upset. Instead, she took a deep breath and asked me where I had heard such a thing.

"My Sunday school teacher," I replied.

"Well, that's simply not true."

"But it's in the Bible, I swear. She even showed me. There are only 144,000 spots in heaven."

"Nothing like that is in the Bible, Gracie. You must not have heard correctly. If you're really convinced of it, show me. Here's the Bible; show me where that is written."

I was too innocent at that age to realize that there were different versions of the Bible – a Catholic version and a jw version. There I was in front of the whole class, flipping pages in the Bible, and desperately trying to find the reference. But I couldn't.

"Where did you read it, Gracie? In the Farmer's Almanac?" snickered someone in the class. I remember the loneliness I felt that day as I was going home on the bus. Who could I go to with this? My parents were too busy to care about such matters. I must have misunderstood Signora Maria. I'd clear it up that Sunday, I thought. My resolve seemed to calm the doubt that was slowly inching its way into my heart.

On Sunday I told Signora Maria what had happened, and she said she would convince me that she was right and my schoolteacher was wrong. She showed me the passage in the Bible again. When I asked why her Bible was different from the one at school, she told me hers was the true Bible, because it had been inspired by God. Who was I to believe? It was a time of confusion and frustration for a child who just wanted the adults to get their act together. Both religions were telling me that there was only one path to God. So both religions fuelled my doubt in God and, sadly, in myself.

Buddhist wisdom says that when you reach the other side of the river, you can discard the rowboat because it is no longer needed. I think religion ought to work like this, too. Religion acts as the rowboat; it's the tool. The "other side" is God. (I like the word "God," but you may be more comfortable using a different word. Whenever I use "God," please feel free to mentally replace it with a spiritual reference you feel comfortable using, for example, Universal Intelligence, Great Spirit, Holy Father, the Other, Holy Mother, Divine Wisdom, Holy Spirit, the Goddess, the Beloved.) Once you find God, you need to focus on God, and not on the rules of the religion. Many of us rejected faith when we rejected organized religion. I, for one, felt I had no right to have a relationship with God because I had turned my back on two religions. I had no rowboat. I was unaware that my spiritual faith was my ticket to God. I, like so many others, had confused religion with spirituality.

GOD IS DEAD

When Zarathustra was done, however, he said to his heart:
"Could this be possible! This old saint in the forest hath not yet
heard of it, that God is dead!"

— FRIEDRICH NIETZSCHE

I don't know when it was exactly that I decided there was no God, but I remember striking God's name out of my diary one day and replacing it with "Sam." I didn't know any Sam – I just liked the name. Writing comforted me. In between chores, I used to take my journal out back to the canal, where I would sit by the pier and write to Sam. How I yearned to understand the complexities of life. I couldn't wait to grow up, because I was convinced that then I would know the truth about everything.

My early teen years were difficult. When I lay in bed at night, a strange image would come into my mind. Some nights I couldn't sleep because the image wouldn't leave me alone. It was of a big fish eating a smaller fish, which was eating another, smaller fish, and so on. The fishes started out big and got smaller and smaller. The feeling associated with the image was that life had no meaning. Why were we all doing what we were doing? If there was only one God, then why so many religions? Why didn't anyone agree? I didn't trust adults. I realized they didn't know what the truth was.

In university I immersed myself in the world of ideas via my philosophy classes and I thrived. I felt I was beginning to scratch the surface of that big-fish-swallowing-the-little-fish scenario. And then I discovered Friedrich Nietzsche, a nineteenth-century German philosopher who had the courage to announce that God was dead and that we had killed him. He was a radical who wanted more to provoke serious thought than to offer formal answers to questions.

Nietzsche believed that we should approach each problem with an attitude of fresh experimentation. He was a brave thinker, passionate and iconoclastic, very much his own man. He hated the herd mentality and rejected the idea of an absolute moral code that everyone should obey. I felt a kinship with him, perhaps because he could articulate much of my religious angst. Perhaps it was because he too was a wounded Christian. Nevertheless, what Nietzsche said made sense to me. I looked around and saw proof that God was indeed dead.

God was dead, I thought, when Christians and Jews and Muslims and Hindus spilled blood in the name of God. God was dead when television evangelists demanded and received millions of dollars so they could increase their empires. God was dead when a lunatic convinced hundreds of people to swallow poison because it was supposed to be God's will. God is dead when the word of God keeps changing (in the past two centuries the Bible-publishing industry has churned out 2,500 English-language versions alone and generated $180 million in sales every year). God is dead when the self-righteous feel it's their duty to brainwash innocent minds. In our hypocrisy we have killed the essence of goodness, the Essence that is God. God is dead and we are responsible.

At twenty-two I became an atheist. It would be several years before faith would visit me again.

FAITH AS A MYSTERY

You know that if you get in the water and have nothing to hold on to, but try
to behave as you would on dry land, you will drown. But if,
on the other hand, you trust yourself to the water and let go,
you will float. And this is exactly the situation of faith.

– ALAN WATTS

My mother is an earth goddess. She grows herbs, veggies and fruit. She makes her own tomato sauce from organic tomatoes. She sows, harvests and preserves. She even makes her own cheese. She adds culture to milk, heats it gently and waits for it to coagulate. After she collects the semisolid curd, she uses the leftover whey to make fresh ricotta. This is the delicious soft cheese coveted by Italian pastry chefs. To collect ricotta, you add more milk to the whey, add some vinegar and heat. Then you wait.

Although it sounds simple, this is a delicate and unpredictable process; with each new batch, the ricotta collected can vary greatly. My mother's ricotta is always abundant, the fresh cheese multiplying at the top as if by magic. Her friends can't quite believe it. They attribute it to luck, better milk, a bigger pot, the humidity, a better cheese culture or whatever. I don't think it's any of those things. I think it's faith.

When the ricotta starts percolating up, my mother turns her total attention toward it. She blesses it, calling on the patron saints of abundance (usually Santo Martino). She closes her eyes, says a few *preghieras* (prayers) and lets her internal Light shine on it. That's why the cheese cooperates – it's rising up to greet her.

One day my mom's friend Paul came over. He owns a pastry shop and he wanted fresh ricotta for a big order of pastries and cakes. He had made cheese before, but never managed to collect much ricotta. Since ricotta is expensive, he decided he needed to learn her secret. I happened to be visiting that weekend when my mom and Paul were making cheese side by side in my parents' basement. Paul was using the same milk and the same heat source and he mimicked my mother's every move, but his pot produced half a bucket of ricotta while my mom's produced three! He couldn't believe it and started cursing his bad luck. It wasn't bad luck. It was his lack of faith.

My mom proved it. She shooed him away and turned to his pot of milk, closed her eyes and blessed it. Then she started saying the *preghieras* under her breath while Paul and I watched from a distance. Soon the milk started to respond. The cheese – which had refused to rise to the top for Paul – was saluting my mother, the goddess of ricotta. She collected an additional two buckets of the soft cheese from Paul's batch of milk. He shook his head in disbelief. "It's true what they say about you, Connie. You're a witch." Then he turned to me and said he wouldn't have believed it had he not seen it with his own eyes. "See, there's the problem," I thought to myself. "Mom's got faith. You don't."

Most people have only conditional faith. That is, they believe in God as long as everything is going well, but as soon as things get difficult they lose faith. One of the most inspirational poems on faith is "Footprints." The author, Margaret Fishback Powers, tells God that she has seen God's footprints beside hers through most of her life, but during a really rough patch there was only one set of prints. "How could you abandon me during my time of need?" asks the author. "Oh, my child," God replies, "I didn't abandon you. The reason you saw only one set of footprints during your difficult times was because those were the times I carried you." (You will find the complete poem in Chapter 10.)

My father showed me the certainty of his faith by refusing blood during a life-threatening pancreatic attack. We knew that his beliefs prevented him from accepting blood transfusions, but my family and I had always figured that when it really came down to it, he would choose to live. But we were wrong. We cried, we begged, but he did not waver. To me my father's faith resembled Abraham's. My father didn't sacrifice one of his children, but he put his own life on the line for his beliefs. Maybe his was a blind faith, but it was, nevertheless, solid. I've always admired that about him.

Faith is a mystery. Faith isn't found in books or arrived at by logical formulas. Faith is found in the heart. It's a feeling, not a knowing. The mind can't "hear" faith, just as the heart can't "hear" logic or reason. There is spiritual faith, like my mother's, and there is religious faith, like my father's. When self-doubt creeps in, faith washes it away. More than anything, having faith grows hope – hope for tomorrow, hope for ourselves and hope for the Love that holds our world together. Faith is not always consistent. It comes and goes like the tides, depending on the events in our lives. Faith is organic, fluid; it changes over time, and that's okay.

MY SPIRITUAL AWAKENING

It is as if God planted a great big kiss in the middle of our spirit and all the wounds, doubts and guilt feelings were all healed at the same moment. The experience of being loved by the ultimate Mystery banishes every fear. It convinces us that all the mistakes we have made and all the sins we have committed are completely forgiven and forgotten.

– FR. THOMAS KEATING

About a hundred of us were ready to experience the "Life-Purpose Guided Visualization Exercise." Our leader, Frank, told us to close our eyes. The room darkened and tranquil music began to play. We began to breathe deeply. "You're in a meadow with wild flowers," said Frank. "In the distance you see a mountain. Walk toward that mountain. At the base of the mountain you'll find a magic carpet, which will take you to the top. At the top of the mountain, there is a temple. . . ."

A white cathedral appeared. We were told to walk toward the source of the white light. White light? And then it appeared at the front, shining down on the altar. At first the "conscious me" thought, "I'm not going any further; I'm not comfortable with altars. What the hell am I doing here?" Then the "relaxed me" said, "Park the skepticism for once. Just go with it and see what happens."

The light was piercingly bright. As I looked up at it, our leader suggested that a being would emerge from this light. It could be our higher Self, an angel or some wise person. I waited for a while and nothing happened. I started to panic. "What if no one appears to me? What if I don't have a higher Self?"

"Park it," said my inner voice once again. I kept looking up, and then I saw it – a face, elusive, then just the eyes – but I couldn't quite make it out because there was mist and cloud.

And then it hit me. "Could this be God?" At that moment another face appeared through the mist, clearly this time. I knew that it was Jesus himself. "Jesus?" I thought. "I don't want Jesus! I want an angel."

For me the idea of Jesus conjured up images of bumper stickers that said "Honk if you love Jesus" or of television evangelists ordering me to touch the screen in the name of Jee-zus and send in my money. Jesus had become a symbol of the perversity and lack of spirituality of organized religions. He was also a reminder of my painful childhood. So no, I didn't want Jesus. "Please send me an angel," I thought, "or my higher Self, whatever that is – anything but Jesus." Sigh. Jesus wouldn't go away. Wearing a garment of white, he descended with his right arm stretched toward me. The image was something like Michelangelo's painting in the Sistine Chapel of God reaching to touch Adam's hand.

He was now about six feet in front of me. He was beautiful. His long, dark hair was parted in the middle and he had a beard. His eyes were piercing and knowing; they radiated so much love. He looked at me. He didn't speak, but he communicated with me in the most poignant way. I felt an overwhelming abundance of Love in his presence. He was sending me so much Love and healing Light that it was almost unbearable. I started to cry. They were real tears, tears that ran down my face like water from a faucet and drenched my lap. Then Jesus spoke, not with words, but telepathically, mind to mind.

"I know it's been hard for you to believe in me. It's okay. I love you. I have always loved you. I will always love you, my child."

Here I was at a self-esteem conference where we were learning to let go of the past and cherish and love ourselves. Yet nothing I had done that week could even come close to the love and acceptance I felt at that moment, standing before Jesus in my visualization. For the first time in my life, I was experiencing unconditional Love.

Frank then told us our guide would give us a gift that would give us insight into our purpose here on Earth. Right on cue, Jesus gave me a gold box. I lifted the lid and a white bird – perhaps a dove – flew out and up toward an opening in the cathedral's ceiling. A little disappointed, I looked questioningly into his eyes. He smiled at me and I got the message to look in the box again.

I found a beautiful crystal ball. It was almost the size of a baseball and fit perfectly into my hand. I rubbed it for a while and felt how smooth, cool and delightful it was. When I looked at it more closely, I saw that the compacted crystal, thousands of years old, reflected all the colors of the rainbow, like a beautiful cut diamond. I looked at Jesus and asked, "Why is this my gift? What does it have to do with my life's purpose?"

"You, my child, can see into people's souls," he said. "You understand people. You can help them heal in your own unique way."

I looked up at the bird that had flown out of the box.

"Yes, that's how you make people feel. Free, limitless, pure. You give people wings."

Again, that engulfing Love. Meanwhile, tears were still pouring down my face.

Then he added, "You will receive a sign in the next few days of your special gift and purpose."

A sign? What sort of sign? And as I was contemplating this, he started to disappear. "Oh, don't go," I begged him. "This feels so good to have you here with me. Please, don't go. I have so much more to ask you."

"I'm here any time you need me. I love you," he told me

again with a look of intense compassion and warmth. And with that, he vanished.

The music stopped, the lights came on and I opened my eyes. The visualization was over. My heart was beating rapidly, and when I looked down, I saw that my clothes were soaked with tears. Frank instructed us to draw what we had seen in our visualization. I spent some time drawing Jesus and the box and the white bird flying out. Already my heart was aching to be with him again. And then I realized that telling anyone else would weaken what I had just experienced. The holiest of experiences can seldom, if ever, be discussed. Perhaps they are holy because there are no words for them. Even Jesus hadn't used words with me, just telepathic feelings.

I got up and started to leave the room, when whom did I see in front of me but a Jesus look-alike. I had been attracted by this man's energy from the moment he had introduced himself to the group, and there he was again, looking just like the Jesus of my visualization: dark hair, beard, square jaw, kind eyes and wearing, of all things, "Jesus sandals"!

"Is this the sign?" I asked myself. The positive energy I felt from him was unbelievable. He smiled at me and said that from the look on my face, I must have experienced something holy. He knew. How could he have known? I hadn't planned on telling anyone, but I found myself opening my mouth. I told him I had seen Jesus and that I'd resisted him at first because of my upbringing and the religious fundamentalism associated with him. This Jesus look-alike – who was, of course, "Kris" – looked into my eyes and said the most amazing thing. "Imagine what Jesus must feel, knowing that all those people and religions have taken out a franchise on his name. Those religions are not what Jesus is about."

Sometimes you will hear something that you know was

meant just for you. I knew that Jesus was speaking through Kris at that moment. His words were liberating. I suddenly realized that what I had been running from all those years was not Jesus, but false and inadequate representations of him. Those false representations had hindered my ability to recognize him, to reach out to him, even to acknowledge him. What I had rejected for so many years – what I had hated, even – was not Jesus, but the trash and tinsel that passes for him.

I had experienced something profound. From then on my doubt began to heal. I began dropping the word "God" into my conversations without feeling uncomfortable. It was not only my visualization experience, but Kris's perspective as well that helped me awaken to the Divine within me.

(If you're wondering about the sign Jesus spoke about, I did receive it. During an emotionally intense exercise at the conference, a woman declared publicly that, of the 120 people she had met that week, she felt most understood by me. It was a beautiful exchange and a cherished moment – and further validation of my life purpose.)

BEYOND SECULAR FAITH

**Faith is potent stuff: It's a generator.
What we believe is the starting point of what we experience.**

– SUSAN L. TAYLOR

After making peace with God, I felt a greater sense of self-love, purpose and destiny. By connecting to the divine Light within me, I learned to truly love myself and my journey. I came to the conclusion that teaching people secular faith – that is, helping them find the confidence and faith in themselves and their abilities – cannot lead to true empowerment unless they go inwards and connect to their God Essence. That's because many of our problems stem not from a psychological root, but from a spiritual root. For years people have been sent to psychiatrists, psychologists and psychoanalysts to have their pathologies labeled and fixed. In all fairness, clinical psychology has tried to help, but it has missed the mark with many people. I think that's because the practice of psychology doesn't allow people the flexibility to discover their own spirituality and connect with God. Relying only on clinical methods of therapy strips us of the ability to discern what is truly sacred in our lives. We are mind, body, heart and Spirit, and secular faith ignores the fact that we are spiritual essences housed in physical bodies. To heal the mind, heart and body, we must also heal the Spirit. You can do this only by reconnecting to the part of you that is divine, that is spiritual, that is most like God.

"At the height of my career," writes Bradford Keeney, author of several classics in the field of family therapy, "I paradoxically began realizing that psychology could not offer the help people needed in their deepest moments of suffering. Its strategies for cure, though intelligent, were not rooted in what spiritual traditions have always known as the great healers: love and compassion."[3]

Keeney knows this from experience. He realized early that the only way to achieve peace within himself was to discover his own spiritual path. He learned his spiritual awareness not from a book, but by living with indigenous peoples of North and South America, as well as the Bushmen of the Kalahari. In his practice as well as in his writings, he acknowledges the Mystery by cultivating a connection to the Divine and appreciating the Sacred in everyday life. Keeney now practises what is called spiritual psychology.

In the book *We've Had a Hundred Years of Psychotherapy*

and the World Is Getting Worse, psychoanalyst James Hillman and newspaper columnist Michael Ventura discuss how psychotherapy needs to change. Hillman asks, "Could the thing we all believe in most – that psychology is the one good thing left in a hypocritical world – be not true? Psychology . . . could that be part of the disease, not part of the cure?"[4] Ventura replies, "There is so much . . . that the West in general and psychotherapy in particular has shunted aside because it simply hasn't had the conceptual framework to deal with it."[5]

Secular faith – the type we've been offering through psychological modalities – is not enough to fill the emptiness felt by many people who seek therapy. Secular faith might get you across the bridge, but it cannot give you lasting peace, joy and fulfillment. That happens when we reclaim our relationship with the Great Spirit that dwells inside each of us. True empowerment comes when we realize that we are not alone, that we've never been alone and that we will never ever be alone. When you can hear the Divine echo in your soul, you are empowered, because you know that you are a child of God. You belong to the human family.

Therapists have been shy of spirituality for various reasons. Some are not trained in the spiritual arena – they have no conceptual framework for Spirit. Some are wary of being perceived as evangelical, and others are simply ignorant of spiritual matters. For our times, traditional psychology has serious limitations. If we're going to help a generation of nonbelievers take the necessary action to heal, grow and contribute their gifts to the world, then we need more than the tools that psychology has given us. Corporate guru Ken Blanchard writes in *We Are the Beloved*, "In confronting my own spirituality, I began to sense that maybe the quickest and most powerful way to significantly enhance one's self-esteem and make ourselves more loving people is a spiritual awakening."[6] We need to embark on our own spiritual journey in order to connect to the necessary faith that will propel us across the bridge.

The field of spiritual psychology is quickly emerging to quench some of the thirst out there. But every day I meet spiritual warriors who are embarking on their own conscious paths, who strive to listen to their authentic voices and see others with the eyes of their souls, who look for meaning in every sacred moment and who cherish mindful and joyful exchanges with others.

This community of spiritual warriors is expanding around the world. They look for God continually and stay connected with each other through books, tapes and the World Wide Web. Together they are healing themselves and the planet.

LOOKING FOR GOD

Cleave a piece of wood, I am there;
lift up the stone, you will find me there.
– THOMAS 95:24

So how does one look for God? In the Sufi tradition there is a collection of teaching stories involving the fictional character Mulla Nasrudin. These stories often portray the Mulla as a fool, but upon deeper reflection he is seen to reveal great wisdom. In one such story, Nasrudin is searching the ground. A man walks by and sees him.

"What have you lost, Mulla?" the man asks.

"My key," says the Mulla. So they both get down on their hands and knees to look for it.

After a time, the man asks, "Where exactly did you drop it?"

"In my house," comes the reply.

"Then why are we looking out here?" the man asks, confused.

"Because there is more light here than inside my house."[7]

This story illustrates how we often look for the "key" in the wrong place. Most of the answers we seek are housed within us, not somewhere outside. We have all the wisdom and resources we need. We have God within us, but we just don't know it. Instead, we look for God outside ourselves because we're attracted by life's illusions, the tinsel. The days pass and we feel alone. We crave meaning; we hunger for spiritual answers but we don't get them. "When the river flows through your own yard, how can you die of thirst?" asks the fifteenth-century poet Kabir. Why do we continue to search for the key outside our house?

Our collective doubt and lack of faith mean that we have become spiritually bankrupt. Some of us want to get close to God and yet we don't know how. But when we realize that our salvation is assured, that there is nothing we need to do to be saved, then we can truly be ourselves. "You and I are nothing but saints in the making . . . there is no fall from Grace, only a very long furlough," says Deepak Chopra in his book *How to Know God*.[8] We are sparks from God's all-embracing flame. We are literally expressions of God – little bits of God pressed out into the world. So why do we keep looking for God and salvation outside ourselves? Because it's the way of the world. Because we're not connected to our own divinity.

So where is God? Does the Divine live in everything around us, or is it some separate entity? It would appear that the answer is "both." Many people get thrown off by this paradox and continue to search for God outside themselves. For too long we have thought ourselves unworthy to have God inside us. But the idea that God is in all things and that we are all One is part of many religions. In John 17:21, Jesus says, ". . . that all of them may be one, Father, just as you are in me, and I in you." This idea is even more emphatically expressed in the Christian Gnostic gospels recovered at Nag Hammadi in the desert of Upper Egypt.

God's Presence is everywhere. Stay open to the idea of a higher purpose, a higher plane, a possibility that there is something beyond the tangible and that this indefinable Presence is in constant communication with us. All we have to do is pay attention. "The words to the next song you hear . . . The story line of the next movie you watch. The chance utterance of the next person you meet. Or the whisper of the next river, the next ocean, the next breeze that caresses your ear – all these devices are Mine," God tells Neale Donald Walsch in *Conversations with God.*[9]

That's how God communicates with us. But we must listen and stay alert. When we have soul moments or angelic encounters or experience extraordinary examples of the sacred, God is making contact. Don't discount these experiences as everyday occurrences or mere coincidences. Stay alive to the Mystery. Be on the lookout for "God moments." They will infuse your soul with faith and Love and the feeling that you're not alone on this journey. In fact, you have never been alone.

KNOWING GOD

I didn't yet understand that God is always unknowable and that as we move closer to Him, God moves farther away, drawing us higher and higher as we seek and search and try to follow.

– ROBIN NORWOOD

One of the most spiritually liberating events of my life occurred when I learned about the secret Gospel of Thomas discovered in the cave at Nag Hammadi in the 1940s. The Gospel of Thomas was not included with the other gospels in the New Testament; for some reason it remained hidden for hundreds of years. I believe, as do many others, that the reason it was put aside by the early Christian elders was that it threatened and made redundant the church middlemen – the papal hierarchy. Why? The Gospel of Thomas is empowering. It quotes Jesus as saying, "The Kingdom of God is inside you. When you come to know yourselves (and discover the Divine within you), then you will become known and you will realize that it is you who are the sons of the living father."10

Perhaps this "Kingdom of God" symbolizes a state of transformed consciousness. You enter that kingdom when you attain self-knowledge. When you come to know yourself at the deepest level, you simultaneously come to know God as the source of your being. Hinduism, Buddhism and Taoism all adhere to the doctrine that we are not separate from God. So if God is inside of us, in our hearts, minds and souls, why do we pray to someone "out there"?

George Fowler, a former Trappist monk who undertook a seventeen-year vow of silence and devoted his life to meditation, says that customary prayer needs to change. We need to learn how to have a mystical reunion with God instead.[11] We must stop praying as if God is in heaven and we're down here. We need to acknowledge that He/She lives within our hearts. This meditative union with God is difficult; it takes practice, devotion and commitment.

Chances are that if you're on a spiritual journey today, you're trying either to find God or to renew your relationship with Him/Her. Find God and you will also find your faith. Renew your faith and you will also find God. Faith is one of the greatest gifts we can give ourselves. People who have a strong faith in God live longer and are happier. Faith allows us to make peace with what is. Faith silences the fear. It heals the wounds from the past. It tells us we are loved unconditionally. With faith we have more courage to cross our bridge. Taking action with faith is more effective than taking action without faith. But how can you embrace faith when all you've known is skepticism and doubt? Well, sometimes a miracle lands on your doorstep that jump-starts your faith or makes it deeper.

EMILIO'S MIRACLE

It isn't the miracle that creates the believer. Instead, we are all believers. We believe that the illusion of the material world is completely real. That belief is our only prison. It prevents us from making the journey into the unknown.

– DEEPAK CHOPRA

"Brain injuries are the worst," the head nurse told me. "We never know who's going to come out of it." It was my cousin Emilio's first visit to America, and while crossing the street near Disneyland in California, he was hit by a truck. By the time the hospital reached his parents back home in Adelaide, Australia, they had already removed two blood clots from his brain. His brother Robbie jumped on the very next plane. When he got to the hospital, he found that Emilio had lapsed into a coma.

We're the only family they have. Emilio is Uncle Jimmy's first-born. He was named after Nonno Emilio, my mother's father, whom I adored. I felt a "call" to go and be with him and support the family. When I arrived in Los Angeles, I was met by a teary-eyed Robbie, who looked like hell. He held on to me for a very long time, breaking down in a torrent of weeping. Robbie, the youngest of Uncle Jimmy's boys, has had a special place in my heart ever since I met him as a child. Actually, all three of them are very dear to me, more like brothers than cousins. And now here was Robbie, the youngest, the rock of his family, dealing with the most difficult challenge of his life. His devotion to his brother was so strong that he did not leave Emilio's side for five days and five nights.

Every day Robbie and I watched as Emilio lay motionless in the bed. We stared at the screens that displayed his vital signs. The most important numbers were his ICPs (intercranial pressure measurements), which monitored the swelling in his brain. If they did not go down to 15 or lower, there would be no hope of survival. At the first family conference with Emilio's team of doctors, we were told that we basically needed a miracle. Every day the numbers hovered between 60 and 80, sometimes reaching scary peaks of 100 to 120. When the alarm bells rang, we'd run out of his room and clutch each other, tensing ourselves against what we feared. Those were the times when I'd tell Robbie to have faith, but I could feel my own doubt creeping in.

One morning, without really realizing what day it was, I proposed we go for a walk before going to the hospital. I thought it would do us both some good. We could have turned left from our hotel, but something told me to go right. After about ten minutes we stumbled onto the grounds of the beautiful Crystal Cathedral in Garden Grove. I did not know that this was the home of the *Hour of Power* televised around the world every Sunday to millions of people. I had seen books by the host, Dr. Schuller, but never before seen the Hour of Power on television. As God would have it, we arrived minutes before the weekly service.

People were bustling around setting up for the broadcast, but what impressed me immediately was the loving kindness in their eyes as they greeted us. Unlike most churches and other places of worship I had visited in the past, they welcomed us with genuine love. They had a luminescence about them that made me feel God's Presence.

Soon 3,500 people were in their seats, ready for the service to begin. The place is massive. It's built of glass, making you feel as though you could fly up and touch the sky. The organ amplified its majestic notes; the singers in the choir added their harmonies. The music, the lyrics and the glorious setting sent ripples of emotion through my entire body. I could feel a wave of gratitude overwhelm me. I looked at Robbie; he was moved, too. I reached for his hand and held it tight. And then, as if that wasn't enough, an extraordinary visiting minister from Argentina stood up and spoke, of all things, about the power of faith to heal!

"Faith," he said, "is like a coupon – it's a coupon from God. It's His promise to us. I didn't have to do anything for that coupon when I arrived from Argentina. It was just given to me. That's what faith is like. You don't have to do anything. God gives you His Grace which is the gift of faith just for being one of his children. Faith is your birthright."

The tears started rolling down my face. I looked at Rob and

he too was sobbing. I knew the sermon was being broadcast to millions of people, but right then I felt that his words were meant for just the two of us. And then I had a thought: If Emilio was going to make it, Robbie and I would have to do a better job of keeping the faith. We couldn't lose hope. We needed to keep praying for him. Even though I teach others to have faith, when faced with Emilio's tragedy, I had wavered. I did not have *enough* faith in my heart. I had let fear over-take me.

I couldn't get over the synchronicity of finding the cathedral on a Sunday morning, minutes before the service. Here was an example of Spirit taking me by the hand and leading me to where I was supposed to be. Now that my faith had been renewed, I told everyone I met to pray for Emilio. I called friends back home and asked them to pray. I e-mailed clients and asked them to pray. People in Australia were praying for him. I went back to the cathedral and submitted Emilio's name to the healing circle that meets and prays for people. Meanwhile, every day I was whispering positive messages into Emilio's ear while Robbie held and stroked his brother's hand. "We love you, Milio. You are so special. You are getting stronger and stronger every day. You are healing yourself perfectly. We have faith in you. We believe in you. We're here for you."

The day before I was scheduled to leave, I witnessed a miracle: Emilio woke up from his coma. The swelling had gone down. Two months later he walked out of that hospital with no permanent damage. Everybody on the medical team said it was a miracle – something they don't see that often. "That's the power of faith," I thought, "and the power of prayer."

Today, almost two years later, Emilio leads a normal life. Other than the scars of forty stitches in his head, he's just fine.

I feel that it was our faith that helped turn things around. I came away feeling closer to God and more committed than ever to shining God's Light and message of Love to people around me. I now know that prayers can heal and that miracles do exist.

Make room in your life for miracles. They will soften your heart. They will transform your soul. Once you've been kissed by the Sacred, you will never be the same again.

THE POWER OF PRAYER

Prayer is as effective from the other side of the world as it is from next door or at the bedside.
— DR. LARRY DOSSEY

In 1984 Dr. Benjamin Carson, one of the world's most celebrated neurosurgeons, was named chief of pediatric neurosurgery at Baltimore's Johns Hopkins Hospital. He was thirty-three, the youngest U.S. doctor ever to hold such a position. Three years later he made headlines by leading a twenty-two-hour operation to separate Siamese twins joined at the head – the first such procedure to succeed for both patients.

He is a legend within the medical community, performing as many as five hundred operations a year, more than twice the caseload of a typical neurosurgeon.

Carson feels that the mind controls much of the body. We are much more than flesh and blood – we are complex systems. Patients do better when they have faith that they're going to do better, he says. That's why he always tells his patients and their families to pray.[12] Studies published in prestigious medical journals such as the *Journal of the American Medical Association* (JAMA) have shown that praying for patients helps in their recovery. The positive results don't prove that God answers prayers or that God even exists, adds the study report, only that prayer be considered as an adjunct to standard medical care.

Scientists have sought evidence of prayer's power for over a century. One of those seekers is Dr. Larry Dossey, whose interest in cures that cannot be scientifically explained led him to leave his medical practice and study the relationship between physical health and spiritual awareness. He writes about numerous studies on the power of prayer to influence health in his book *Healing Words*.

I'm convinced that prayers worked on Emilio. According to one of his nurses, when the ambulance brought him in, he had what they call "neuro-breath." I smelled it myself the day I arrived. It was foul; at the time I thought it was the smell of infected wounds or dirty bandages, since one of his arms and both hands had been badly hurt in the accident. Nurses know that a patient who comes in with neuro-breath usually dies within a week. Then the smell disappeared and no one noticed. "In fifteen years of nursing," a nurse told us, "I've only witnessed one other miracle like this."

MAKING PEACE WITH PRAYER

Many people pray and receive the answer to their prayers, but ignore them – or deny them, because the answers didn't come in the expected form.
– SOPHY BURNHAM

Because of my background, I had always been skeptical about prayer; I used to feel uncomfortable about praying. After making peace with God, I had to make peace with prayer as well. Praying was such an alien thing to me, especially since the only prayers I knew about were petition prayers, where you're always asking God for something as if he were Santa Claus. I think of what John F. Kennedy told the American people: "Ask not what your country can do for you. Rather, ask what you can do for your country." Sometimes I think we should be asking what we can do for God.

I had a moment of epiphany about prayer because of my husband's older sister, Grace. A devout Christian, she belonged to groups that prayed regularly for the sick or needy. "What exactly do you do when you pray?" I asked her one day. She told me that they joined hands and collectively asked God to send His blessing and His divine light to a particular person. I was surprised; it was so similar to what I had been doing in my Visualization Circle. I never thought that I was praying, but praying and visualizing are similar in that they both use the power of thought to affect the external world, usually across some distance.

Visualization is done by concentrating, focusing, intending and repeating. Successful athletes use this technique all the time. When I interviewed participants in the 1988 Calgary Winter Olympics for CBC Radio, I learned that many of them had what they called a "head-coach." The head-coach was someone trained in mental imaging and visualization techniques – the "faith expert" who helped them see in their mind's eye the performance that would give them the gold medal. Some would visualize a perfect program, others a fast time and still others a clean landing. I began studying visualization the following year and learned a variety of techniques that I used to develop myself both personally and professionally. I was quite good at it. I found that through mental imagery not only could I diagnose other people's health problems, but I could also help them heal.

My husband and I decided to join a visualization group. Each month members brought in the names of people who were sick, so it was very much like my sister-in-law's prayer groups. To protect the subjects' privacy, the only information we were allowed was the first name, the city where they lived and their particular health challenge, for example, "Mary, San Francisco, tumor in left breast." Then we'd quiet our minds, go into deep relaxation and collectively focus on Mary in San Francisco, sending positive intentions and healing Light to her left breast.

Sometimes we'd work on the tumor itself, visualizing vacuum cleaners sucking it up or magic erasers rubbing it out or some other tool shrinking it down. The energy in the room was exhilarating. We were like laser beams all focusing on the same thing. I know we helped many people that way, for we frequently heard reports of complete remission. Until my talk with my sister-in-law, it had never occurred to me that what I was doing was a form of prayer. I realized that although I was visualizing and she was *praying*, we were both doing the same thing.

Do these prayers work because there is a God? Or do they work because focused, concentrated, positive mental energy from one individual to another can heal? The mental imaging we were doing to help others heal was a secular form of prayer, or what I call spiritual intention. You could argue that it was also a religious prayer: The healing Light we were sending each patient was divine, and therefore of God, even though we didn't use God's name. The visualization exercises became a bridge between me and prayer – and one way in which I began to heal the doubt of my childhood.

I use this spiritual intention all the time. When my friends have big days or special events that I can't attend, I tell them,

"I'll be thinking of you and sending you white Light at that time." Now when I have important keynote speeches or seminars, they reciprocate by sending me their good thoughts, their Light. Those mental beams are pure, positive energy emanating from their minds, hearts and souls. Even my children get into it. As soon as I walk into the house, Kajsa or Jasper will run to hug me and say, "I sent you Light, Mommy. Did you get it?" or "We put white Light around your airplane, Mommy."

Do you remember the worldwide mourning when Diana, Princess of Wales, died a few years ago? We were united in grieving, praying for Diana's soul, for her children, for the legacy she left behind. So many people, especially on the day of her funeral, were thinking about her and praying for her and feeling for her children. I am convinced that if we had taken a rocket ship into space that day, we would have seen our planet throbbing with Light.

I find that people who have heightened self-awareness and a greater spiritual consciousness achieve the best results when praying or sending Light. We know that our thoughts carry energy. In Chapter 8, I will discuss further the power of thoughts and their influence on us.

TYPES OF PRAYER

Dear God, Is this hellish mess for my spiritual advancement?
- JULIA CAMERON

There are all kinds of prayers. The most common are petition prayers – the kind in which we ask God for something. Those are the ones I used to be uncomfortable with. Across religions, the most common petition is a request for ultimate happiness, bliss, nirvana or enlightenment. When we ask God for something on behalf of someone else, those are intercession prayers. For example, "Please help my friend Janet cope with and heal from the death of her spouse" or "Please help Emilio pull through." Prayers of gratitude are called thanksgiving prayers. Those are our personal family favorites, and my husband believes they are the most powerful prayers of all. He gives thanks for what he has, but also for what he doesn't have yet. Thanksgiving prayers (and not just for the meal) are a ritual around our dinner table.

There are also formal forgiveness prayers, when we ask God for forgiveness. Those are like reconciliation prayers. Confession prayers ask God for a sign about a specific problem. My friend Sandra is famous for these. She asks God for signs all the time – and she gets them. Asking for illumination or a divine Presence in your life or a stronger bond with God are all invocation prayers. And finally, when we surrender to God's will, when we acquiesce to the Wisdom and Light, we are offering submission prayers.

Which type of prayer attracts you? Which one is calling your name right now? Which one could bring you peace and healing? Which one could help you connect to the unconditional Love of God?

To develop a stronger spiritual connection to God, we need to talk to God.

In one of the most entertaining, straight-talking books ever written on religion, author and creativity expert Julia Cameron says she writes love letters to God all the time and stuffs them in her "God jar." In *God Is No Laughing Matter*, she writes, "I sit down, scrawl out: 'Dear God and Higher Forces,' and then I report in."[13] She also says, "My experience of God is of a benevolent, listening interactive Something, and when I communicate with It, I feel better."[14]

I've met many people who tell me they feel better when they communicate with God. Prayer allows us to connect to God, and when we do this we feel more optimistic and hopeful about the world. In other words, connecting to God through prayer generates faith. And it is faith that sustains and nourishes us through our darkest hours. A few years ago the magazine *Mother Jones* did a special issue on the state of faith and emerging spirituality. Editor Jeffrey Klein said in his introduction to the issue, "In my own life, when repeatedly faced with the grave illness and subsequent death of those closest to me, I've found faith the most sustainable, healing resource. Personally, I'm grateful when I find faith in something larger than myself."[15]

Nietzsche announced that God was dead in 1883, but in 2001 God is very much alive. The newly emerging spirituality means that people are seeking together. They're looking for meaning, for soulfulness, for a connection to the divine Mystery. They yearn to belong. We have the careers; we've made the money; we've bought the toys. We thought they were enough, but we were wrong. "Marx did not recognize that our desire to connect with a transcendent power runs even deeper than our drive for economic satisfaction," Klein continues in his *Mother Jones* editorial. Today, as we face the fragmentation of families and the decay of innocence, we look to faith as a way out of the despair and loneliness we feel.

If you're looking for answers in your life or if you're looking to connect to your own Spirit, talk to God – directly. You don't need any middle-people and you don't have to belong to a religion. Just think it and God will hear you. Be honest. Share your feelings. Praying will deepen your relationship with God and strengthen your faith. When do you pray? How do you pray? Perhaps you need to start some praying rituals in your life or, if prayer is not an option for you, perhaps you need to visit a holy site.

MERYEM ANA EVI

**On the summit of a mountain near Ephesus there are four walls
without a roof. John lived within these walls.**

– GREGORY OF TOURS

High up on a mountain in Ephesus, Turkey, a tiny chapel is said to be the place where the Mother of Christ spent her last days with the Apostle John. The Turks call it Meryem Ana Evi, or Mary's House. The Bible says that Jesus asked John to take care of his mother. Initially they probably lived in Jerusalem, as did the other apostles, but as persecution grew, the Christians began to disperse into Judea and Samaria. Around that time – in approximately the year 40 – John left for the Roman province of Asia (now Ephesus), taking Mary with him.

Sometimes you need to connect to holy ground, a shrine, a monument, a relic – a meaningful place – in order to connect to your faith. Nearly ten years ago I visited Mary's home and it made a deep impression on me. We were in Istanbul, visiting our friends Fatih and Melek, whom we had met at university. One day, out of the blue, Fatih announced, "I want to take you to this place, Grace. I know you'll like it." So we got in the car and drove to Ephesus.

A big white sign greets visitors to the site and explains the story of how this holy place was discovered. A German seer, Katharina Emmerich, saw Mary's house in one of her visions. She described it to Clemens von Brentano, who wrote about it in his book *The Life of the Holy Virgin*. In 1891 four men set out to see whether such a place existed. After searching for days, the travelers were about to give up when they stopped to ask some women working in the fields where they might find fresh water. The women pointed the way to a "monastery" that had a fresh spring. After they had refreshed themselves, the travelers looked around and saw "the ruined house, a mountain behind the house, the sea in front of them" – exactly as Katharina had described.

Soon word of the discovery spread. Scholars, archeologists, Catholic authorities and other experts visited the site. In 1950 the Turkish government built a road so that vehicles could drive up to the chapel. Since then, millions of pilgrims and tourists have visited the house of the Virgin Mary.

As I walked around that sacred place, I was overcome with emotion. I wondered about the woman the world calls the Virgin Mother. What was she like? I imagined how she must have suffered to see her son crucified and then to have to live in hiding for the rest of her life. For the first time I could connect with her as a real woman and not some religious icon. Although the Vatican has not yet recognized the shrine as authentic, it didn't matter to me. I knew in my heart of hearts that this was where the Virgin Mother spent her last days. Some truths have to be felt rather than known. The experience was one of a series that helped to heal the doubt in my heart.

HEALING THE DOUBT

The shadows of doubt are part of the spiritual experience.
They visit all of us. Priests, nuns, rabbis, metaphysical teachers
and channelers all confess to seasons of darkness in which they doubted the
very message they carried.

- JULIA CAMERON

Doubt is part of life and it happens on many different levels. Having doubt is the opposite of having faith. Doubt is insidious, fearful and contagious. On the micro level, we may doubt ourselves – as in "I doubt my abilities." But it also happens on the macro level – "I doubt there's a Higher Power, a reason for it all."

A business leader hired me to give his group a two-day personal growth workshop. He asked whether I could be available for private coaching if people had questions or issues they wanted to discuss in confidence. I agreed, so we extended the lunch break by an extra hour to make time for those who might need to talk to me. I was overwhelmed when I saw a long lineup forming outside the room I would be using. Immediately I was gripped by doubt. How was I going to help all those people in just one hour? I wanted to give all of them the time they deserved and not rush them. How was this going to be possible? And then a quiet voice inside urged me on. "Shh, it'll be fine. Just have faith."

Each person who came to see me seemed lost. Invariably their questions betrayed deep uncertainty and despair; they talked of failed marriages, stalled careers and conflict in their relationships. Most of them became emotional as soon as they began speaking. Tears began to flow. It struck me that we all carry so much pain and that we're so good at hiding it. My heart was filled with compassion. I absorbed their stories one by one, forgetting about the lineup outside my door. It seemed I *could* give each person what he or she needed. For some it was a different perspective, for others validation. For still others it was a question that helped produce a healing shift. To some I suggested books to read. Many of them needed a hug. No one seemed rushed, yet I got to everyone. Even though my doubt was still present, each grateful embrace helped me to push it aside. To this day I don't know how I did it, but I know I didn't do it alone. God was with me. By taking action even though I was feeling self-doubt, I grew my faith.

There have been numerous times in my life when self-doubt has plagued me – writing this book, for example. For years I thought, "Why would anyone want to publish it? It's all been said before." Even the most illustrious geniuses have moments of doubt. Granted, some of us have weeks and months of doubt rather than moments. We doubt our brilliance and our magnificence and our talents and we fall victim to a darkness that seems to rise up and swallow us. Doubt is a close relative of fear.

The way out of the darkness is through courage: Take action; do it anyway! The other way out is to silence doubt with the gentle voice of faith, which sweeps in and says, "Shh, it'll be fine. I am here with you."

Some of us walk around feeling as though we're impostors and that we will be found out at any moment. These are the people who harbor self-doubt even though others may believe in them. Some of my clients have admitted feeling like impostors at work and in their personal relationships. Their bosses believe they can do the job, but they don't. So they walk around every day in fear that the truth will be discovered and they will be exposed for the frauds they really are.

This impostor feeling is very stressful because it means we're on guard all the time. Why is it that others can see our magnificence but we can't? Feeling like an impostor comes from doubt, and doubt comes from fears that we're not enough, or that we're too much. This arises because the lack of faith in ourselves is programmed at a deep level in our minds. It may be connected to feelings of unworthiness from our past. Most adults I coach or counsel seem to have this lack of faith in some area of their lives, and I'll be addressing this issue in the next few chapters.

The other thing to keep in mind is that doubt is contagious. I know this from experience. While I was in Los Angeles a few years ago with a dear friend, we were awakened one night by a violent shaking. We were experiencing our first earthquake, and it was happening in the middle of the night! We were unsure what to do, but I got a strong feeling that everything was okay – that the earthquake was actually over. That intuition gave me the faith to remain calm even as aftershocks continued to shake us up every twenty or thirty minutes.

My friend, on the other hand, grew more and more agitated with each tremor. After a while I encouraged her to come and sit with me so we could pray together. As time passed and the sporadic tremors continued, her fear got worse. She was clutching on to me so hard I could feel her nails digging into my skin. I began to doubt my original feeling. Soon the internal voices began: "You fool! That wasn't the earthquake. It's still to come. These are warning tremors, and here you are in bed! Idiot!" Panic gripped my heart. Fear and anxiety were swallowing whatever faith I had left. Yet I couldn't break down in front of my friend. She needed me to have faith. For three hours we held on to each other, waiting for morning to come and the tremors to subside.

In the morning we learned that the earthquake had happened in Joshua Tree National Park, 250 miles away, and that there had been no deaths or major damage other than a train derailment. My initial feeling of faith had been correct, but I had betrayed it when I allowed doubt to sweep over me. Doubt is contagious. Fear is contagious. It takes resolve and strength to stay true to the faith you may feel inside. When do you absorb doubt in your life, and from whom? What do you typically do about it? What would happen if you trusted your instincts and let faith lead you?

Remember the saying, "If you have but the faith of a mustard seed, you shall move mountains." Faith is powerful. It's a journey – a dynamic and fluid journey. Let faith take root in your heart. Nourish it and soon it will help you move your life forward – beyond your wildest dreams.

Some Questions to Think About

1 When did you lose your faith?
2 Were you religiously abused?
3 If you have faith, have you always had it? How do you nurture it?
4 What makes your faith strong? Weak?
5 What soul moments or spiritually significant experiences have you had?
6 Did you discard them?
7 Do you believe in miracles?
8 Have you confused spirituality with religion?
9 What will it take for you to believe?
10 What would having more faith in your life look like?

7

Heal the Past

BEGIN THE HEALING JOURNEY

You are caught by what you are running from.
— SAM KEEN

"Grace, he finally cried. It was all because of that movie. I never knew it would have such an impact on him!" Judy had been complaining to me about her husband's indifference and lack of passion for quite some time. Now she couldn't wait to tell me how the movie *My Life* had triggered Bill's healing journey.

The main character, played by Michael Keaton, has been diagnosed with terminal cancer and has only a few months to live. His wife, played by Nicole Kidman, is pregnant with their first child. He begins to record himself on video talking to his unborn baby, making a record of his life for the son he might not live to see. He desperately wants to be a father to this child, so he tells him about his heritage, where he was born and where he grew up. But when he gets to pictures and home movies of his childhood with his parents and brother, buried emotions – anger, disgust, shame and hurt – begin to surface.

At his wife's insistence, he sees a Chinese doctor who supposedly cured a friend's father of cancer. He is skeptical, but goes anyway. The doctor tells him he has a lot of anger and that the tumors will go away when he learns to forgive. As the doctor is performing a healing-energy massage on his chest, Keaton's character sees a white light and has a strange experience. Frightened, he bolts off the table and leaves. "What did the doctor say?" his wife wants to know. "He says I'm angry and that I have to forgive. Stupid quack! I'm not angry! Who do I have to forgive?" he yells.

This is the story of a man coming to terms with his bottled-up past, the feelings of hurt and anger that he felt as a child but never voiced. He finally does make peace with his parents and forgives them, but it is too late. Although he now has faith in alternative medicine, the tumors have spread to his brain. He spends his last days at home surrounded by his wife, his parents and his brother, and that's when he makes peace with his family and with himself.

In one scene the dying man's father gives him a shave. Obviously touched, the son slowly reaches up to touch his father's hand, pauses and whispers, "I love you, Dad."

That's when it happened. Bill's lower lip began to quiver. He started crying softly at first, but then the dam broke. He sobbed as Judy had never seen him sob before. He collapsed on the floor with his head on her lap, and she held him tight. He cried, he moaned. The sounds that tore from his throat were primitive and full of anguish. His body shook with the force of the wails that came from deep within him. The tears kept coming and coming; sorrow swept over him like a blanket, engulfing them both.

Judy said later that it felt as though she were giving birth – to his tears, to his pain, to his healing journey. He kept quivering, shaking, one contraction after another, one moan after another as she held on to him, whispering words of encouragement.

When the trembling finally subsided, her chest and lap were completely soaked from his tears. Judy had been Bill's midwife, helping to usher in his tears.

Then Bill began to speak. "All I wanted was his touch, his love. I just wanted him to be my dad. But he ignored me. I was invisible. I was robbed! I hated him – and *I turned into him!*"

With this realization, his body went into spasms, vibrating with energy fueled by his disbelief and shock. He howled in agony.

And then it was as though an arrow had pierced his heart. His pain climaxed and he was left limp and wasted. However, the wound of Bill's realization went deeper and deeper, until he lay curled up on the floor.

Judy lay on the carpet with him, soothing him and loving him. He was soaked and spent, and so was she. As she lay there, stroking Bill's hair, she heard a sudden patter of rain-drops outside. There was no thunder or lightning – just a lot of rain, a gentle, cleansing rain. She opened a window and let the spray of that cleansing rain wash over Bill's face. Her husband had lost his father nearly twenty years earlier, but only now was he finally grieving his death and, more importantly, the relationship he never had with him. Bill had finally reached a point where he could begin to heal the past.

In this chapter I will tell you about some ideas and practices that I have used to heal myself and people who have come to me with the same need. Ultimately, the best advice I can give you is to follow your own heart. Trust your instincts. Try the approaches that speak to you. Some people advocate leaving the past alone, but I believe that healing and learning from our past are necessary to remove the obstacles to faith in who we are and what we can achieve.

Buddhists use a phrase that means "no escape." Sometimes

when life becomes unbearable, we want to run away – so we leave our families, move to a different city, change jobs, remarry and start over again. And then, sooner or later, we find ourselves dealing with the very issues and people and problems we thought we'd left behind. "No escape" means that what we run from follows us. What we don't heal will always be with us.

HEAL THE INNER FAULT LINES

> Running away from suffering intensifies it; denying suffering intensifies it; wallowing in suffering intensifies it; blaming our suffering on others intensifies it. Anesthetizing it will work for only so long. And emotional shutdown is ultimately destructive to mind and body.
>
> – GABRIELE RICO

Most people at first glance seem happy and together. They're competent in at least some areas of their lives. They've learned how to play the game, they juggle their many roles and responsibilities and most of the time they appear to keep it all under control. But what the outside world doesn't see is the fault lines on the inside, which are susceptible to pressure.

Earthquakes occur along fault lines. Pressure builds beneath the earth's crust until the tectonic plates "slip" along a fault line and an earthquake results. In human terms, once sufficient stress has built up over time, the fault line will lead to a dramatic life event. The event could be, for example, a heart attack, diagnosis of a disease (the disease develops over time, of course, but its detection can be a shock) or the breakup of a marriage. By healing the fault line, however, we can pre-empt the dramatic event. If there is no fault line, no earthquake can happen.

Like Earth, we are riddled with internal fault lines. Unlike Earth, we have the potential to heal our fault lines one by one. What are these fault lines? They could be an abusive past, spiritual emptiness, feeling unwanted or unloved, clogged emotions, low self-esteem, anxiety, depression or loneliness.

In her book *Pain and Possibility*, Gabriele Rico talks about the death of her mother in a bombing raid when Rico was only seven years old. For many years she imagined there was a long, jagged crack across her heart, and she wondered if she would ever heal from it. As an adult Rico concludes, "we're all damaged somehow, somewhere – the real issue is not whether, but how, we learn to deal with our damage."[1]

When his parents divorced, my client Marco was only ten years old. For reasons that are still unclear to him, he was sent to live with relatives in Spain. They were mean to him. Both his father and mother remarried in his native Nicaragua, but they never sent for him. He grew up feeling abandoned and unloved.

It's always when we're at the threshold of change that the question of healing our past emerges. "Cross that bridge," the nasty demons warn you, "but deal with us."

"No, not today," you reply. "I can't face you today." So you turn back. But Spirit grows impatient. It pushes you to take that step toward your destiny. Somewhere deep within you, you hear the voice saying, "It's time." As you look inside, you see a tarnished mirror reflecting back all the tears you've never cried, the hurts that never healed – an infinite well of sadness. No Band-Aids will work. The wounds are still fresh, even now, after so many years. They've been waiting for you, waiting for the day when you have the courage to face them and heal them. Your soul has a special destiny. It wants to fly, but it can't fly if the emotional wounds of the past are not healed.

We must make friends with our past and take responsibility for it if we are to heal and reclaim our power. We all have "stuff" from our childhood locked in that Pandora's box deep inside us, stuff that needs healing. But most of us are unaware of it.

The healing journey is deeply personal, and there are many paths one can take. Every experience we bring into our lives becomes an opportunity to grow our souls and heal the past. Those experiences are the stepping stones on which we build our lives. They are the ladders to healing and fulfilling our mission here on earth. But while the paths are as varied as the individuals, there is a common destination. People want rich, meaningful lives filled with deep spiritual connections and loving relationships.

Meaningful healing takes place when there is a change of heart, expansion of consciousness, letting go, forgiveness, release of emotion, acceptance of something previously denied or reconnection. Healing the past can happen on many levels. It is not only a cure of the body, but a cure of the Spirit as well.

YOUR JAGGED EDGES

*Everyone is a moon, and has a dark side
which he never shows to anybody.*

– MARK TWAIN

One morning I woke up with a curious phrase on my mind: "Don't deny your jagged edges." I didn't understand it at first. Was this some message seeping up from my unconscious? And then I remembered – the night before I had been listening to the song "You Learn" by singer-songwriter Alanis Morissette. In the song there is a line about "the jagged little pill." "Swallow it down," she recommends. Her song is wise. To me the jagged little pill can be anything unpleasant in your life. By embracing it, swallowing it down, you learn.

Your jagged edges are the things you hate about yourself. Psychologist Carl Jung called them your shadow. Everyone has a shadow. It is the sum of the aspects of your Self that you deny, repress or disown. It's those things that made us feel shame or brought us punishment when we were children. We would rather hide that part of us in the closet or sweep it under the rug. But to be truly authentic and to reclaim our wholeness, we have to allow the qualities in ourselves that we love and accept to coexist with the parts of ourselves that we hate and disown.

Poet Robert Bly says the shadow is "the long bag we drag behind us." It is filled with character traits, emotions and talents that were unaccepted by our family and friends. Bly believes we spend the first twenty years of our lives filling up our bags, and the rest of our lives trying to empty them.

When we are moving strongly toward abundance and positive thinking, why would we want to bother with the shadow? Why would we want to illuminate the monsters in the darkness? Why would we want to open that Pandora's box? The reason is this: Who you are is a totality. Over the years you have played one side more than the other and you have lost your balance. In an effort to regain equilibrium, you have attracted into your life people and experiences that reflect the aspects of yourself you've disowned.

Here's an example.

Rita is kind, giving and accommodating. But she has disowned her anger – the part of herself that can stand up for her rights, the part of her that can say no, the courage to roar like a lion if necessary. Consequently Rita keeps attracting selfish and aggressive people who take advantage of her.

When we bring our wholeness to a relationship, we attract others who are whole and balanced. We can see the sun because we have experienced the darkness. We know peace because we've experienced war. We know love because we've felt the fear. When we embrace all that we are, we're healing all that we pushed aside in the past.

"A soulful life is never without shadow," says Thomas Moore in his book *Care of the Soul*. In fact, "some of the soul's power comes from its shadow qualities."[2] Embracing our shadow allows us to live authentically and purposefully. When we have the courage to say yes to all our moods, all our emotions, all our qualities, then we've entered the realm of possibility. We have a wide range of options from which to create our lives. When we can express the totality of who we are and live from our depths – passionately, intensely, soulfully and without fear – then we come into the power that is our birthright. We become spiritual warriors, ready to take action and move our lives and our communities forward.

OPEN THE DOORS IN YOUR CASTLE

Within every human being there are gods and goddesses in embryo with only one desire. They want to be born.

– DEEPAK CHOPRA

"When you understand that you contain everything you see in others, your entire world will alter," says Debbie Ford in her book *The Dark Side of the Light Chasers*. "The key is to understand that there is nothing we can see or perceive that we are not."[3]

What she is suggesting is a holistic model of the Universe. It teaches that each of us is a microcosm of the macro, that we contain every aspect of the Universe. We are all that we see, all that we judge, all that we admire.

Just imagine what that would be like – to realize that within you is every quality, every emotion, every attitude, every state of being, and that you can choose to call forth whatever you wish from within yourself. What a concept!

Ford borrows John Welwood's analogy of a castle to illustrate the world within us. Imagine being a beautiful castle with thousands of exquisite rooms. Each room is beautiful in its own way, each possessing a special gift. These rooms represent different aspects of your Self. As a child you loved each room. In fact you were altogether carefree and fearless, and regardless of what kind of room it was, you always found something that made it special. Your castle was full of light, love and wonder.

Then one day someone arrived and told you that one of your rooms was ugly. They suggested you close it off and lock the door. Since you wanted their love and approval, you agreed. Eventually more people arrived and started complaining. Everyone had his or her opinion about the rooms. To accommodate them, you shut the doors on more of the rooms in your castle. Eventually it became a habit and you closed rooms because you were afraid they were becoming ugly. Sometimes you compared your castle to others and decided that some of your rooms didn't measure up. Soon you found yourself living in just a few rooms.

You forgot that you lived in a castle with thousands of rooms. You stopped taking risks, stopped believing in your magnificence and stopped feeling joy.

MEET YOUR SHADOW

We are not there until we can say "yea" to it all.
- JOSEPH CAMPBELL

You can illuminate your shadow in a variety of ways. There are many avenues to the past. The castle metaphor shows poignantly how we begin the cycle of disowning who we are. When we embark on our healing journey, we need to throw open the doors to all of the rooms in our castles. But how can we go into those rooms when we're afraid? How can we reclaim the things that make us uncomfortable or that we would rather not look at? You know – the rooms called "stupid" or "selfish" or "arrogant" or "lazy." Surely we are not really like that. If you're serious about changing the direction of your life and healing your past, you must go into each room and find the positive potential of each quality.

What do I mean by the positive potential? If stupidity is something you disown (your shadow self), ask yourself, "What is the positive potential of stupidity?" In other words, how do you need to view stupidity in order for you to reclaim your wholeness? For example, contrast these two ways of being:

- I do something stupid. My co-worker screams at me and calls me stupid. I feel bad, accept the label and now think that I am stupid. I start working hard never to be stupid again. My motivation for love and acceptance is so great that I disown this part of myself. (This is a person who has closed off the "stupid" room of his castle.)
- I do something stupid, but I won't accept the label. I accept that I *did* something stupid, but not that I *am*

stupid. I don't disown stupidity – I just allow myself the possibility that I will do stupid things sometimes because I'm human. In other words, I accept that there is a room in my castle called "stupid" that sometimes, intentionally or not, I may visit.

One way to meet your shadow is to start off by finding the positive potential of your disowned selves. In other words, what else did you give up when you closed that room of your castle? How might it have put pressure on your fault lines?

In your journal make three columns. In the first column, write down six of your positive qualities, using words that best describe you and those qualities that you're proud of. Then in the second column, write down the opposite of each quality in the "positive" column. These opposites don't have to be an exact antonym according to the dictionary, just what you would say in your own words. So, for example, if you wrote down "loving" as one of your positive qualities, ask yourself what would be the opposite of loving. For some people it might be "callous," for others "cold," for others "mean." It's important to write down *your* opposite. Be aware of any repeat words or patterns you see emerging. Column 2 represents your shadow. These are the rooms in your castle that you've closed off for whatever reason. One way we can open them up again is to tell ourselves that our shadow holds the key to our healing.

Positive Qualities	Shadow Self	Positive Potential (The Gift)
1 smart	stupid	
2 loving	cold	
3 fast	slow	
4		
5		
6		

Column 3 is where you become creative. Take the disowned quality and reinterpret it in a positive way that makes sense to you. For example, three of my positive qualities are that I'm smart, loving and fast. For me the opposite of *smart* is *stupid*, the opposite of *loving* is *cold* and the opposite of *fast* is *slow*. I have certainly disowned *stupid*; all my life I've generated esteem by being smart. Because I was the oldest child in my family, my parents depended on me to solve problems and be a role model for my brothers. Once I was able to give myself permission not to know it all, not to be the "consummate seminar leader" (as a friend once called me), to make mistakes and not have to educate the entire world, then I could see *stupid* in a positive way. When someone presents me with a problem, I don't have to jump to solve it. I can say I don't know and refer them elsewhere. Your positive potential gives you permission to embrace the opposite so you can come into balance with yourself.

As for *cold*, I really disowned it. *Cold* was a room in my castle I'd shut down for good. My family, especially my mom's side, are all very loving. I was taught to show respect by hugging and kissing everyone who came to the house. I'm naturally warm and compassionate, so that wasn't hard for me. In my workshops and keynote speeches I talk about love. I greet all my friends with hugs, and sometimes my clients, too. After my workshops I usually have a long line of people waiting to hug me.

So what could possibly be the positive potential of *cold*? Well, I could learn to stop being judgmental about myself when I don't feel like chatting to a stranger on the plane or when I don't feel like being nice or friendly. I need to tell myself that I don't always have to be caring and nurturing and compassionate with everyone. Sometimes I need to say no and take care of myself first. Sometimes I need to detach and restore my energy. I didn't used to be good at this, often giving too much and then later resenting it or feeling drained. But now I no longer disown *cold*.

I had disowned *slow*. Everything about me is fast. I think fast, make decisions fast, drive fast and walk fast, and consequently I used to get impatient frequently. I'm also a doer and can't stand indecision and inaction. So whom do I marry? A slow and thorough man. This is the Universe's way of balancing me. I love life and have this greed for living and experiencing everything I can. This is not a bad thing, but what did I need in order to become more whole and balance my energy? I needed to learn to just *be*. I've learned to meditate, do yoga, be still and pray. I've learned not to beat myself up for just staring out the window and daydreaming. I no longer try to jam-pack my day. I've embraced my *slow*ness and I'm a better person for it.

If you get stuck on the positive potential, ask yourself what gift your shadow has for you. What do you need to give yourself permission to be or do? How can you bring your life into greater balance? The positive potential of any disowned quality is an interpretation – there are no wrong answers. Think about it; talk about it. If it makes sense to you, that's all you need to meet your shadow. By allowing yourself to be what you have disowned, buried or pushed aside, you are healing those parts of yourself that you don't yet love or accept. Open the doors in your castle and let the sun shine in. It's time to celebrate all that you are, to reclaim your wholeness. Carl Jung once said that he would rather be whole than good. What part of yourself have you sacrificed in order to be good? What masks have you assumed to please others? Know that the world needs *all* of you.

WRITE DOWN YOUR PAIN

Spilling your pain onto the page is healing; holding it in is as unfruitful as holding your breath. Letting go leads to life.

– GABRIELE RICO

Soon after giving birth to my first child, Jasper, I decided to take a creative writing class. During that class we were encouraged to meditate on some aspect of our childhood and then to pick up our pens and start writing. The instructor was irreverent, funny and intense. "Anything at all," she'd say. "Let the story bubble up. Just keep writing until I say stop." It was then that I became aware of some of my "stuff" – childhood stories, unexpressed emotions, memories that had slipped out of consciousness. They were rich and textured, and brought me face to face with my past.

I am a little girl about seven years old, sitting on the outside steps at the side door to my house. It's dark and cold. I'm crouched down, hugging my knees to stay warm and rocking back and forth. I'm alone. I'm waiting for daylight so I can go to school. My father has already left for work. I'm too small to lock the door myself, so he locks the door and leaves me outside. My mother is in hospital. She had my little baby brother a few weeks ago, but now she's in the hospital again. When the sun comes out and I see people walking, that's my cue to walk to school. I'm not scared.

In the back of my mind I had always known this story, but I was not aware that I had unexpressed emotions around it. Reading it out loud to the class, I started to cry. I had found a wound.

Slowly other childhood stories and emotions began to bubble up. It was time for me to deal with my stuff. My healing journey started then and continues today. We don't always understand why people do the things they do, but healing leads you to greater intimacy and truth in your relationships. Because my dad has always been fiercely independent, I know now that it wouldn't have occurred to him to leave me at a neighbor's. I was given responsibility at a young age. I am the person I am today because of my parents' confidence in me.

Many people advocate the therapeutic value of writing down your pain. Gabriele Rico is one of them. She teaches workshops on how to use writing as a way to confront your repressed feelings. She says in her book *Pain and Possibility* that "writing is a gateway to healing and personal transformation" and that when we "can explore our pain or despair through language, we see ourselves in a new light. Best of all, we discover the enormous satisfaction that comes from putting our feelings onto the clean white page of healing."[4]

Do you keep a journal? Look at some childhood pictures. Close your eyes, take a deep breath and visualize a memory from your past. Don't judge it, just go with it, whatever it is. Then pick up a pen and let the memory guide you. Write about it. Use writing as a vehicle for healing and self-discovery. Make connections, see the patterns and reconnect with your memories. The act of writing loosens the pain encrusted on your emotional walls. It will help you unearth the disowned parts of your Self. It will help the stories of your past percolate up. It will throw open the doors in your castle.

LET YOUR STORIES OUT

Love me, love my story.
Human intercourse is an intermingling of flesh and story.
- SAM KEEN

Our lives are stories, and by expressing our stories we heal. That's why we seek out therapists, friends and family members who will listen to them. We have all at some time or another been wounded emotionally, psychologically or physically. The stories that make up our lives comprise our identity, our history, our individuality. Stories are the language of the heart. They connect our human drama. We need to be heard. We need someone to bear witness to our lives. I feel blessed because people trust me with their stories. My husband teases me that I have "Compassionate Therapist" branded on my forehead. Why else would absolute strangers pour out their intimate stories to me in grocery checkout lines, on airplanes and at my seminars (though it's more understandable at my seminars). They've heard me speak and they feel they know me, like the woman who wrote me the following letter:

Dear Grace:
I feel compelled to write to you. Last week when I heard you speak I had been feeling an endless despair. Needless to say, I am feeling better. My whole marriage has been spent trying to conceive a baby. It didn't happen, and probably won't now, and I do not want to adopt. I am in turmoil but in spite of it all my heart still whistles a tune and I really do not want to leave this earth. It was comforting to hear your hopeful and empowering words.

The paradox in all of this is that I feel as though I am going through labor to give birth to myself and it hurts so much. I don't mean to be so self-centered. I just wanted to share my story with you.

Our stories tell people who we are. They reveal secrets, hopes and dreams. They express our deepest longings. It's our stories that make us real. When we express them, we heal. What stories may be percolating up for you? Your stories are rich threads woven together to make the tapestry that is your life. Choose to remember the stories from your past. Share them. Do it tonight over dinner. Tell your beloved a story about your childhood. Tell your children, tell your staff, tell a friend. Or tell it to the white page that is waiting to help you heal.

HEALING SHIFTS

**Hidden wounds have hidden agendas
that hold us hostage to the past.**
– PAUL FERRINI

I'm convinced that sometimes an "aha" moment, or what I like to call an SFI (Sudden Flash of Insight), can let you make a quantum leap of healing. I've had such moments in my life and I've also shared the experience as other people "get it." Sometimes it's when I teach workshops or seminars, other times it's when I'm coaching or counseling. I see it on their faces, in their eyes. Their posture shifts. Frowns relax and illumination appears. It's almost as though you can hear their souls say, "Ah, I see." It's one of my biggest professional highs. When you suddenly see another way or a different perspective or a reason for something, it's like all the puzzle pieces finding their spots at once. Everything clicks and a shift takes place. These shifts are healing; they change our perception. They're like laser beams of awareness that burn their healing marks on our consciousness.

"Miss Cirocco, I'm wondering if you have a few moments to talk to me," I was asked just before a seminar. The woman speaking to me was Theresa, a relative of the person who had invited me to speak. I looked at my watch. It was almost time to begin my presentation, but I sensed a real yearning and need, so I found us a quiet corner and said, "Sure, what can I do for you?"

"It's my life. It's coming apart. I don't know what to do . . ." – and then she burst into tears.

Offering her a tissue, I asked, "What's the problem?"

"I've been married three years and I have a two-year-old son, but I don't know whether I can stay with my husband."

"Why? Is he hurting you?"

"Oh, no, he's kind and gentle and wonderful."

"Well, then, what's the problem?"

"He has this mental disease – he takes pills – he's manic-depressive."

"Does his disease get in the way? Does it hurt your relationship? Does he ever hurt you or the child?"

"No, it's not like that. He takes his medication and he's okay."

"Well, then, what's the problem?"

And finally Theresa got to the root of her worries.

"Everyone knew about his problem before we got married except me. Nobody told me."

Oh, now I understood. "So you're feeling betrayed, deceived, tricked?"

The tears streamed from her eyes. I could see the depth of pain she had been holding inside and I hugged her.

"I can't talk to anyone about this. All my friends and family were in on it," she told me as we continued to embrace.

"They must have felt this man was the right choice for you and that if you knew the truth you might have passed him up," I rationalized for her.

"Yes, that's what they say now, but I still should have known."

"So what do you want to do about it?" I asked her.

"I don't know. I'm confused. I feel as if I've made another big mistake – this is my second marriage. Now I have a child with him and I feel like I've really messed up my life. I can't sleep, I can't eat. No one understands. I don't know what to do."

I looked at the clock and saw that there was no time. Suddenly I got an inspiration. "Betrayal hurts a lot," I told her. "You have a right to feel hurt. Your family had their reasons, but it still doesn't make it right. You wanted to marry him with all the cards on the table. But now you're married and you have a son with him, and you tell me you love him. Let me ask you this: Had you known about his illness before your marriage, would you still have gone through with the wedding?"

By her reaction I knew this was the question Theresa needed to hear. This was the question that would pierce her heart and give her the illumination and peace she so desired. She paused and her jaw dropped. It was a blessed moment. She looked deep into my eyes and a tiny smile came to her lips. Her eyes were moist with tears. She was ready to give me the verdict.

"Yes," she said. "I would still have married him." And then she let out a huge sigh of relief and asked incredulously, "Oh my God, how did you do that?"

"I didn't do it, you did!" I replied.

"Thank you, thank you, thank you," Theresa repeated over and over, throwing herself into my arms. "I just knew I had to talk to you as soon as I saw you. I knew you were the person I needed to talk to about this. You're the angel I've been waiting for. I feel like I'm out of jail!"

When people heal, their hearts fill with gratitude. They are transformed. They become abundant thinkers. For the rest of the evening, Theresa was floating, interacting with others in a carefree, happy-go-lucky way. Her husband arrived after the workshop to pick her up, and she introduced me to him. I could see his gentleness immediately from the way he helped her with her coat, the way he looked at her. "She is blessed with a good man," I thought.

Sometimes forgiving or letting go of the past seems like it can take forever. And sometimes, as in Theresa's case, it can take five minutes – if the right question is asked.

In the Arthurian legends, Sir Perceval loved asking questions, but by the time he became a brave knight of King Arthur's Round Table, he had been convinced to curb his questioning. By listening to others, he lost touch with his own authentic voice. One night while at the Grail castle, Perceval dines with the wounded Fisher King. As the king and the knight converse, a procession passes before them carrying the fabulous Holy Grail. Perceval is being tested. If he asks the right question – "Whom does the Grail serve?" – the Fisher King will be healed and the surrounding wasteland restored to a paradise. He fails and as a punishment is placed under a spell. Perceval spends five years wandering alone in the wasteland, not knowing who he is or how to cure his malaise. One day, exhausted and spent, he stops to ask a stranger, "What day is it today?" At that moment the spell is broken. Apparently the act of asking a question did it. Perceval is healed and free to rejoin the rest of the knights of the Round Table.

Like Perceval, I think we're all suffering under a spell. We seem to be drifting in our own personal wastelands without a compass and without our souls. Healing ourselves and our planet will come when we learn to ask the right questions. Beware of the army of experts out there that are ready to tell you what's wrong with you and to prescribe a medley of solutions. Sometimes all you need to do in order to heal is to ask the right question. What question do you need to be asking? What question can, as in Theresa's case, help you heal your heavy heart?

DARK NIGHTS OF THE SOUL

The dark night of the soul comes just before revelation.
- JOSEPH CAMPBELL

Healing the past brings us face to face with our "dark night of the soul." In the sixteenth century the Spanish mystic St. John of the Cross coined this phrase to designate the part of our journey in which we lose our inner compass and fall victim to fear, loneliness, depression and pain. The dark night of the soul can be our worst nightmare, but it can also be a rich time for learning and spiritual growth.

Spiritual growth means growing our souls, and growing our souls means becoming better at being human beings. But when we're in the throes of the dark night of the soul, we feel hopeless. This is the valley that Theresa was living in before her "shift" in thinking. This is the wasteland that Perceval was sent to during the five-year spell. Our minds start playing tricks on us and we fall deeper and deeper into a chasm of despair. We ask, "How can it possibly be a positive experience?"

I have had clients who I knew were not ready to heal because they hadn't experienced their dark night of the soul. Therapists call this "hitting rock-bottom" – you can't come up until you've gone all the way down. You can't heal your pain until you've had the courage to embrace all of its raw intensity. Mystics and sages of the past taught us that pain brings us closer to God, that it can fuel the fire of purification, taking us further along in our spiritual journey. For them suffering intensified the search for what is most sacred.

Generations ago, pain was not something to be avoided; it was simply a part of life. And the more pain you endured, the more respect people paid you. In my grandparents' village in Italy the people who were most respected and most called upon for wise counsel were those who had suffered the most. My maternal grandmother was one such person. The thinking went that the more suffering one did, the more one was blessed with wisdom.

When I was twenty and away at university, I got a telephone call that rocked my world. "Your father has been in a car accident," the voice said. "He's hurt pretty badly. Doctors say there's a fifty-fifty chance he'll survive the night. I think you'd better come home." The voice belonged to a neighbor and longtime friend, Zia Natalina. The accident had happened while my mother was in Europe visiting her parents. As I boarded the train for the five-hour journey home, my heart was full of terror. So many questions came to mind. What if he died? What if Mom couldn't make it home on time? How were my brothers, John and Tony, coping? Why did Mom have to go away? How was I going to do this alone?

My mind was racing while the train seemed to crawl from one town to another. I was feeling overwhelmed, alone and frightened. "Hurry up, train, I want to see my Daddy alive," I sobbed. I stared out the window, trying really hard not to let the other passengers hear me crying. Then out of nowhere a woman sat down next to me. We hadn't made a stop to pick up new passengers – she had just been walking up the aisle and had decided to sit next to me. She saw my tears and invited me to share my suffering.

"Some day, Grace," she said, with love in her eyes, "this experience will feed your art." They were strange words, but they were exactly what my soul needed to hear. Her words had the same effect on me as the question I posed Theresa. Sometimes God sends us angels when we most need them. I know she was sent to comfort me in my moment of darkness just as I was sent to Theresa.

I interpreted her statement to mean that my pain would transform itself to make me a stronger, wiser Grace. I would grow and the strength and wisdom would someday translate into my "art." In *The Heart Aroused*, American poet David Whyte alludes to a similar concept when he says, "It is the embrace of failure and grief, harrowing as these are, that forms the vessel for the joyous votive flame of creativity."[5] Many of his own poems were created that way.

Carl Jung spoke of an archetype called the "wounded healer." Perhaps each wound we suffer and eventually heal from has the potential to grow us as humans so that we can, with time, participate in the healing of our world. I know that my suffering has made me a better counselor, workshop facilitator, mother and friend. And yet sometimes I don't think I've suffered at all. I think about the unbearable cruelties and torture that are going on right now on this planet, and I weep. I watch movies, read books and hear stories of personal hardship, and I grieve along with them. It seems that some people are cursed with more than their share. That seems wrong.

But a different point of view might suggest that those sufferers are the chosen, the blessed. They have had an opportunity to heal and grow their souls. They are the enlightened ones, further along in their journey. Medical doctor, researcher and psychologist Joan Borysenko says in her book *Fire in the Soul: A New Psychology of Spiritual Optimism* that "even the most painful and seemingly senseless events can be understood as grist for the mill of soul-making and deep healing," and "part of the value of suffering . . . is that it initiates or intensifies the search for what is most sacred."[6] Pain is our birthright. If we deny it we're robbed, we're cheated out of being human.

I have always loved the work of Christiane Northrup, a medical doctor and expert on mind/body wellness. In her best-selling book *Women's Bodies, Women's Wisdom*, she quotes an old Sufi saying:

> Overcome any bitterness that may have come to you because you were not up to the magnitude of the pain that was entrusted to you. Like the mother of the world who carries the pain of the world in her heart, each one of us is part of her heart and therefore endowed with a certain measure of cosmic pain. You are sharing in the totality of that pain. You are called upon to meet it in joy instead of self-pity. The secret is to offer heart as a vehicle to transform cosmic suffering into joy.[7]

Our pain feeds our art. By transforming darkness into luminescence we become better poets, writers, storytellers and seekers. We become better people. We learn to make a work of art of our lives. When we have room for our pain, we have room for the pain of others and we can actually help bear the suffering of others. Our suffering is a gift.

Through our suffering and healing we help to enlighten humanity as a whole. Healing comes about through a change of consciousness, a change of heart, through forgiveness of others, forgiveness of ourselves, forgiveness of Life and forgiveness of God. Healing comes when we let go of how we *think* our life should have unfolded and instead accept our life the way it is. Through sorrow you will bring more meaning, joy and fullness to your life.

"NUMBING OUT"

I want to know if you can sit with pain, mine or your own, without moving to hide it or fade it or fix it.
- ORIAH MOUNTAIN DREAMER

Instinctively we try to shrink away from pain. Pain is messy and ugly. We don't have the time for it, and what will the neighbors think? So we pop a pill, we numb out, we coast. We've become experts at easing our pain, erasing any jagged edges, pretending that dark nights of the soul don't really exist.

In the 1950s, when people visited their doctors because they couldn't bear the burdens of life or were feeling an emotional malaise, they were given the "feel-good" drug – Valium. There were so many people hooked on Valium that it became part of our culture. There were jokes about Valium and it was talked about in the popular media. Today Valium is still part of our culture, although the antidepressant drug Prozac is now threatening to supplant it.

Not too long ago I read an article on depression in a national magazine. The writer's focus was on the new drugs available to curb this devastating disease. While some people have legitimate biochemical disorders of the brain, I think we need to consider that others may be experiencing their dark nights of the soul, and have been increasingly so over the past two decades. There is enormous pressure to do more, be more, make more. We spend more time commuting to our jobs and less time with our families. It's a fast-paced world, and every day we're reminded that we've got to stay current, flexible and positive in order not to become obsolete. It's no wonder then that depression is on the rise. We've reached rock-bottom. And we're choosing to numb out with powerful drugs.

While I know that drugs have saved many lives, I also feel that as a society we're hooked on them – both the legal and the illegal kind. "We get the message of pain all wrong," says Norman Cousins. "Instead of addressing ourselves to the cause, we become pushovers for pills, driving the pain underground and inviting it to return with increased authority."[8]

Drugs are disempowering. And they are addictive.

Perhaps these heart-wrenching experiences come to teach us that joy and sorrow are two sides of one coin. You can't say "yes" to one without also saying "yes" to the other.

Open your eyes to your dark nights of the soul. What is their lesson in your life? What wisdom do they bring? What healing do they offer?

A HELPFUL EXERCISE

When you have a moment to reflect, take out your journal and answer the following questions:

1 What dark night of the soul have you experienced?
2 What signs are there in your personal or professional life that may be symptoms of a dark night of the soul?

3 What dark night of the soul might you be going through right now?

4 What do you think the "gift" is?

5 How might the dark night of the soul feed your art?

RESPECT AND RELEASE YOUR FEELINGS

We know too much and feel too little.

– BERTRAND RUSSELL

One February several years ago I could not get out of bed for three days. Sadness engulfed my heart. I felt I had been betrayed by a friend and all I could do was cry and stay in bed. The depth of my sadness was so real and so overwhelming that, quite frankly, part of me thought I was going crazy. I could hear a voice in my head saying, "My God, Grace, get a grip!" But when I tried to deny how I felt and force myself to get up, I would fall back into bed, completely limp with sorrow. Eventually a deeper voice – my higher Self – reassured me, "It's okay, you're not going crazy. Just stay with it. Respect your sadness. You'll figure it out."

I did figure it out eventually. Yes, I was upset and hurt by the incident, but I came to realize that most of the emotion I had felt and released in those three days had been an "old" betrayal from my childhood that had been locked away in my body. When I was two years old, my parents left me with my grandparents in southern Italy so they could take advantage of employment opportunities in Switzerland. They had felt extremely guilty about leaving me, so, to avoid the pain of separation, they had left after putting me down for a nap. When I woke up they weren't there. Intellectually, I've always understood why they did it. But emotionally, I felt tricked, deceived, betrayed. I had carried all that childhood sadness inside my heart until the day my sense of betrayal was triggered again, this time at a deep level.

Swiss-German psychotherapist Alice Miller says it is not childhood trauma per se that engenders problems later in life, but our repression of the feelings associated with the trauma. Feelings are repressed when the child has no one to name, listen to and validate their feelings. Given no language and no voice, the fear, anger and rejection are banished to the realm of the subconscious. "But they will, nevertheless, stay in her body, her cells, stored up as information that can be triggered by a later event," writes Miller in *The Drama of the Gifted Child*.[9]

We must overcome this disease of repression. We need to respect our feelings, not hide them. We need to release them, not bottle them up. Once we become conscious of our pain, we must go through it and cry our tears, express our anger. When your feelings come out in full force – whether directed at yourself, your partner or your children – know that old feelings from the past are asking to be healed. Pay attention to them.

Expressing feelings is as natural as walking or eating. But we've been conned. Too often we are told that men shouldn't cry and that women shouldn't get angry. What the mind represses, the body expresses. Unexpressed feelings from the past stay locked in our cells and block our vital energy flow. Research suggests that many conditions and illnesses are linked to an inability to express feelings and emotions.

Releasing emotion is a blessing; it's an opportunity to heal the past. After my workshops people will sometimes hug me. I usually let Spirit guide me and will often offer some words of encouragement or inspiration. That's when I see their eyes getting moist. Embarrassed, they stare at their feet. They apologize. I tell them, "Never apologize for your tears. Your tears are my gift to you." Every time you respect and release your emotions, know that you are healing a part of your past. You can let go of what was holding you prisoner and look forward to taking the step toward your future.

RESCUE YOUR HEART

Keep knocking, and the joy inside will eventually open a window and look out to see who's there.

– RUMI

Imagine a treasure buried deep beneath the earth. In order to get to it you must dig a tunnel straight down. You must work and sweat. Your fingers will bruise and bleed. You must burrow beneath the clay and the rocks. But the effort will be worth it because you will find what you were looking for at the end. You'll find a treasure chest, and inside the chest will be your heart, bursting with infinite Love and Light. You were given this heart by your Creator to show love. But your fault lines, your dark nights of the soul and the wounds from your past have prevented you from sharing your heart with others. It has been waiting for you to rescue it.

What makes this effort hard is that you must dig through five layers of old emotions and heal them before you can get to the love in your heart. Each layer of rock and sediment you clear away represents a different level of healing. The five levels of healing are anger, sadness, fear, longing and forgiveness. You will come to know each level intimately by naming it, feeling it and expressing it. Every time you shed a tear, express your anger, feel your fear or admit a longing, you are getting closer and closer to being able to express your love. But in order to love, you must rescue your heart. Healing happens when we embrace all of our emotions, feel them and then let them go.

It's easier to move through those five layers if you can think of a specific example that triggers each feeling. Is there a relationship that needs healing, perhaps with your mother or father or a past lover? Is there a trauma you must deal with? What is a burning issue in your life right now? What relationship would you like to heal?

Many people can't heal because they try to take shortcuts to get to their treasure. They're fooling themselves. They think they can forgive before venting anger. It doesn't work that way. The laws of the Universe dictate that healing happens from the top down, not the other way around. The only way to free your heart and make it whole again is to do the necessary work. If done with integrity and respect, the process can be life-changing.

HEALING THE FIRST LAYER: ANGER

You will not be punished for having anger.
You will be punished by it.
— BUDDHA

"Anger is your personal jet fuel," says Christiane Northrup. Healing the past cannot be done without respecting and releasing your anger. Anger is the top layer of dirt and clay. You can't get to any other level of healing without first cleansing your body of anger. Writing about your anger is one level of expression. But you also need to voice it. Scream, yell, swear, growl, roar. Let your anger free itself through your voice. Find a private place and trust your process. Next it must come out of your body. It's been locked in your tissues and your cells. It's been clogging your energy. There are many ways to move anger out of the body – beat a rug, drive your fists into your pillow (in anger-release workshops, we use a punching bag).

How do you know when all the anger has been cleared out of your system? You'll know when your recall of the event or trauma no longer triggers your rage.

Clearing anger is not a quick fix, though. As with all emotions, be aware that you can spend any amount of time at each level, depending on the event or relationship you are trying to heal. For example, a friend of mine who was making peace with her abusive childhood spent two years feeling angry about everything. Don't judge yourself. Give yourself time. You may be digging for a while.

Women often skip the anger stage, despite the fact that most of them carry enough rage inside to blow up a football stadium. I have participated in anger workshops and I've led intensive weekend retreats where people do deep process work. A room full of people releasing anger and pain through the voice and the body can often resemble a maternity ward! It always amazes me how people who appear to be quite meek and mild-mannered can store enormous amounts of anger within. It's those people who take longest with this first layer.

I like what Julia Cameron says about anger in her book *The Artist's Way:* "Anger is a map. Anger shows us what our boundaries are. Anger shows us where we want to go."[10]

Make anger your ally. It will not betray you. Rather, it will tell you when you have been betrayed by others. It will tell you when you have betrayed your heart. It will show you which rooms of your castle you have closed off. To get in touch with your anger now, get out your journal and think of a person or event that really bugs you, and then start writing.

Here are some statements to help you with the dig:

1 I feel angry when _____.
2 How dare you _____.
3 I hate it when _____.
4 I resent that _____.
5 I'm fed up with _____.

In the book *Anger Kills*, author Redford Williams says that by being angry with others you're killing yourself. We know that anger can hurt your health, but if left unexpressed it can also hurt others, sometimes those we love most. Angry people are hostile and belligerent. As a society we've paid a high cost for uncontrolled anger. It has shown up in our neighborhoods, classrooms and homes. Listen to your anger and learn to express it in a healthy way.

HEALING THE SECOND LAYER: SADNESS

We remember sadness so that we can ignite and enhance life.
– BRIAN SWIMME

To penetrate this layer, we must cry. We must feel sad. Unfortunately, this is the stage that most men avoid and where most women hang out. When women feel frustrated and angry, they cry. Men get angry. "Losing it" for women means crying. For men, it's a fit of temper. Men don't want to feel sad because they've been trained to equate tears with weakness. If women must get in touch with their rage, then men must shed a few tears.

I had a client once who was so unaware of his feelings that he didn't have them in his vocabulary. He was a member of

Mensa and prided himself on his intellectual abilities, but he had also been severely abused as a child. He had shut down his heart and his capacity to feel anything. I counseled him for years. When he cried his first tears, it was an epiphany. We had finally broken through the concrete wall surrounding his heart.

Think about the incident or relationship that you expressed anger at and now express your sadness about the same situation. Do this exercise in private, when you know you will not be interrupted. Don't let anything interrupt your tears. Let them flow out of your body like a peaceful river. Put your shame on the shelf and feel compassion for yourself. Hold your heart in your hand and envelop it with kindness. That's how you heal your pain.

I couldn't talk about certain events in my life without my lower lip quivering. That's how I knew I still had sadness left inside me. When you have cried all of your tears around a certain event or relationship, it's over. You're ready to move to the next layer.

1 I feel sad about _____.
2 It makes me sad when _____.
3 It cuts like a knife when _____.
4 I feel let down about _____.
5 I'm hurting because _____.
6 I feel sorrow over _____.

HEALING THE THIRD LAYER: FEAR

Fear is what blocks an artist. The fear of not being good enough. The fear of not finishing. The fear of failure and of success.

– JULIA CAMERON

I talked about fear in Chapter 5, but the fear you are releasing at this stage is specifically about the situation you have selected to heal. Many of us have lots of fears that we are not conscious of. I was helping Claire, one of my clients, dig for her treasure. She had been abandoned by her mother when she was two years old and she grew up not knowing who her parents were. She had so much anger and hurt about this that she couldn't wrap her brain around fear. "Fear?" she would remark. "I don't have any."

It took a while, but Claire at last became aware of childhood fears she had experienced around the abandonment. "I was scared of being alone. I was afraid I wasn't good enough." And then she began to cry. I recognized that Claire still had sadness to express, tears to shed. Healing in one stage may trigger another, and that's okay. Some people while expressing their fear get in touch with their anger, and that's beneficial too. That's why it's important that you don't rush through the process. Right now, focus on fear. Express it with your voice and with your pen.

1 I'm scared that _____.
2 I was afraid of _____.
3 I'm frightened about _____.
4 I'm fearful when _____.

HEALING THE FOURTH LAYER: LONGING

It doesn't interest me what you do for a living. I want to know what you ache for, and if you dare to dream of meeting your heart's longing.
— ORIAH MOUNTAIN DREAMER

We all have deep longings, aches that yearn to be satisfied, depths that crave to be filled. When our desires and longings are not met, we grow bitter and resentful. This layer is an opportunity for you to state your heart's longing without compromise and fear. When you think about your relationship with your parents, what didn't you get? In your relationship with your ex, what did you want but never received? What do you need now from the significant people in your life?

Have you forgotten the longings of your heart? When my children were younger and I was away teaching seminars, I would call every night to speak to them. Those phone calls weren't always easy for me. As soon as Jasper and Kajsa came to the phone, their precious little voices would get straight to the point. "I want you, Mommy." That's all they'd say, over and over, like some sort of mantra.

"Tell me what you did today, my darling," I would ask my daughter.

"I want you, Mommy."

"How was school, Jasper?"

"I want you, Mommy."

The pain of their longing would cut right through me. I ached desperately to hold them, to smell them, to kiss them. Their longing for me was so strong and direct and they could express it in such a straightforward and healthy way.

Most adults can't do this because they're ashamed of their

longings. They feel they don't have the right to them. In order to heal and get to your heart buried deep in the rock, you must awaken your deepest longings and desires. You may have shut down your longings as a child. What did you want but didn't get? This layer of healing is about acknowledging your unmet needs. Think about the situation you're working on and complete these sentences:

1 All I ever wanted was _____.
2 I would have wanted you to _____.
3 I want us to _____.
4 I yearned for _____.
5 I wish _____.
6 I desire _____.

HEALING THE FIFTH LAYER: FORGIVENESS

*When we forgive, we set a prisoner free
and discover that the prisoner we set free is us.*
- LEWIS SMEDES

Years ago I was invited to speak to a group of women who had been sexually abused. The workshop was called "Journey to the Self" and I talked mainly about personal empowerment and developing self-esteem. At one point I was speaking about the importance of forgiveness when a woman in the back row stood up and started yelling, "Forgiveness! You obviously know nothing about being sexually abused. I can never forgive that bastard for what he did to me. Forgiveness! How dare you come here and speak to us about forgiveness!"

I was horrified. I was still so green that I couldn't respond to her attack, so I backtracked and tried to suggest something else.

Today I would have gone over to her with love and compassion in my heart and said, "You don't have to forgive. Forgiveness is for him. Letting go is for you. I am here to help you heal so you can move on with your life. When you've expressed enough anger, enough sadness, enough fear, then you'll be ready to think about letting go."

Life is filled with hurts, both large and small. The only way we can walk away from the pain inflicted by others is through extending forgiveness. If you can't forgive, then let the hatred and pain go.

This is the last layer to dig through before you can rescue your heart from inside the treasure chest, and it's the most challenging. Why is it so hard to forgive? I think it's because it's difficult for our Egos to let go of the power that comes from being wronged. As long as we feel hurt and damaged we give ourselves the right to blame and judge. We are the victims. Ego can point the finger and feel a certain power. Forgiveness takes great strength because you are extending unconditional love to the person who wronged you. Unconditional love is possible only when we put Ego on the shelf.

There is also a difference between forgiving and forgetting. We may forgive, but that doesn't mean we forget. Forgiveness is an act of compassion and compassion is holy. Forgiving someone's trespasses against us doesn't mean we forget about them; it just means there's no longer an emotional charge from remembering. Forgiveness doesn't mean the event goes away forever. It's still very real. It just can't hurt us anymore.

Forgiveness is not just a gift you give the other person – it's a gift you give yourself. Open your Self to the possibility. Begin by completing these statements:

1 I forgive you for _____.
2 I forgive myself for _____.
3 I understand why you _____.
4 I'm letting go of _____.
5 It's okay that _____.

Once you have rescued your heart, you can use it for its intended purpose – to love yourself and others. I offer this healing process as a way for you to release old emotion and heal your life. When we heal past hurts, we can cross any bridge – obstacles vanish and confidence is restored. The following are the most common questions I get from people about how it works:

How long does it take?
It depends on the issue or relationship you're working on. Core relationships (parents/siblings/spouses) take longer. To heal each layer it's necessary to remember specific events, and this may take time. Start the letter-writing process and see what comes up for you. Sometimes childhood wounds are buried deep within the emotional brain. Healing the past takes time, energy and courage. At my retreats, it usually takes about three hours to process a "core relationship" from the letter to experiencing all the feelings, but I've had about eighteen hours to set the stage. If you're on your own, this work is rather difficult. You cannot do emotional surgery on yourself and then make dinner. I recommend taking an anger-release workshop, or finding a professional who will help you release old emotion. This investment may just be the most valuable thing you will ever do for your peace of mind and quality of life.

What should I choose to work on?
Make a list of events or relationships that require resolution and
healing. For example, you may need healing in your relationship
with one or both of your parents, a spouse, a child, a sibling, a
teacher or an employer. Events that need healing include your
parents' divorce, your divorce, a death, a loss, a change, a trauma,
an accident, a tragedy, abandonment, betrayal and abuse. Choose
an event or a relationship that you would like to work on first and
go through the five layers of feeling.

What's the difference between writing it and speaking it?
What should I do first?
I suggest expressing the emotion by writing it down first. This
brings the specific painful memories to the surface, from the
unconscious to the conscious. Only when you've written the whole
letter should you go somewhere private and read it out loud. When
you hear yourself speaking the words you wrote, the emotion in
your body is triggered and it comes pouring out. You've got to feel
the emotion and heal the pain in order to leave it behind you. For
the anger stage, writing and speaking it is not enough. You must
move the negative energy called "anger" out of your body. Pick up
a plastic bat and beat a pillow, the couch or the bed while shouting
key phrases that will support your release of negative energy. You
can also use a punching bag. Even if you feel silly, just do it. The
key is to release the memory (i.e., the words) at the same time as
you physically punch or beat the object.

What if I can't get angry?
This is more of a concern for women than for men. Women
have not learned to get in touch with their anger, even though
many of them harbour intense rage. You've got to remember
and write down specifics about the hurt or the trauma to access

your repressed anger. If you still can't get angry, go back to some of your anger statements and start saying them out loud: "How dare you not protect me!" "How dare you abandon me!" "I hate your cowardice!" "I hate you!" Choose a point on the wall, or something that represents the person you are talking to. By saying "How dare you? I'm so angry with you!" the anger will start floating to the surface. As soon as you feel it, start hitting the punching bag or the pillow!

If you're still having trouble with the anger stage, be patient. You might have to get over your shame at feeling anger. Women at my retreats often confess that they would never have had the courage to do this work alone or even one-on-one with a therapist. It's just too intimate and scary. In small groups, there is a sense of safety and solidarity. I am always in awe at the tremendous transformation that happens to men and women after they've allowed their anger energy to flow out of their bodies. Getting anger out of your body is the best thing you can do for your health and personal happiness. As the Buddha said, you will not be punished for having anger; you will be punished by it.

What if I don't express anger, but I express everything else?
Then the healing is not complete. Most anger is unconscious, stuck in our Emotional brain, especially the anger we felt as children. We've had to store it away because it was not appropriate or, in many cases, not allowed by our caretakers. Left unexpressed, that childhood anger is still there and is activated by the people or events in our adult lives, especially those closest to us. Remind yourself that your anger is legitimate. Give yourself permission to release anger without judgement. Move that negative energy out of your body and reclaim your life!

But what if the object of my anger is my elderly parent?

I know it doesn't seem kind to express anger towards aging parents. They did the best they could to raise us, but the truth is everyone makes mistakes and everyone gets angry. You don't express your anger to your mother in person, only in therapy. Do it alone, or at a retreat or with a therapist, but express it. Get that toxic energy out of your body, otherwise it's always there, acting as an unconscious block between you and your parent. Your relationships will be richer and more rewarding once you move the negative energy out of your heart and body.

How often should I work on this process?
After you're finished writing the letter, leave it alone for a few days. Then come back to what you wrote and re-read it out loud and see if it produces the same reaction. Releasing your anger is physically challenging, so you have to pace yourself. It all depends on how you feel. Some people like to do it all at once and get it over with and others prefer to take it slowly. You will know by how you feel.

How long do I beat the bed?
It is healthy to release anger when it flares up inside you. The worst thing you can do is store anger because it will eventually "leak" out, usually at the wrong people. To heal a core relationship can take hours of physical release before you feel cleansed and free. Pace yourself. Take breaks. Drink water. You will know you're done when reading your letter produces no more angry charge, just sadness. That's how you'll know you've entered the next stage of the healing process.

Should I undergo this process alone?

The writing is usually done alone, but when you speak your words out loud, especially when you're expressing the anger, you should do it with a professional or someone you trust with your secrets. I encourage you to find someone to work with to help you with this.

Why is it so important to express these negative emotions?

Emotions are energy in motion. For us to stay healthy, all emotions need to move freely within us. When negative energy is stuck inside us, it creates imbalance, stagnation and disease. If you are feeling "stuck," take a look at the emotional toxins that have accumulated inside you. Each trial, tribulation, hurt or betrayal carries with it emotional energy that must be released. Many of us have pent-up emotions from the time we were infants. All this repressed energy causes emotional, spiritual, psychological and, in some cases, physical blockages. The process I'm suggesting is a tool I have found to be useful with clients. Everyone who has done this work with me has walked away feeling liberated. When you're ready, the right teacher will come so that you too can free your heart.

HEALING OUR PAST RESTORES OUR FAITH

All your past except its beauty is gone,
and nothing is left but a blessing.
- A COURSE IN MIRACLES

Tom put up his hand to talk about his marriage. He was worried that he was heading for divorce and wanted some advice. The seminar leader looked at him and said, "Well, my friend, the solution is easy – just love your wife." His argument was that *love* is a verb, not a noun, so all the distraught husband had to do was love her. Tom said that he couldn't, that he had nothing left to give. Again the seminar leader advised, "Just love her." Tom sat down again, embarrassed and confused.

The seminar leader's intentions were good, but Tom probably can not love his wife because his love is buried deep beneath layers of hurt, anger and fear. Before he can feel love, he needs to rescue his heart. And to rescue his heart, he needs to express and acknowledge the layers of hardened and forgotten feelings. If Tom wants to save his relationship, he must first learn how to heal it. Until he can dig through all the layers of hardened emotion, he cannot rescue his heart. His love for the woman he married will remain dormant, buried deep beneath the layers of rock and earth.

The truth is, we've all got emotional scars, but until we can look our past in the eye, it will always be telling us to be less than we can be. The Spiritual Age has a place for you to begin that healing process. Books beckon. Courses and workshops call out your name. Kindred spirits surround you.

We carry our own pain but also part of the cosmic pain that binds our Spirits together. We're one family. When we have room for our own pain, we have room for the pain of others and we can actually help to bear their suffering. Only then can pain be transformed into joy. When an individual heals, so does the rest of humanity. And when humanity heals, so will the planet.

In order to grow your faith and walk across that bridge toward whatever is calling you, you must heal the past – and rescue your heart. That is our greatest work, because that is how we nurture faith – faith in the Great Spirit, faith in others, faith in our dreams and faith that the bridge will be there as we move toward our destiny. Emotional healing helps us restore our self-esteem. It helps us heal our bodies, our minds and our Spirit. It allows us to cleanse our souls from the inside out, to throw open the doors in our beautiful castles. When we heal, we reclaim our magnificence. Our Spirit takes flight.

Healing past hurts can happen anywhere, any time. It can be triggered by a line in a book, a scene from a movie, a song on the radio or a question from a stranger, if you're open and willing. Trust your intuition. When the time is ripe, you too will experience those holy moments, moments that heal the past, transform your present and shine light on your future.

8

Esteem the Self

ST. PETER'S FOOT

> We are unhappy because we no longer believe we are
> a special miracle . . . we have become cattle, numbers, punch cards, slaves
> . . . we look in the mirror and no longer see the
> God-like qualities that once were so evident.
> We have lost faith in ourselves.
>
> – OG MANDINO

Should you ever visit St. Peter's Basilica at the Vatican in Rome, you'll find the tomb of St. Peter himself, the humble fisherman from Galilee who was one of Jesus' apostles. In front of the tomb are ninety-five tiny lamps that stay lit the year round. The basilica is enormously captivating, and the first time I was there I was awestruck by the grandeur of it all. The building houses one of the world's most celebrated art collections, which includes paintings, frescoes and wonderful sculptures such as Michelangelo's *La Pietà*.

"Follow this path and turn right. There you'll see a bronze statue of St. Peter. That's the starting point for the official tour, which starts again in half an hour," I was told by a Vatican tour guide. As I approached the statue, I noticed that St. Peter was truly majestic. He was sitting on a throne raised about four feet off the ground. He was cast in bronze, with exquisite detail, and wore a glorious crown studded with jewels and a robe made of red and gold silk. It was obvious that this was his church. As I got even closer, I noticed that below his robe his feet were not symmetrical. His left foot was perfectly formed, the toes intact, but the other foot, which jutted out a bit more, was totally worn away.

I remember thinking how strange this was. Why the imperfection? And then, I stood back and watched as pilgrims and visitors from every corner of the world came to pay their respects and homage to St. Peter. They did this by kissing or patting St. Peter's foot! They needed to touch him, to hold on, to feel connected to this great saint. And then I was struck by how many millions of times St. Peter's foot must have been touched. Can you imagine how many rubs that foot must receive in a day or a year? The power of these constant caresses, like drips of water on rock, is so great that they can over time shape a substance like bronze or marble or granite.

When we're born, we're all given a huge rock of self-esteem. As children we love ourselves, we have faith in our abilities and we know there isn't anything we can't do. There's not one tree we can't climb or sport we won't try or activity that's too hard. We jump fearlessly into the deep end of life. Kajsa's first word was "Self." I'd show her how to do something and she'd say, "No, Mommy. Self, Mommy, Self!" Indeed, children do have a strong sense of Self. It is powerful and magnificent to behold. But then they start to grow up and people come into their lives, just like the pilgrims in the cathedral, except that they don't all come to celebrate the child. Some come – unknowingly – to erode her rock. Some people rub just a little, so a bit of dust comes off but there's no immediate damage. However, years of that subtle rubbing can do a great deal of damage. Others are more blatant; they come with their hammers and chisels and take big chunks out of the rock. That's called child abuse.

For many of us, the older we get, the smaller our rock. Bit by bit, day by day, our rock has eroded away. For some people, the big rock they were given at birth has been ground down to the size of a pebble.

WHAT IS SELF-ESTEEM?

**Self-esteem isn't everything;
it's just that there's nothing without it.**
— GLORIA STEINEM

What is self-esteem? Research done over the past thirty years has shown that self-esteem is our most important psychological resource. It is a powerful filter through which our experiences and perceptions pass. If that filter reflects a core of high self-worth, then the perceptions and experiences the individual has will be empowering and positive. If the filter reflects low self-worth at the core, then all the individual's experiences will be tinged with a sense of victimization and negativity. Self-esteem is like the moon. It waxes and wanes depending on our moods, the events in our lives and how we handle them.

The man who first alerted the world to the importance of self-esteem, the father of the self-esteem movement in America, is Nathaniel Branden. In his book *The Power of Self-Esteem*, he defines it as "the experience that we are appropriate to life and to the requirements of life. More specifically, self-esteem is (1) confidence in our ability to think and to cope with the basic challenges of life; (2) confidence in our right to be happy, the feeling of being worthy."[1]

I was first introduced to the importance of self-esteem by

Jack Canfield, coauthor of the *Chicken Soup for the Soul* series. Through his company, Self-Esteem Seminars, Jack had been bringing the message of self-esteem to corporations and schools and to professionals in the field. Every summer he held week-long intensives for practitioners and facilitators who were interested in learning more about self-esteem. I attended the program during the summer of 1994.

Jack belonged to the first-ever task force convened in California to promote self-esteem and personal and social responsibility. I was impressed that politicians were behind the self-esteem movement, at least in some places. I learned that California was one of the few states to recognize the importance of teaching self-esteem to children and young adults. The task force had found that almost every problem of society, including violence, family breakdown and drug and alcohol abuse, can be traced back to low self-esteem. Its research showed that between eighty and ninety percent of five-year-old children have high self-esteem, but that by the time those children are ready to graduate from high school, their self-esteem has taken a dramatic fall. Only five percent of adolescents feel sufficiently worthy and confident to handle the challenges that life presents.

In other words, kids are born with huge rocks of self-esteem, but by the time those kids have grown up into adults, their rocks have been crushed. The result? Only one out of three adults has positive self-esteem.

This information produced a strong emotional reaction in me. I was simultaneously sad and angry. "What happened to those kids? Why did they stop believing in themselves? How did they lose that sacred connection to their magnificence?" I wondered. How could I teach adults to get it back? How could I teach teachers and parents and corporate leaders to enhance self-esteem in people rather than tear it down? I felt the call to do something. Life is too short not to have the self-esteem we need to do the things we want. I wanted to help those who felt beaten down by life, discouraged and perhaps lost. I wanted to reach out to all those who felt broken and teach them that they could feel whole again.

When I got back home I was excited. I learned everything I could about self-esteem. If I was going to empower others, I had to understand it myself. What I learned is that self-esteem is a huge topic and everyone has an opinion on it. But to me self-esteem has two components: self-confidence and self-respect.

Self-confidence is the part I link with the idea "The bridge will be there." This is the faith that no matter what life sends you, you'll be okay; your bridge will be there. It is a deep knowing or belief that at the core you are a beautiful, radiant and worthy human being who deserves love and happiness.

Self-respect I link with "Take the step." This is the *action* we need to take in order to move our lives forward. This is where we act on what we know, we walk the talk, we take risks. We respect ourselves when our actions are congruent with our thoughts and beliefs. Without action, no integrity. No integrity, no self-respect. And no self-respect means no self-esteem. We need both self-confidence and self-respect in order to have self-esteem.

Perhaps one of the reasons that the self-esteem movement has received some negative publicity is that the focus has been too much on building self-confidence at the expense of building self-respect. That is the greatest challenge for teachers every-where. How do you get people to apply what they know? This is my challenge when I give workshops and training seminars. I have found that for the most part we know what to do, but we don't do what we know. Learning isn't learning unless we can integrate it into our lives and take risks, make changes, do something different that will move our lives forward.

For example, we all know about the dangers of cigarettes, yet we smoke. We all know that junk food is not good fuel for the body, yet we eat it. We may believe we deserve happiness and love, yet our actions betray us. We all know the benefits of exercise, yet we don't exercise. The betrayal of integrity and the guilt we feel when we don't do what we know feeds into the negative cycle. We feel bad for not taking action and then that bad feeling keeps us stuck.

I always have a sheet called "Action Steps" in the handouts I give to my workshop participants. I encourage them to make a commitment to doing one or two things differently after they leave. I tell them that taking one or two action steps, stretching outside their comfort zones by only one percent, can translate into huge, lasting, positive life-changes that will get them closer to the person they want to be. Then I get them to share their action steps with the person next to them, because I have found that our commitments are stronger when we declare them publicly.

You can grow your rock of self-esteem by either working on your thoughts (faith) or by taking risks (action). It's a bit of a catch-22. You need to take action to feel good about yourself, but you need to feel good about yourself before you will take risks. There may be some situations where you're comfortable about taking risks, but in others you might have to do some mental preparation beforehand. Remember the dream that opened this book? I tried to scale the sheer marble wall, but I couldn't do it by action alone. I kept trying, but I kept failing. I changed tactics. I paused, thought about it, then visualized and psyched myself up. Then my action was effective and I got to the top. Action and faith must work together to grow self-esteem if we are going to be able to secure the future we want for ourselves.

What happens when we fail? I find that for some of us, if we take action and fail, the setbacks make it harder and harder to get back up and try again. Self-doubt is insidious. The only way to deal with self-doubt is to build a bridge of faith. You do this by changing the pictures inside your head, by challenging your core beliefs and your mental maps. The other way you deal with failure is by stumbling forward, not backward (I talked about this in Chapter 5). Let failure help you refine who you are. Don't let it stop you from taking action or taking risks. If you fail and learn from it, you're still moving forward. That's what is important.

HOW THE ROCK IS CRUSHED

So long as we are blind to our inner tyrant we blame an outer tyrant, some person or some system that is victimizing us.
– MARION WOODMAN

Before we work on improving our thoughts and growing faith, let's examine that "inner tyrant." Do you criticize yourself incessantly? Do you have a negative tape inside your head that keeps repeating such upbeat remarks as "How can you be so stupid?"; "You'll never amount to anything"; "You'll never lose this weight"; "You're such a loser!"; or any other self-empowering thoughts? The fact is that many of us have childhood wounds. If our role models shame us, criticize us and abuse us when we are children, it is difficult to feel worthy as adults. In *Everyday Enlightenment*, Dan Millman says, "Nearly all of us have lost touch with our intrinsic goodness –

allowed it to be covered over by memories of a thousand transgressions, real or imagined, so that we feel only partly deserving of life's blessings."[2]

We all have emotional "stuff" deep inside us from our childhood that affects our outer lives. Some of us – most of us – don't even know that stuff is there. When I was in my early twenties, I knew people who liked to immerse themselves in tranquility tanks to meditate on their stuff. I was intrigued. I used to think, "Wow, I wonder what stuff I have that I'm not aware of?"

Let's face it, we've all got scars. Many of us come from dysfunctional families. People who can nurture self-trust and self-respect and self-love in their children are mature, responsible and secure. They love and accept themselves and feel safe and secure in the world. But some parents, though full of good intentions, can place appalling roadblocks in the way. While you were growing up, did you ever hear these encouraging words?

You're stupid.
What will people think?
You're no good at anything.
So you got ninety on the test. What happened to the other ten percent?
Bad girl! Bad boy!
How come you're not as pretty as your sister?
You'll pay for this!
Why would anyone want to give you a job?
I told you so!
You'll never be happy.
Why can't you be more like your sister, or the neighbor's children?
I wish you had never been born.
I wish you would just shut up!

You better stop eating or you'll never attract a husband.
You're just a girl.
You're too much! I can't handle you!
You're driving me crazy!

Do any of these comments resonate with you? These are rubs on the rock of self-esteem. Over time they will erode a child's confidence and make them believe they are less than the spiritual beings they are. And what of the children who have more than verbal abuse heaped on them? Those are the children who are threatened and beaten regularly, who are shamed publicly, violated sexually – who have had to experience what I call the ugliness of life. The ugliness of life is what Oliver Twist experienced – hardship, cruelty, darkness, hunger, cold, loneliness and betrayal. If this is what happened to you, then your rock of self-esteem has been torn asunder by a jackhammer.

Maybe you've said some of those things to your kids. People repeat patterns of speech and behavior they have learned. Patterns are repeated if there is no awareness there to defeat them. Don't beat yourself up about it; focus on the future. A very wise woman once told me that with children, every day is a fresh page. You can create new memories by deciding to behave differently tomorrow.

Parents aren't always the villains. Sometimes the experts of the day are to blame for how children are treated. In Barbara Goldsmith's biography of Gloria Vanderbilt, she writes that the most eminent child psychologist in the 1930s was recommending total detachment in child-rearing – no hugs, holding or kisses. Toilet training was to be completed at six months and "spoiled" babies who did not comply were to be force-fed castor oil. Such "experts" help to erode our rocks. Parents who have healthy self-esteem have a strong sense of Self.

They listen to and value their own instincts rather than blindly following the advice of experts.

When our rocks of self-esteem are small, we haven't the necessary faith to cross our bridges. We don't believe in ourselves. We don't think we can do it. Sometimes we get brave and head out for the bridge, but the fear-monsters inside our heads are too loud. They hold us back and, month after month, year after year, those dreams on the other side of the bridge lie there dormant. We wait. "Maybe one day I'll have the courage." "Maybe one day I'll win the lottery." "Maybe one day Mr./Ms. Right will find me." "Maybe one day I'll be happy." And so we fool ourselves into thinking that by waiting for others, our happiness is secured; by waiting for others, we might eventually get the outside validation that we're okay. We don't take the step across the bridge because our belief systems are flawed. We have lost faith in ourselves. We believed them when they called us stupid and bad. Bit by bit they clipped our wings and we stopped flying.

BROKEN ANGEL

Why have you valued yourself in pennies when you are worth a king's ransom? Why did you listen to those who demeaned you . . . and far worse, why did you believe them?

— OG MANDINO

My friend Caroline and I were out shopping one day when we noticed some items on a half-price table. Immediately our eyes went to a stunning Serafin angel that had been marked down. I picked it up and noticed a label: "Broken – half-price." "Wow! It's beautiful," we thought. Though we looked carefully, we couldn't find the flaw. We took it to the counter and asked the sales clerk to show us the break. She too could find nothing.

"Maybe it was put on the table by mistake," I said.

The clerk went to the back room to ask her manager. When she finally returned, she said, "My manager said that if it's on the half-price table, then it's on sale."

"What about the break?" we asked her.

"My manager says if it's marked 'broken,' then it's broken. Do you still want it?"

"Yes, yes, we'll take it!"

Were you labeled "broken" at some point while growing up? Were you humiliated and dumped on a half-price table for all to see? Were you awkward at something? Not good enough? Too much trouble? Did some adult calculate your worth and give you a price tag? Those labels are rubs on your rock of self-esteem. Who was ignorant of your magnificence?

Sometimes we may feel like broken angels, but we're not really broken at all. There's nothing wrong with us, but the labels from the past are a heavy burden. We've convinced ourselves that they were right after all. Those labels bruised our spirits. They were the voice of authority that as children we felt we couldn't challenge. But you can now. "Never in all the seventy billion humans who have walked this planet since the beginning of time has there been anyone exactly like you," writes Og Mandino in *The Greatest Miracle in the World*. "Never, until the end of time, will there be another such as you."[3] Appreciate that you are unique. Even your flaws and imperfections are unique. That is what esteeming the Self is all about. It's about realizing that you've had wings all along. You, my friend, can fly.

Dannion Brinkley was clinically dead for twenty-eight minutes after lightning struck a line to the telephone he was speaking on. It took him two years to learn how to walk and feed himself again. Fourteen years later he had another near-death experience when he had emergency open-heart surgery. While he was "clinically dead," Brinkley had some amazing insights. He wrote *Saved by the Light* and *At Peace in the Light* to share the wisdom he received while on the other side.

> Once we begin to really understand that we are not from Here, we are from There, that we all chose to come Here and were chosen to come Here, that we were somebody and something long before we came Here, only then do we comprehend that we are not poor, pitiful, stupid human beings. We are all great, awesome, powerful, and mighty spiritual beings![4]

If you could connect to your spiritual genesis, to the fact that you have wings, you would no longer suffer from low self-esteem or lack of self-worth. You would realize that who you are at the core cannot be harmed by anyone. That is what I think Jesus meant when he said in the Gospel of Thomas, "If you bring forth what is within you, what you bring forth will save you. If you do not bring forth what is within you, what you do not bring forth will destroy you."[5]

If you could bring out your intrinsic worth, your Light, your divine Essence, then you would be forever empowered to take the step and cross whatever bridge needs to be crossed in your life. Your rock of self-esteem would be solid. Sometimes a near-death experience, a spiritual encounter or a wake-up call of some kind is enough to show you that you are an angel sitting on a huge rock of self-esteem. All you have to do now is fly.

Remember that when you put yourself down, whether consciously or unconsciously, you are denying your magnificence, denying your spiritual origin. And when you deny your magnificence, you give others permission to do the same. Self-esteem is plastic. If we become aware of our hurts, learn to feel our pain and heal it, we become whole again. And when we're whole, we feel worthy. Your rock of self-esteem is your birthright. It is your ticket to everything you want in life. It is the foundation of your happiness. Once you love yourself and feel worthy of love, you will know who you are; you will understand your divine origin. The miracles of the Spiritual Age will start to shower stardust over your head.

YOUR THOUGHTS CREATE YOUR REALITY

Everything we are is the result of what we have thought.

– BUDDHA

Thomas Jefferson, founder of the University of Virginia and the third president of the United States, was also the principal author of the Declaration of Independence, which was signed on July 4, 1776. His good friend John Adams (the second president of the United States) defended the declaration before Congress. Both men proclaimed that they wanted to be alive for the fiftieth anniversary of independence. It was their vision and their dream. They nurtured this desire by returning to it often in their thoughts. Some would say it was a miracle, but on the morning of July 4, 1826, fifty years after America's Declaration of Independence, both men were still alive. Jefferson, who was eighty-seven years old, died after lunch that day, and Adams survived his friend by just a few hours.

This story amazes people. How was that possible? In order to reclaim our perfection and esteem the Self, we need to be aware of our thoughts. You are what you think. The Bible says it more eloquently: "As a man thinketh, so shall he become." So what do you think about?

Your thoughts have created the life you're living right now. Every single thought, whether positive or negative, the vision you hold of yourself or of your world – whatever you spend time thinking about – is the person you become. I don't want to say "the person you are," because who you really are is Light, Divine, Spirit. But negative thoughts can pollute this reality until you begin to doubt who you are and create a reality that says you're no good, unworthy and unlovable. Whatever you consistently focus on mentally you will eventually call into your life. Your thoughts may not be realized immediately, but eventually they do come to pass.

The creators of the movie *What Dreams May Come* explored the power of thoughts even after death. Robin Williams plays a character who dies in a tragic accident, as do his children. His wife cannot handle the grief, so she takes her own life. During the rest of the movie Williams tries to rescue his wife from herself, from the hell she has created inside her head. While Williams is in Spirit form, whatever thoughts he has are instantly realized. The movie suggests that on the spiritual plane, where there is no body or physical mass to slow things down, as soon as you think it – *poof*, thought is realized. Thought is pure energy. In the movie the new souls who arrive daily in this spiritual dimension quickly realize the speed with which their thoughts are actualized. They learn to monitor them carefully lest they have an outcome they do not want.

Think about the thousands of thoughts you have on a daily basis. Are they positive visions of what you want or negative, fearful visions of what you don't want? Suppose that everything you thought of, you experienced? Not next year, not next month, not tomorrow, but today. Right now. Would that motivate you to change your thinking?

Some research I read a while back suggested that on average we think fifty thousand thoughts a day, many of them automatic, programmed and unconscious. What are you thinking about right now? According to the late John K. Williams in his book *The Knack of Using Your Subconscious Mind*, "Positive, constructive, purposeful, confident thoughts will gradually reproduce themselves in the actual conditions of a person's life."[6]

Throughout history all sorts of mystics, philosophers and spiritual elders have warned us about the power of our thoughts. In *Conversations with God*, God tells the author, "It is the time lapse between thought and creation – which can be days, weeks, months, or even years – which creates the illusion that things are happening to you, not because of you."[7] That is why people don't connect their thoughts with what happens to them: It's because of the time delay. They feel victimized by the events in their lives, not realizing that their thoughts could have contributed to the outcome. At another time God says, "Thought control is the highest form of prayer. . . . Therefore, dwell not in negativity and darkness. And even in moments when things look bleak – especially in those moments – see only perfection, express only gratefulness, and then imagine only what manifestation of perfection you choose next."[8]

People are indifferent to their thoughts because they underestimate the power of thoughts to influence us. The truth is that negative thoughts not only block our energy, they block our ability to stay conscious and alert to the miracles of life. Gary Zukav writes in *The Seat of the Soul*, "When you release a negative thought, you release lower frequency currents of energy from your system, and this, literally, allows an increase in the frequency of your consciousness."[9]

KINESIOLOGY AND THE POWER OF THOUGHT

Take charge of your thoughts.
You can do what you will with them.

– PLATO

In some of my workshops I do kinesiology demonstrations. I find these a very effective tool for showing people how powerful their thoughts really are. I've done them with all sorts of different groups, including once with a team of people whose members weren't getting along. They had many unresolved issues that led to manipulation and plenty of back-stabbing. Trust was very low, but the senior managers needed the team to get along in order to ride out the many changes the organization was experiencing.

At the beginning of my workshop I asked for eight volunteers to come to the front of the room. I told them to stand in a line facing the rest of the group and hold hands (a challenge in itself!). As I usually do in this exercise, I put a strong, hefty male at one end of the line to show that negative thoughts can disarm and weaken even the toughest of us. Then I proceeded to test his strength by having him extend his arm outward and telling him to resist my touch. I then pressed on his arm with only two fingers. His arm bounced up in a healthy display of power and vitality. I acknowledged his strength and told him to hold on, that I would be back.

Then I went to the person at the other end of the line and whispered in her ear, telling her to close her eyes and think one negative thought about someone in the room. She looked at me with a smile and whispered, "Ha, that's easy." I asked her to keep thinking that thought until I told her to stop.

While she was focusing on the negative thought, I went to

my strongman at the other end of the line. Because they were all holding hands, an energy exchange was happening. I told him I wanted to test his strength again while the woman at the other end of the line, seven bodies away, was thinking a negative thought about someone in the room.

That was when his Ego became thoroughly deflated. He held out his arm, I pressed with exactly the same pressure and his arm was visibly weaker. You could see the shock on his face. His look said, "What have you done to me?" In some demonstrations I have done, the change is so visible that the audience gasps. It really is powerful.

I then asked the woman to erase that thought and to think of a positive thought about herself or someone in the room. I asked her to focus on that thought so that it would become emotionally charged. While she was doing this, I went back to the muscleman at the end of the line and tested his strength again. He was, of course, once more brimming with strength, but the look on his face was still one of confusion. I then sent them back to their seats and asked them to discuss in small groups what they thought had just happened. What do you think happens to your strength and vitality when you focus on negative thoughts?

THOUGHTS LEAD TO DESTINY

You must declare who you are in public.
Public declaration is the highest form of visioning.
— NEALE DONALD WALSCH

As I was explaining the power of thought at a seminar I was teaching in New York City, a woman in my audience got very excited, throwing up her hand and crying out, "Oh, oh, oh! I get it, I get it! Oh, oh, oh!" She stood up and told us that she had heard something really powerful on the car radio that morning, so powerful that she had to pull over and write it down. She said she had never done such a thing before, but what she heard was so compelling; she knew she had to capture it in writing. And now, after hearing me speak about the power of thought, she understood what she had written so much better. She was so excited that she could barely keep from jumping up and down.

By now all of us were curious, so I asked her if she wouldn't mind sharing it. She reached into her purse and proudly pulled out a crumpled piece of paper, then stood up in front of two hundred people and read:

Be careful of your thoughts, because your thoughts become your words.
Be careful of your words, because your words become your actions.
Be careful of your actions, because your actions become your habits.
Be careful of your habits, because your habits become your character.

And be careful of your character, because your character becomes your destiny.

There was a hush in the audience. It was a powerful moment. She looked up at me and said, "Thank you, Grace. I get it. It all starts here," pointing to her temple. "It all starts with my thoughts, and I can change my thoughts."

This was obviously a major shift in her thinking. It was one of those perfect teaching moments, when someone sees the light and shares it with others. Everybody wanted to write down the wisdom she had heard that morning, and I've been using it ever since. If you want to change your life, change what you say to yourself. Change the pictures inside your head. You can do this by activating your imagination.

Activate the Power of Your Imagination

Imagination is the first step toward action. You have to be able to hope before you move forward. Otherwise you are always acting out of fear.

– GLORIA STEINEM

Imagination is a powerful tool. Take for example, falling in love. When love is new, we spend endless hours imagining what to wear, how we will be seen, what they will think of us, etc. We see the world through the filter of our lover. Everything we do, see, touch, taste or experience, we experience through our beloved's eyes. We consume endless energy thinking, musing, wondering what it will be like when we are together. After a date, imagination embellishes and enriches the experience. This is imagination's role – to make life richer and more textured. A compliment can be turned over and over in our imaginations until it becomes an empowering mantra. A look or a gesture can nourish us for weeks, a deep, penetrating kiss for months and months. I know people who can still remember – that is, imagine – their first kiss. Even the thought of it can produce a flushed face and embarrassed looks. That's the power of imagination. Then when we fall out of love, it's because reality has in some way contradicted our imagination.

When I was traveling through India, I met a gentleman from England. He was visiting for the first time since moving away as a young boy. With tears in his eyes, he told me how disappointing his trip was proving, how betrayed he felt. It seems the India he remembered as a boy – the India he had spent hours boasting about to friends back in England – was nothing like the India he was experiencing during his visit. Reality didn't match the pictures inside his head.

The uncle of a friend of mine was reunited with his only sister after forty years. The visit back home to Greece was an experience he had imagined and looked forward to for a lifetime. He had lived in South Africa for most of his life and had told his children endless stories of his sister – of how they had grown up with no mother, of their trials and tribulations. The only family history he could give his kids was stories from his imagination, from what he remembered of his childhood and growing up with his sister.

Imagine then the disappointment when experience didn't match what he had pictured. He had never considered the possibility of a personality conflict between his sister and his wife. He had never imagined the worst heat wave in twenty years, which made being outdoors unbearable and tested everyone's patience. He had never imagined his sister arriving late at the airport to greet him. It was an unfortunate series of events, but the visit that was supposed to be the trip of a lifetime, the long-awaited reunion with a beloved sister, ended on a sour note. After he returned home my friend's uncle fell into a deep depression from which he never quite recovered. Sometimes when reality doesn't match our imagination, we feel cheated, betrayed. Our enthusiasm for life wanes. But sometimes imagination can also save us. It can be the only vehicle we have to escape from unbearable circumstances and painful memories.

CREATE A NEW VISION

The primary function of the human being is to imagine, not to stand up straight, not to make tools and fire, not to build communities or hunt and till and tame, but to imagine all these other possibilities.
– JAMES HILLMAN

The musician Ray Charles was totally blind from glaucoma by the time he was seven years old. If that wasn't enough of a hardship, he was orphaned by the time he was fifteen. He started playing the piano when he was five years old, and while at the school for the deaf and blind, he spent hours teaching himself to play by ear. He dropped out of school when he was fifteen and started performing with small bands, doing gigs in local bars and hotels.

When he was sixteen, Ray Charles borrowed six hundred dollars and took a bus to Seattle. When people later asked him why he chose Seattle (it wasn't exactly the music capital of the world), he replied that he had wanted to get as far away as possible from Florida, perhaps because he had so many bad memories of the place. So he consulted a map and chose Seattle because it was the farthest away. When he got there, he used the last of his money to hire a few musicians and formed the Ray Charles Band. One year later he hit the big time. Today his CDs sell on average half a million copies. Many people have asked him how he did it, considering all the obstacles he had to overcome. You know what he says? "I saw myself as a recording-artist star. It was the image inside my head that pushed me forward and kept me going. I saw myself as a star and so I became one."

Ray Charles' imagination helped him create another reality for himself. Sometimes our thoughts come in the form of pictures. What picture of yourself do you carry around in your head? This picture is called your self-image or self-concept. The image is influenced by how other people treated you at an early age and the conclusions you made about that treatment. Psychologists believe that by age four you have a clear sense of whether the world is a nurturing or a hostile place, whether you are loved and whether you're smart or dumb, capable or incapable.

Some people were treated badly and drew negative conclusions: "The world is a bad place and I'll never get what I want because life is a struggle and I'm not very worthy." Others were treated badly and yet for some reason they took it as a challenge. Their conclusion was "Okay, so life is tough. But I'm not going to give up. I'll show them." They focus instead on what they want, and the pictures inside their heads support their final goal. In Ray Charles' case, his goal was to be a star, and that's what he became. What you must realize is that who you are today is not just a result of the way you were treated, or the obstacles you faced, but of how you internalized it – what you told yourself about what happened to you – and how you behaved as a result. Think what would have happened if Ray Charles had thought, "Wow, I'm blind. I guess I'll never amount to much."

Decisions we make at an early age about who we are end up being strong indicators of our personalities later in life. Unless we consciously challenge the pictures of ourselves that we have inside our heads – in other words, our self-image or self-concept – there can be no personal growth. What about you? Were you listened to? Did people respect your opinion? Were you treated like someone special or were the people around you indifferent to your magnificence, your talents? Was your community of friends and relatives loving and accepting? Were you trusted? Were you loved for who you were? Were you celebrated?

Imagination is wonderful. It nourishes us spiritually. It creates dreams and fantasies that we have every right to. It feeds our souls. And while it's important to dream big, to focus on positive thoughts and outcomes and to have faith in endless possibilities, we need to remember that sometimes our imaginations will let us down. But that's only because we have expectations. I know it's difficult not to enter the realm of expectation when you dream up futures for yourself, but leave yourself open to something better, God's plan, destiny, endless possibilities or however you wish to think of it. Ask the Universe what lesson is there for you if the future is less than what you imagined. Imagine the *you* that you would be if you had the necessary self-esteem and faith to cross your bridge. Conjure up the highest thought you can think about yourself and then cradle it in the palm of your hand. That is who you really are. Forget the rest. Forget the fears and the voices from the past. You have the opportunity to take the step and become the *you* of your imagination.

TAPPING INTO THE SUBCONSCIOUS MIND

The conscious mind may not know how the subconscious works or feels, but the subconscious knows, to the last detail and shade of feeling, just what is in the conscious mind.

— JOHN K. WILLIAMS

It's only in recent years that we have come to appreciate the importance of the subconscious mind and its role in our creativity, energy and success. By learning to tap into this underused resource, we can take action toward our goals, feel more confident and relaxed and enjoy greater creativity and well-being. We know that important discoveries and works of genius seldom come from the conscious mind. The German scientist Hermann von Helmholtz, speaking to a group of friends on his seventieth birthday, said, "Happy ideas come unexpectedly, without effort, like inspiration . . . they have never come to me when I was at my working table." Henri Poincaré described the same phenomenon when he said that his creative ideas did not come to him while he worked at his desk, but frequently flashed into his mind while he was engaged in other activities. Charles Darwin, who developed the theory of evolution, wrote, "I can remember the very spot in the road, whilst in my carriage, when to my joy the whole solution came to me." Albert Einstein recalled that the unique relationship between time and space and the nature of reality sprang into his mind while was confined to his bed because of illness.[10]

The subconscious mind is a huge reservoir of all our past thoughts, attitudes and desires. Into its trillions of pigeonholes go the things we read, hear and observe; the pictures we see; the impressions we receive; the thoughts we entertain; our dreams and our feelings. It is on duty twenty-four hours a day.

It has immense powers to solve whatever problem the conscious mind gives it. The subconscious mind is there to help us cross the bridge. It is our silent partner in life. It can help us achieve any objective.

Two key aspects to remember about the subconscious mind are that (1) it has the power to create and (2) it can learn to obey the conscious mind. Unlike the conscious mind, it has no power of choice. It does what it is told. Its purpose is to create whatever is desired by the higher, conscious mind.

Our personalities are not static. We are not limited by the kind of person we were yesterday. We are constantly changing and we can create ourselves anew each day. We can use the subconscious mind to give us greater faith in ourselves by directing it toward positive thoughts. "The first requisite of creative mental life," says John K. Williams in *The Knack of Using Your Subconscious Mind*, "is positive thinking. Aspiration molds the mind in a stronger way than does fear or trepidation. Appreciation is more creative than aversion. Confident thoughts are more powerful than questioning doubts."[11] By being aware of our subconscious self-talk and reframing our thoughts to be more abundant, more hopeful, more positive in nature, we can create miracles in our lives. It's those thoughts that create the bridge to our dreams.

What do you say when you talk to yourself? What do you think about? That tape in your head, is it positive or negative? Most of us are not aware of our negative subconscious self-talk. It has been programmed since birth – even, some say, since the time of conception.[12]

Your subconscious mind hears everything you say or think. At the University of Michigan, researchers flashed information cards for a thousandth of a second and then asked the hundred people who were participating in the study what they saw.

Each person was hooked up to a monitor in the next room that measured brain activity. At the precise moment the information was flashed, even though no one felt they "saw" anything, their charts registered brain activity. What this tells us is that the subconscious mind is an incredible sponge. It soaks up impressions, messages and information without our even knowing it. So even when the hundred participants couldn't recall an image, their brains picked up information. An imprint had been made.

Advertisers know how the subconscious mind works. That's why they pay networks big bucks, sometimes millions of dollars, to air their television commercials. Print ads are just as powerful. And if you think that magazines, newspaper ads and billboards don't affect you, think again. There's something called subliminal messaging and it's very powerful. While I was at university I attended a disturbing presentation by Jean Kilbourne. She had just completed her Ph.D. on the subliminal effects of advertising and was on the lecture circuit to share her amazing research. That's when I first became aware of how subliminal advertising seeps into our subconscious mind and contributes to our core beliefs and values – without us even realizing it.

It's critical that we learn how to harness those thoughts that go astray, that are self-defeating, critical and negative. What negative core beliefs have limited your growth and stunted your potential? If you can convince yourself of your limitations, your negative qualities, your less-than-human attributes – congratulations, they're now yours. Your subconscious mind listens to everything you say or think about yourself, and then works really hard to make it happen for you.

CONQUERING NEGATIVE SELF-TALK

If everything you tell yourself about yourself becomes a directive to your
subconscious mind, then any time you make a statement about yourself that
is negative you are directing your subconscious mind to make you become
the person you just described – negatively!

– SHAD HELMSTETTER

The following are just some of things that we say or think
about ourselves. You may think that they are innocuous
thoughts, but I would like you to consider the person you
might be today if you reframed some of these limitations to be
less restricting and more empowering. How different would
your life be? Put a checkmark beside the statements that relate
to you.

I'm just not a patient person.
I will never learn that.
I can't seem to get organized.
Today just isn't my day.
Nothing ever goes right for me.
That's just my luck.
I'm so clumsy.
I'm just not creative.
I can't do that.
Everything I eat goes right to my thighs.
It's just no use.
I can't remember names.
I'm not very good with details.
I can't function without my first cup of coffee/cola.
I will never lose these extra pounds.
I never have enough time.

I can never afford the things I want.

I just can't seem to get anything done.

Why should I try? It'll never work. I've never been any good at that.

I never win anything.

I feel like I'm over the hill.

Nobody likes me. Nobody respects me. I'm a loser.

I never get a break.

That's too complicated for my simple brain.

I get sick just thinking about it.

Sometimes I just hate myself.

I can't speak up. I'm shy.

I never know what to say.

Nobody wants to pay me what I am worth.

I always get a cold this time of year.

I'm just no good at math.

I'm just not a salesperson.

I hate my job/boss/co-workers/teachers.

REFRAMING NEGATIVE PROGRAMMING

Become a possibilitarian. No matter how dark things seem to be or actually are, raise your sights and see possibilities – always see them, for they're always there.

– NORMAN VINCENT PEALE

Why is it that our minds turn toward negative thoughts more easily than to positive ones? Why do people gossip? Why do we like to read about grisly murders, slow down to look at an accident or watch violent TV programs? Our ancestors enjoyed gladiatorial games in which people butchered each other in the name of sport. As a journalist I was amazed at the appetite people have for negative news. In fact, if it wasn't negative it wasn't considered "hard news." If you were a serious journalist, the last thing you wanted to report on was "fluff," those feel-good stories that I always seemed to gravitate toward (that's how I knew I wasn't a "serious" journalist).

Some people believe that we grew into our negativity over the course of human evolution. It may be a survival trait, because it can help us prepare for potential dangers. The problem is that the pendulum has swung too far. Some people have let a pessimistic attitude overwhelm their lives; all they see, all they look for is the negative outcome. However, this perception can be changed with intentional awareness. You don't have to throw up your hands in despair when faced with negative voices from the past.

The answer is "reframing." Reframing changes the way we perceive what happens to us. We learn to give the events in our lives a different interpretation so that we can call upon healthier ways to respond to our environment. You might be thinking that would be difficult to do, but it can be quite simple. Here's an example:

A client of mine suffered stress from his highway commute to work. He drove over two hours every day during rush hour. The problem was that he would stress himself out over all the "bad drivers" on the road. By the time he got to work he was in a foul mood and his staff had trouble relating to him. Not only that, but his wife was worried about what the aggravation was doing to his blood pressure. His inability to control his perceptions of the other drivers was stealing quality from his life.

Reframing for him meant that he had to tell himself something different about the bad drivers so as to produce fewer stress hormones in his system. So he learned to perceive them with new eyes. When a driver cut him off, he would have the following internal dialogue: "Okay, buddy, I know, I know. You've got to get to the hospital because your wife is having a baby. Hey, I understand. I'm a dad myself."

Every bad driver was rushing to some emergency. Once our brains perceive a different reality, we experience different emotions. He could forgive the other drivers more easily when he gave them reasons for their mistakes. The result of this exercise was that he started to calm down and began letting go of his road rage. He stopped looking for the bad drivers.

Reframing is powerful. It can change your life. Think about a challenging relationship or situation you are dealing with right now. Ask yourself, "What attitude shift can I make that will allow me to see this situation in a different way, in a more positive light?"

Think about this question. Ponder it. If you don't get an immediate answer, that's all right; the answer will come. How you see the world affects what you get from the world. If what you've been getting is not what you want, then you need to change your perceptions. Examine your filters. Do you have an optimist's filter or a pessimist's filter when you look at life? If you want to influence your level of happiness and inner peace, you must be willing to look at the way you perceive reality.

$$L + P = HQ$$

What is replenishing? What is depleting? What takes? What gives? What wrings you out and truly, what rinses you with happiness?
– FRANCES MAYES

L stands for Life, P stands for Perception and HQ stands for Happiness Quotient. Life happens to us. Think about the things that happened to you today. Were you late for work?

Did you yell at your kids? Were you stuck in traffic? Did you celebrate a birthday? Were you criticized or praised? Was your plane on time? Did the meeting run late? Did someone stand you up? Did you make love? Have a fight? Shop? Pay a bill? Meet a friend for lunch? Play with the kids? Cut your finger? Give birth? Divorce your spouse? These are just some of the events that happen to people every day. You can't always control *life*.

HQ is the happiness quotient. Are you content or are you wanting? Are you satisfied with the decisions and choices you've made or do you feel an ambiguous emptiness in the pit of your stomach? Do you feel connected to your joy and your Spirit? Have you accomplished your heart's desires? Think about it – are you happy? The happiness quotient is the outcome, the bottom line. It changes over time; we have good days and bad, valleys and peaks. How we feel about what's happened to us depends on the P in the formula.

P stands for perception, the way you perceive what happens

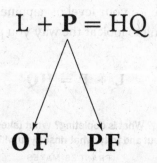

$$L + P = HQ$$

OF   PF

to you. This is where you have the power and ability to influence your happiness quotient. We know that stress is not the event itself but comes from how you perceive the event. Therefore you have the power to control your stress levels by altering your perception, by reframing what happens to you. You can choose to see the world through an Optimist's Filter (OF) or a Pessimist's Filter (PF). If you see the world through an OF, you approach life from the point of view of abundance. You believe the world is a good place. Before reacting to events you stop and think and decide on the best course of action. You feel empowered and proactive. You know that life is a series of choices and that the word "responsibility" means the ability to choose a response. You don't blame the outside world for your problems; rather, you look within and ask yourself, "How can I avoid this mistake next time? What can I do now to make it better?" Optimists can have bad days, but they bounce back quickly. They are future oriented.

On the other hand, if you see the world through a PF, you react negatively to everything. You believe the world is a hostile place and you spend a lot of time being afraid and angry. You perceive the events of your life through a "poor me" filter. You exhibit the classic victim's outlook, blaming everyone and everything around you for your troubles. Because of your negativity you look outside yourself for validation, and when you don't get it, you feel unworthy and afraid to take action. When a pessimist has a bad day, it can turn into a bad week, a bad month, even a bad year. Pessimists have trouble shaking off misfortune.

Which of these filters you have makes a huge difference in how you perceive the events of your life. It's what we tell ourselves after the fact that causes the stress or the negative feelings. In other words, it's not the experience but what you choose to do with the experience. So many of our problems are unnecessary. We cast events as problems when they don't need to be. If only we knew how to come up with different interpre-tations of what happens to us. That is the secret behind stress management – indeed, behind life management. Event control is about interpretation, and interpretation is based on how we perceive the event. As the philosopher William James said, "The greatest discovery of my generation is that humans can deter the courses of their lives by altering the attitudes in their minds." Your attitude is your interpretation, the spin that you put on the events in your life. Your happiness depends on you. When reframing the events life has sent you, keep the follow-ing ideas in mind:

1. THINK POSITIVE ABUNDANCE

**Why gaze down the sewers
when there is loveliness all around us?**
- PARAMAHANSA YOGANANDA

When you think abundance, it means that you focus not on what you don't have, but rather on what you *do* have. This thinking is at the core of a positive attitude. Canadian artist Doris McCarthy, who is ninety years old, says, "I keep my eye on the half of the bottle that is full and ignore the half that is empty. The half that is full is so rich, so rewarding, so happy, that I would be stupid to regret the things I haven't had."[13]

Choosing to look at your glass of water as half full rather than half empty is not about denying the truth; it's about shift-ing the focus to an attitude of abundance rather than an atti-tude of lack. Abundance thinkers are optimists; they have a higher threshold for change, transition and stress. Further-more, they live longer than pessimists.

Thinking abundance is simple for some people. They automatically see the silver lining in every cloud. Sometimes we make fun of those people, thinking them unrealistic, stupid or naïve. Optimists have their bad days, too. They grieve, they cry, they get angry. But they eventually bounce back because they're resilient. Unlike pessimists, they refuse to stay stuck in the problem and blame the past. They would rather focus on the future and figure out what action they can take.

Job placement agents tout a positive attitude as a necessary survival skill for the future. Realize that stress is a perception, not an event. Whatever the situation, reframe it to focus on abundance – on what you have, rather than on what you don't have. Keeping a gratitude journal may help to get you in an abundance mindset.

2. FOCUS ON WHAT YOU WANT

When I have forgiven myself and remembered who I am,
I will bless everyone and everything I see.
– A COURSE IN MIRACLES

Reframing the negative things you think or say to yourself is not about denying reality; it's about focusing on where you want to go. If your job requires you to remember names, for example, and you're not very good at it, telling yourself that you're bad at it will not help you. Something more empowering would be to think, "Remembering names is sometimes difficult, but I am getting better and better at it" or "Remembering names is hard, but I can do it."

This attitude moves you from "stuck" to "unstuck." It's breakthrough thinking.

Psychologist James Loehr helps to train athletes, among them tennis great Martina Navratilova. Loehr has studied what tennis players do during a match in the twenty-second break between points. He found that mediocre players use that time to scold themselves for mistakes they've made during the game. Champions spend the time focusing and preparing their minds for the next point. One group focuses on the past, one on the future.

Tell your brain what you want. Create the vision and see it in your mind. Don't think of all the things that could go wrong; that is called "catastrophizing." Focus instead on how you want it to turn out. Let's say you have a job interview, an important meeting or a big event coming up. Instead of anxiously thinking about everything that can go wrong, focus on how you want things to go. Use all your senses to see the final result. Feel the emotions you want to feel. Talk to yourself in a way that will support the end result you want. Avoid using language that is fearful, self-deprecating and self-defeating.

3. WATCH YOUR LANGUAGE

And I made a rural pen,
And I stained the water clear,
And I wrote my happy songs
Every child may joy to hear.
— WILLIAM BLAKE

When reframing negative thinking, you must realize that the subconscious mind does not register negative words such as "don't." For example, if I said to you, "Don't think of a purple turtle," what would immediately come to mind? A purple turtle, right? The subconscious brain works this way too. It ignores "don't" and focuses on the other words. So if you say to yourself, "Don't be stupid," "Don't get angry" or "Don't be late," what have you just programmed yourself to do? Be stupid, get angry and be late, of course.

At the playground with my kids, it used to break my heart to hear the adults saying, "Jimmy, don't break your neck"; "Don't fall down"; "Lizzie, Don't hurt yourself." What was even harder to bear were the negative statements predicting some dire outcome." You're going to fall from up there!" or "You're going to kill yourself and give me a heart attack!" I'm sure I must have sounded like an alien, because I was yelling things to my children like "Focus"; "Be careful"; "Concentrate"; "You can do it!"

Pay attention to the language you use with others and yourself. What negative words or thoughts may be sabotaging your efforts?

4. CHALLENGE YOUR CHILDHOOD ECHO

Each of us has the right, the possibility to invent ourselves daily.
If a person does not invent herself she will be invented.
Be bodacious enough to invent yourself.

– MAYA ANGELOU

Think back to your childhood and some of the things that were said to or about you. Were they positive or negative? Adults are not always enlightened. I think we get too caught up in describing behaviors we dislike rather than communicating the vision we want. One of my clients, Bob, recently told me that he didn't like school when he was a kid. One day his principal came to his home and told Bob's parents, "This boy will never amount to anything." Luckily for Bob, he didn't let that opinion decide his future. He went on to teachers college and eventually became a school principal himself. Twenty-five years later, at a class reunion, he met his old principal and had the last laugh.

What were you told when you were growing up? Perhaps you remember wonderful things being said to you. Those positive statements may have planted seeds that you are today reaping. Maybe you weren't so lucky. Perhaps, like Bob, you were given negative pronouncements, prophecies of how badly you would turn out. Did you let them come true or did you defy them? Sometimes, by becoming aware of childhood statements – the echo from the past – and challenging them, we can plow through our fears and anxieties and take the necessary action.

Here's an example. When I was a kid my mother used to say to me, "You'll never find a hat for that crazy head of yours." I guess she was trying to say I was too intense, too much, too restless. The message I received was that I would never be happy: I wouldn't be able to find a man I could have a family with, or the right career, and so on. I have defied this message and found many hats to wear, and I feel blessed to be who I am. I also realize that when I was younger I might have been offended by the word "crazy," but not now. To me it's a compliment. It means that I am creative, energetic and passionate. I think outside the box. I recognize this and take pride in it. Think of an echo from your childhood. If it was positive – great! Affirm it. If it wasn't – challenge it by looking at it from a different angle.

5. RAISE THE BAR

We ask ourselves, who am I to be brilliant, gorgeous, talented. . . .
Actually, who are you not to be? You are a child of God.
Your playing small does not serve the world.
— MARIANNE WILLIAMSON

I once heard a story about a rug seller. A man who had taken part in looting a city tried to sell one of the precious rugs he had acquired. "Who will give me a hundred gold pieces for this rug?" he cried throughout the town. He found a buyer, and after the sale was completed, a comrade approached the rug seller and asked, "Why did you not ask for more?"

"More?" replied the rug seller. "Is there a number higher than a hundred?"

How often have you set your sights too low? So many of us are capable of so much more, yet we don't even know it. We have set these self-imposed limits on ourselves. In many cases we have sold ourselves short. When you think about yourself, raise the bar. Use your imagination to create the grandest, most magnificent vision of your life that you can possibly have.

I once had a client in sales who hired me to motivate her team. She kept saying over and over that she believed that the bar was set too low, that their results could be higher. Even though she believed they could do better, most members of the team felt there wasn't any more they could humanly do. She was convinced that if they could just remove the limit inside their minds and raise the bar higher, they could jump over it into new possibilities and more success. She was right. We found that what was holding her people back were assumptions made by their previous boss who quit when the organization restructured. Slowly, with awareness, they pushed beyond those assumptions and, with her help and faith in them, generated more success.

Be open to trying on new glasses, new hats and new ideas. Stretch yourself. Take some risks. Aim higher. Don't settle. So many of us settle, like the eagle that hatched with a bunch of chickens. Every day he would walk out with his adopted brothers and sisters and play in the dirt. Occasionally he'd look up and see one of his relatives flying high in the sky. "Wow, I wonder what kind of bird that is? I wish I could fly like that." He was born with wings made to soar, but he never knew it. If he had flapped them around a bit and taken a risk, he might have realized he could be something more than a chicken. That's what happens to so many of us. What a tragedy to die not knowing we have wings.

Esteeming the Self is about treasuring your infinite depths. It is about celebrating and releasing your splendor. It's about connecting to your beauty, your intelligence and your radiance. When you believe in yourself, you feel invincible. If life sends you challenges, you bounce back; you find another way. Esteeming the Self is about believing in yourself, about living your life with more faith. "For self is a sea boundless and measureless," says Kahlil Gibran in *The Prophet*.[14] When self-esteem and positive self-worth rise within us, our mental bridge becomes real. Once we can see the bridge and feel it there beneath our feet, we step across it with confidence. We take action *expecting to succeed*. Expectation is a critical component when we take action. If you act expecting to succeed, you will. If you act expecting to fail, you will. When we esteem the Self, we strengthen our ability to expect excellence from ourselves, and our action steps become effective. Action – that's what it's all about – not just dreaming our dreams but *act*-ualizing our dreams.

Suggestions and Helpful Exercises

Do not allow your life to represent anything but the grandest version of the greatest vision you ever had about Who You Are.

— NEALE DONALD WALSCH

Learn to Reframe

1. Choose some negative statements about yourself that you checked off on pages 275 and 276. Write them down in your journal.
2. Now ask yourself what underlying message each statement supports. What core belief lies beneath this negative statement?
3. Ask yourself how this core belief may be sabotaging you. How is it stopping you from having faith in yourself so that you can take action? If you can think of specifics, great!
4. Rewrite the statement, keeping in mind the pointers on how to reframe negative self-talk (think abundance; focus on what you want, not what you don't want; use only positive language). Your reframing statement should sound empowering but ring true for you. You don't want to deny your reality, but rather to suggest another possibility for your brain to consider. Play with it.

Example 1:

1. Statement: "Nothing ever goes right for me."
2. Underlying message: "I'm a loser; I can't do anything right."
3. How does it sabotage me? It prevents me from taking risks because deep down I believe I won't succeed.
4. Reframing statement: "I attract positive experiences that add value to my life," or "Everything happens for my highest good," or "I learn and grow from every experience."

Example 2:

1 Statement: "I can't seem to get organized."
2 Underlying message: "I'm out of control; I can't cope. Help!"
3 How does it sabotage me? I'm constantly stressed and overwhelmed by life. I'm tired, crabby and impatient with everyone.
4 Reframing statement: "I am becoming better organized day by day," or "I have enough time to accomplish my priorities," or "I am in control of my time."

Write the reframing statements on index cards (these statements can also be called affirmations). Writing them down gives them more weight in your subconscious mind. Remember how teachers used to make us write lines if we misbehaved? I once knew a boy who had to write "I will not speak out in class" one thousand times. I'd like to meet him today! Visualize the pictures that accompany your reframing statements. Hear the statements inside your head when you need them most; they will become your invisible cheerleaders. You can also tape-record your positive statements and listen to them as you're drifting off to sleep. This is very effective for subconscious reprogramming.

The most important thing is that you create the vision of the person you want to be. You are in charge of your destiny. Make a commitment to empower yourself. Erase the negative programming from the past. Tell yourself, "I am attracting people and experiences that celebrate me and that allow the best version of myself to emerge. I am a magnet for all good things. I draw to myself abundance and opportunity. I radiate love and goodness to all I meet. I am a channel for divine Love and divine inspiration."

Choose Your Theme Song

What soundtrack is playing inside your head? Do you have a theme song, like Ally McBeal in the popular television series, that starts playing at odd times? Depending on your level of self-esteem, your theme song might be upbeat and cheery or dark and somber. Is it serious music or inspirational? Is it the theme to *Chariots of Fire* or *Rocky*, *Star Wars* or *Friday the Thirteenth*? Is it a jazzy instrumental or pop? Classical or reggae? Sometimes we play scary *Friday the Thirteenth* music when we're having a *Chariots of Fire* day. Why is this?

Music has the ability to cut through to the subconscious mind and release endorphins. It can be used as a tonic to affect your mood and it can also assist you with your goals. I recommend choosing a piece of music that makes you feel invincible, that is the best version of you. I need to immerse myself in music so that it penetrates my every pore. I can't bear to hear my favorite songs reduced to background music.

Crank it up. Let it seep into every part of your body. Let it make love to your soul. Close your eyes and connect to your power, your magnificence, your invincibility. Then turn the song off and think about that undone that is beckoning you from across your bridge. Is it a conversation you need to have with an ex? Is it a new job? Is it starting over with someone new? Is it public speaking? Whatever it is, close your eyes and imagine it. Feel the sensation in your body. Once you've got it firmly in your mind, turn your theme song back on. Associate the feelings of your theme song with the difficult thing you have to do. Imagine facing your demons and doing that thing with courage, magnificence and Love. Imagine the outcome you want – not the one you fear might happen, but the one you desire – all the while listening to your song. Eventually, any time you experience a crisis of faith, you will be able to close your eyes and connect to your theme song.

Connect to the Future You

Sit in a comfortable chair and close your eyes. Take three deep breaths and relax. Spend a few minutes breathing deeply and imagining yourself on a beach, relaxing under the sun's warm rays. Then visualize yourself in the future when you're old and gray, the day before your death. Imagine that you have lived a great life filled with rich experiences and adventure. Your heart is filled with compassion and wisdom. Then think of a situation or problem in your life right now that you can bring to your future self for illumination and guidance. Ask the older version of you for help with this problem or issue. Be aware of the first thought that you have. If you don't understand it, ask your future self to explain. Engage in a dialogue. There's no telling what insights you might gain from an older, wiser version of you. Capture it afterwards by writing it down.

Make a Habit of Gratitude

Keep a special journal next to your bed just for your gratitude thoughts. Before retiring each night, write down five things you were grateful for that day. For example, "Today I am grateful for (1) the telephone conversation I had with my parents this morning, (2) the surprise tulips from my friend Meranda, (3) the warm wind in my hair as I walked Jessie tonight, (4) the hugs my kids gave me when they got off the school bus, and (5) the delicious dinner my husband prepared."

By making a habit of gratitude you start to reveal the magnificence that is your life. Gratitude is healing. It helps us connect to what is really important. It helps us stay grounded in Love. It grows faith.

The Worst Thing Someone Could Say to You

Write down the worst thing someone could say to you. Ask yourself why it hurts so much. What part of you does it violate? Then create a statement that not only contradicts it, but enhances it. For example, if the most painful thing someone could say to you is "You're out of your league. You can't do this," write down "I can compete with the best. I can do it. I can do anything!"

Some other examples: "You're stupid!" transforms into "I'm brilliant. In fact, I'm a genius!" "You're a loser" becomes "I'm a winner – everything I touch turns to gold!" These positive statements will eventually influence your core beliefs about who you are.

Exercising Your Rights

People with low self-worth have limiting or restrictive core beliefs. In some cases, they don't even allow themselves basic human rights, such as the right to be happy, the right to make mistakes, the right to create one's own life. They feel they don't deserve a second chance or don't deserve to be loved. These irrational thoughts are based on a poor self-image. In order to esteem the Self and grow faith, we need to examine and become conscious of our core beliefs. One way to do this is to become aware of our rights. The rights we allow ourselves determine the action we take.

For example, if you don't give yourself the right to make mistakes, then your actions will be characterized by perfectionism. You will work hard to make everything around you perfect. We all know that striving for perfection is a self-defeating exercise. I always tell people to strive for excellence, not perfection. Perfection is an unattainable and self-defeating goal. Not allowing yourself to make mistakes will eventually become a burden and a curse. Joy will be sucked out of your life.

Take a look at the list below. Which of these rights do you honestly feel you allow yourself? Which ones do you not allow yourself? Write down any other right that occurs to you. Then ask yourself, "Are these rights based on rational, realistic, empowered thinking or on irrational, unrealistic, self-defeating thinking? Which rights encourage self-worth?" The ability to be loving and kind to your Self is one of the first steps toward healthy self-esteem.

I have the right to

change my mind	be moody
be outrageous	be impatient
choose my own life	have my own opinions
create myself	hang out with whom I please
have a bad day	color outside the lines
have a bad hair day	play
be grouchy	cry
make a mistake	feel free to be me
be wrong	be loved
look awful	have feelings
feel like not caring	feel tired
choose my friends	lose my temper
be authentic	take a day off
relax and do nothing	speak out if I don't agree
seek meaningful work	

Create a Collage of Your Passions

This exercise is a lot of fun. If you have kids, get them involved. Start collecting words, pictures, images, anything that speaks to you. Get a huge piece of bristol board and decorate it with your pictures, images, colors or poems. Arrange them any way you want. Then post it where you can see it every day. Remind yourself of your splendor, your magnificence and your Spirit.

Be Vigilant About Sights and Sounds

Avoid watching the television news just before going to bed. It pollutes your subconscious mind. It hammers at your rock of self-esteem. If you're that much of an information junkie, get your news earlier in the day via radio or print, which are weaker media. It's not necessary that you see and hear the wacko who raped and killed an eleven-year-old girl. It's not necessary that you see people running from bullets in war-torn countries. Those stories pollute the Spirit and subconsciously challenge our faith. Native cultures believe that we are all One, that the human family is connected on a spiritual level, therefore we are psychically affected by the actions of others. How can our souls feel good when we hear such stories? I'm not saying that you should lock yourself in a closet and hide from the world around you. Just be vigilant and proactive about the media content you and your family decide to take in. Young children are spiritually pure and very impressionable. Let's prolong their innocence for as long as possible.

9

Practise Love

WHO WE ARE IS LOVE

We are all born for love; it is the principle of existence and its only end.

– BENJAMIN DISRAELI

"I hate math, I hate math, I hate math."

Over and over again, Jim told us how much he disliked his worst subject in school. "I hate math, I hate math, I hate math."

"Okay, Jim," I said, "you sound pretty convinced. Let me test your strength."

I was teaching a workshop and Jim had volunteered to do an applied kinesiology demonstration with me. When I pressed down on his arm with two fingers, it collapsed and went limp. His eyes bulged out. "What did you do to me?" he gasped.

"Nothing. You were in a state of hate. Let's try this again with you changed to a state of Love."

I instructed Jim to close his eyes and repeat "I love math" over and over again until he felt convinced.

"But I don't love math," he protested.

"I know that," I told him, "but let's see what happens when you say you love it."

The two hundred participants watched as Jim began his mantra. "I love math, I love math, I love math, I love math. . . ." But his tone didn't match his words.

"Say it like you mean it," I urged him.

"I *love* math, I *love* math, I *love* math."

"How much do you love it?"

"I love math a lot, a whole lot. It's the best. I really LOVE math."

The audience applauded. He sounded really convincing.

"All right," I said. "Open your eyes. Let's test your arm strength again."

He lifted his dominant arm and again I used the two-finger technique to press down on it. This time his arm sprang up with power. He looked at me, confused but nevertheless pleased that his strength had been restored.

Jim sat down. "Any conclusions?" I asked the group. There was a pause, and then the response began like popcorn starting to pop, one kernel at a time. The *aha*'s and moments of illumination began to appear on their faces.

The first response was, "So those mornings I'm stuck in traffic and I tell myself how much I hate this city, I'm actually zapping myself of energy?"

A collective sigh of understanding rose from the audience. Another person spoke up. "No wonder I'm exhausted on Mondays. I always tell myself how much I hate them."

And then a woman said, "So when I struggle with the kids' snowsuits every morning, I shouldn't be telling myself how much I detest winter. Do you mean to tell me that it wouldn't be such a chore if I told myself how much fun winter is . . . even if I don't believe it? No wonder I'm tired before my day even begins."

Finally Jim asked, "So how come this works?" And I explained about the power of Love.

The reason we have strength when we come from a place of Love is this: *Who we are is Love.* Our core Self is fundamentally made of Light. This Light is part of a universal Light – the part of us that is most like God. Some call this the soul or Spirit and others just call it Light. The Greeks called it *psyche* and the Romans the *animus*. We are creatures programmed to love, not hate. When we're aligned with our true Essence – which is Love – we are mentally, physically and emotionally stronger. Our energy flows. Our strength is restored.

Every soul was sent to earth for one mission only – to learn to love and to receive love. This information was programmed early on. But after that soul took on a body, an Ego and a personality, depending on its past karma, the path of Love became obscured. Imagine a vast, boundless sea. Its Essence is Spirit and unconditional Love. Now imagine a bucket dipped into this beautiful Essence. The essence of the water in the bucket is the same as that of the ocean, but the walls of the bucket separate the water from its origins. The life we live is contained in that bucket. Over time we have forgotten who we are: We have forgotten our spiritual origins and that the purpose of our soul's journey is to love.

Love is synonymous with God. "Love is the threshold where divine and human presence ebb and flow into each other," writes John O'Donohue in *Anam Cara*.[1] Love is the most powerful energy in the world. It has the ability to heal our deepest wounds, and when we lose faith, it brings kindness, compassion and understanding to requite our sorrows. Love is the compass of life. It adds meaning where none existed. It is water to the desert rose. In its highest extreme it is a fountain of euphoria and ecstasy; when it is lost, blocked or denied, it leaves a bottomless well of despair.

In this chapter I talk about Love – Self-love, romantic love, parental love, brotherly love and friendship love – and how we can become intimate with life. By facing our fears and relinquishing the allure of Ego, we let Love blossom in our lives. Once we have reconnected on a spiritual level to that sacred ocean, we will make the practice of loving a habit. The German poet Rainer Maria Rilke said that to love another human being is "perhaps the most difficult of all our tasks; the ultimate, the last test and proof, the work for which all other work is but preparation." By opening ourselves to Love we can take the step across the bridge with greater joy, convinced that we're traveling down the right path. By remembering our soul's purpose, we can make the journey home.

LOVE AND ACCEPT YOURSELF FIRST

**Do not go to the garden of flowers! O Friend! Go not there;
In your body is the garden of flowers. Take your seat on the thousand petals
of the lotus, and there gaze on the Infinite Beauty.**

– KABIR

Learning to love begins with learning to love who you are, for you are the source of Love. Access Love for yourself and you'll be able to shower it on others. Learning to love ourselves is spiritual work; it's reconnecting with our inner beauty and our spiritual Essence whence we came. It's also difficult work. Silencing the inner critic and loving our rough edges is the work of angels. Angels love us the way we are. God loves us the way we are, but we don't. We put conditions on ourselves.

Psychologist Carolyn Hillman writes in her book *Recovery of Your Self-Esteem*, "Do you command yourself: Do something impressive, then I'll approve of you? That behavior works about as effectively as telling a plant, 'First grow, and then I'll water you.'"[2] The problem is, for whatever reason, many of us think this way. "First do something spectacular, and then I'll approve of you." Or "First get someone else to love you and then I'll love you." Or "Get a good job and then I'll accept you." Throw away those conditions!

In order to connect to our true Essence, we must learn to love and accept ourselves without conditions. When you offer yourself kindness, compassion and acceptance, you start a success cycle. You feel good about yourself; you can take bold steps that will lead you across the bridge toward whatever you want to accomplish in your life. Think about it. Typically, when do you take risks? When you're feeling invincible or when you're feeling beaten up by life?

Remind yourself that you are a miracle, perfect as you are. You have a magnificent Light within you that is meant to emanate Love and compassion to the world. The way out of the darkness is not by climbing the tallest mountain, winning an Olympic medal, getting a Ph.D. or finding approval from outside your Self. The only way out of the darkness is to accept yourself unconditionally, just the way you are right now. When you do that, you start a positive cycle of self-esteem and success in your life. I've seen amazing things happen to people when they let go of worrying about their faults and failures and embrace themselves unconditionally.

When my children were younger, at dinner they'd spend several minutes thanking God for everything imaginable while we listened attentively and watched our food get cold. Some nights they'd go on and on, wanting to make sure they hadn't left anything out. At the end of each prayer came the line, "Oh, and thank you, God, for me. Amen." Children are connected to their Spirit in a way many adults are not. Children know they are part of that infinite ocean of divine Love. Adults, it seems, have become disconnected from their Source and are unaware of their magnificence.

There is nothing you have to do to earn your self-love and self-acceptance. You are already good enough, smart enough, attractive enough, talented enough. You aren't broken and you don't need to be fixed. You're fine just the way you are. But herein lies the paradox. If we are perfect just the way we are, then why are we on the self-improvement treadmill, taking courses, attending workshops and reading books on how better to "sharpen our saws"? Why the toil and trouble to become *more*, *better* and *smarter*? Are we indeed perfect or do we need to be fixed? This is not a contradiction, but a paradox. Let me explain.

A client of mine had been trying to lose weight forever but just couldn't get motivated. Then one winter, while suffering a bout of flu, she lost five pounds. People noticed and paid her compliments. She felt good about herself. This gave her the motivation to take two steps: She stopped eating junk food just before going to bed and she started going for half-hour walks with a co-worker during her lunch hour. Within a month she had lost another five pounds. We need to feel good about who we are *first*, and then we will take action toward our goals. That's how motivation works. Self-acceptance allows us to feel good about ourselves where we are right now.

In order to accept yourself without conditions, you must realize that you were born the person God wanted you to be. You are unique, and your qualities, whether you see them as strengths or as weaknesses, were given to you so you could fulfill your mission on Earth. Look at your flaws through different eyes. Consider them as aspects that make you original. Embrace all of you; only then will you be motivated to grow your beautiful wings so that you can fly to even higher altitudes. I love what Gabrielle Roth says: "How can we love another if our own heart is stuck? How do we let someone in if we won't let ourselves out?"[3]

We can add to our beauty when we realize we're already beautiful. We can learn great things when we appreciate our own wisdom. We can cross the bridge when we give ourselves credit for all the bridges we've already crossed. Only when you truly practise self-acceptance can you push yourself beyond your limits and reach for the stars. Only by showing yourself compassion can you overcome obstacles that may be preventing you from moving your life forward. So first accept yourself where you are, then you can move forward.

PUT YOUR OXYGEN MASK ON FIRST!

If I am not for myself, who will be for me?
If I am only for myself, what good am I?
And if not now, when?
– HILLEL

One way to love yourself more is by learning to put your oxygen mask on first. If you have traveled by plane, you'll recall the information you're given at the beginning of the flight. "In the event of an emergency, oxygen masks will drop down in front of you. Please put your mask on first and then assist others with theirs." The logic behind this is not to promote selfishness, but to ensure maximum safety for all concerned. How can we help anyone else if we're gasping for air and keeling over? How often have you attended to others when you yourself were tired and wanting? How often have you filled someone else's cup when your own cup was empty? It doesn't make sense, and yet we do it. Sometimes we're running too fast on the treadmill of life to realize the futility of this behavior.

And yet we've been conned into believing that attending to ourselves first in life is selfish and unkind. For the most part we're taught to put the needs of others before our own. Where did we get this idea that martyrdom is holy? Most world religions recommend that we be magnanimous and selfless, and we admire those who can be so. Yet even Mother Theresa had to eat, sleep, pray and do what else was necessary to stay centered, positive and healthy. How else can we stay focused on our vision? There is something to be said for appropriate selfishness. We must become better at defining our boundaries, learning to say no and reconnecting with our centers. And defining your boundaries is about figuring out what's most important to you.

I hope you had a chance to do the exercises in Chapter 3. If you're saying yes to unimportant requests, then you're letting someone else define what's important for you. If because of guilt you're allowing yourself to be manipulated by others, pay special attention to Chapters 7 and 8. Saying no to people is not about being selfish. It's about filling your cup so you've got more to give everyone else. It's about putting your oxygen mask on first. But how can you do it and not feel guilty or manipulated?

HOW TO SAY NO
AND NOT FEEL SELFISH OR GUILTY

STEP 1. ACKNOWLEDGE THE REQUEST WITH KINDNESS

This is simply an opportunity to pause before giving your answer. It lets the listener know that you heard and understood the request.

Examples
- "Thank you for letting me know about that meeting. I'm sure it's important . . ."
- "I would love to help you celebrate this occasion . . ."
- "I love your kids, and they're welcome here any time . . ."

STEP 2. SAY NO

If you already know that the answer is no, then make it clear. Most people who aren't assertive feel uncomfortable stating their boundaries. Inevitably they make their answer ambiguous so they won't offend anybody. Later, because the requester walked away with the impression you said yes, you're put in the uncomfortable position of having to compromise either your friendship or your sanity. If at this stage you are genuinely unsure of whether you can do what is being requested, say "I'll let you know by tomorrow" or "Can I check on that and let you know?" If you know the answer is no, Step 2 sounds like this:

Examples

- " . . . unfortunately, I won't be at that meeting."
- " . . . unfortunately, I won't be able to attend your birth-day party."
- " . . . unfortunately, tonight I won't be able to babysit."

Use the language of intention, not victim language such as "I can't make it."

STEP 3. GIVE REASONS

This step is for the relationships you wish to keep, not for those one-time requests from strangers. This is the step that allows your heart to connect with their hearts. If you do it right, the person will accept your turning down their request without feeling hurt or slighted. How honest do you have to be? As honest as you wish to be. You can also be ambiguous, without going into details.

Examples

- "The problem is that I've got two clients coming in from out of town at that time. They are very busy and travel a lot, and this was the only time I could meet with them."
- "The problem is we're out of town that weekend." (You can give more details if you like, such as "It's my mother-in-law's birthday and all the children are giving her a surprise party.")
- "The problem is my children are sleeping over at their friend's house this evening and my husband and I have planned an evening out."

STEP 4. SUGGEST ALTERNATIVES

This is optional. You do not have to offer this step as part of saying no effectively. But in some cases you might suggest ideas or alternative solutions to help them out. It's a way to say, "I'm sorry I can't help you out right now, but I care about you."

Examples
- "However, I can send Jim in my place. He can tell me about the meeting and I will give you my feedback by Friday."
- "However, I really want to celebrate with you. Let's get together next week sometime."
- "However, I'd be happy to take the kids for you some other time."

Another reason we hesitate to put the oxygen mask on first is that we have too many personal and professional roles to balance. There's never enough time to do it all, and when we do, we spread ourselves too thin. When we ignore ourselves and attend to everyone else first, we grow bitter and resentful, not to mention unhealthy. To make matters worse, because we try to be everything to everybody (and women are especially guilty of this), we lose the connection to who we are and what our authentic Self wants. When we perform our many roles and responsibilities, we forget that it's *our* drama, *our* story, and that we came here to play the lead role in our own lives. Ask yourself, "What have I been neglecting in my life? What do I need to do or be in order to feel nurtured and whole?"

Once when I was talking about this principle at a stress-management seminar, a woman in the audience put up her hand to share one of her strategies for putting the oxygen mask on first. "Every night between 9 and 10 p.m., I schedule 'person time,'" she said. "During my sacred hour I'm not anyone's mother, wife, sister, friend, sex-goddess, manager, little-league coach, cook, taxi driver, daughter or maid. I am me – a person." The audience broke into applause. People really seemed to like the idea of "person time."

Give yourself one hour every day. Schedule it if you have to. Be true to it. Plan what you will do with your hour of person time. If you can't find one hour right now, aim for twenty or thirty minutes. Find time to nourish and nurture your soul. Self-nurturing is not a luxury, it is a necessity. By nurturing yourself you are showing yourself acceptance and love. When you feel validated and whole, you will be able to extend that love and kindness to others.

So ask yourself, what do you need in order to feel balanced, whole and nourished? You might take a weekend off from the kids, go for a walk under the full moon, spend a day golfing or skiing or go out on the town dancing. You might want to luxuriate in an aromatherapy bath, indulge in a slice of decadent chocolate cake or drink champagne in bed while your beloved reads you poetry.

There are a million ways to soothe an aching soul. Start making a list of ideas that speak to you. Then act on one every week. Whatever you do, don't feel guilty about it. Tell yourself, "I'm putting my oxygen mask on first." Try something new every week, making sure you put it in your planner. If we all took time to nurture ourselves, we'd be more empowered to take the step toward our bridge. And we'd have a kinder and gentler world.

LOVING EACH OTHER

*We are each of us angels with only one wing.
And we can only fly embracing each other.*
- LUCIANO DE CRESCENZO

Aristotle declared that man is a social animal, and two thousand years later we're still trying to learn how to love each other. The late Leo Buscaglia, in his book *Loving Each Other*, writes of a woman who was an invalid and very much alone. In order to maintain some human contact she would dial the numbers for information and the time at intervals during her day, just so she could hear another voice.[4] Some people keep the radio or television on all day for company. Many people in my workshops have confided that they feel lonely and isolated. We want to belong in a meaningful way. We yearn for Love.

Studies reported in *The Language of the Heart* by Dr. James Lynch show that lack of human companionship, chronic loneliness, social isolation and the sudden loss of a loved one are the leading causes of premature death in the United States. Evidently millions of people are dying, quite literally, of broken hearts. The death rates – for both sexes and all races – of single, widowed and divorced (or unhappily married) people range from two to ten times higher than those of happily married individuals. We crave contact and human interaction.

Government workers in remote areas get a special bonus called "isolation pay." We punish prisoners who misbehave with solitary confinement. And there are people who live together in committed partnerships yet still feel alone. There is among us a persistent sense of inner isolation. We busy ourselves. We travel down different paths. We lose emotional connection.

Dr. Dean Ornish, in his book *Love and Survival: The Scientific Basis for the Healing Power of Intimacy*, says that the most powerful healing doesn't come from exercise, diet or clean living, but through love and intimacy and the emotional and spiritual bonds we form with people. He argues that love and intimacy, or their absence, are at the very root of what can make us sick and what makes us heal. He cites countless studies that show our survival depends on love, intimacy and relationships.[5]

There is a fascinating body of research emerging in a field called "energy cardiology" (or "cardio-energetics") that argues that the human heart thinks, feels and emanates a powerful energy field that communicates information about who we are – our "code" – to all our cells. Observations and experiments discussed in *The Heart's Code* by Dr. Paul Pearsall, also show that the heart can and does remember. Pearsall interviewed hundreds of patients who had received heart transplants and found that, along with the heart, the recipient also received the donor's special "heart's code" that told them of the donor's loves, fears and fantasies.[6]

It seems that science is finally catching up with what we've always known spiritually – that the heart is the control center of the body and that the powerful energy that emanates from the heart can nourish, heal and transform even the most despondent of individuals. Loving relationships help us connect to everything that is real, beautiful and profound in the world. The path of relationship is perhaps one of the biggest challenges we face as human beings, but it is also the way out of the darkness and into the Light.

ROMANTIC LOVE
AND THE PATH OF RELATIONSHIP

What is that you express in your eyes?
It seems to me more than all the words I have read in my life.

– WALT WHITMAN

Romantic love is one of the most magical experiences in the world. Falling in love means that your beloved's Essence has been planted in your soul, and as it takes root it consumes your every waking moment. Your desire and longing to merge as one flesh know no bounds. Being far away from your love is like internal hemorrhaging. You mourn, you cry, you wait and suffer. There is no joy until you can have complete communion of heart, body, mind and spirit. From this union is born the Other – the divine spark that ignites in Love. The vision of how God sees you is reflected in your beloved's eyes – beautiful, radiant, alive and magnificent. When we're *in love*, we feel acknowledged, whole, complete and full – in short, blessed.

Naturally, when we meet a kindred spirit or a soulmate, someone who reflects who we really are, we want to hold on to that person forever. Why wouldn't we? They've introduced us to parts of ourselves we had forgotten about. Through their eyes we see ourselves as the beautiful, warm, intelligent and passionate creatures that we are, and we fall in love with ourselves as well. Through their eyes we catch a glimpse of our divine magnificence. "Love is not a cool arrangement or a night in bed," says Marianne Williamson in her book *A Woman's Worth*. "Love is angels hovering, circling, calling us to seek the sky together. And when we do, we change our patterns. We become new women; we become new men."[7]

Those who fall in love with us see the possibilities in our lives before we do. They complete our dreams. They hold a vision in their hearts for who we are. A while ago, I found a love letter I had sent to my husband in our student days. It was neatly folded in one of my philosophy texts, something I had been studying at the time. I had written, "I love you, Sant. I love you because when I'm with you I feel 'full' to the brim. I feel *more* Grace, *more* the person I was meant to be."

Love is born in a glance, a knowing, a feeling, a soul connection, a synchronicity – and then it burns deeply inside us, like flames consuming wood. We cannot sleep, we cannot eat, we cannot think of anything but the object of our desire, our beloved. It is said that the experience of falling in love happens when one heart falls into energetic synchronization with another. It's as if both hearts begin to beat synchronistically, with the same pulse and rhythm. When this heart-to-heart connection between two people happens, they feel an overwhelming attraction, almost a magnetic pull. They "fall" in love.

The emerging field of cardio-energetics says that the brain is ill equipped to translate this powerful magnetic energy between two people, but we do our best. "How do you know you're in love with her?" I asked my client Rob, who was passionately in love with a woman for the first time in his life.

"I know I'm in love with her because she's my first thought when I wake up in the morning and the last thought before I fall asleep, and pretty much every other thought in between."

When destiny couples you, then you embark on the hero's journey – the path of relationship. Some of us are terrified of true intimacy and of merging our hearts, souls, bodies – and pocketbooks – with someone else's. It's uncomfortable having to give up our sense of separateness and our individual rhythms. And that is precisely why relationships fail – because we haven't been able to keep our separateness sacred.

There's a man in Ireland who has an unusual hobby. He compares photographs of newlyweds with pictures taken ten years later, and he has found that most couples grow to resemble one another. He can also usually tell which people in the relationships have given up more of themselves – who has been more accommodating. Poet and Catholic scholar John O'Donohue calls this phenomenon a "subtle homogenizing force." In his book *Anam Cara* he says, "One of the most precious things you should always preserve in friendship and in love is your own difference."[8]

Love is a dance between connecting and disconnecting, coming together and drawing apart. If this equilibrium can be maintained, the path of relationship brings with it intense joy and happiness. If it cannot be maintained, the path will bring us heartache and pain.

Sometimes Love arrives and there are no complications; the path to each other's embrace is direct and unhindered. The two can walk hand in hand into the sunset. But sometimes it comes when it's not convenient. It's the wrong time, the wrong color, the wrong religion or the wrong geography, and so we make excuses and turn away. We tell ourselves, "It's too far"; "It's not right"; "It'll never work." We take refuge in logic, conventional rules and the moral code of the day. And the more we deny, the more delirious and weightless we feel. The more the mind rationalizes, the more bitter and resentful the heart becomes. When Love lands on your doorstep, what will you do? If you have not allowed yourself to be ripped open by Love, then you have not lived. If you have not been drunk on passion, you have not touched the cheek of God. If you have not used your heart to love, then you don't know who you are.

LOVE AS A SPIRITUAL AWAKENING

Through you God touches me at the sweet core and changes that which I was, the rock of the earth, into the body of communion.

— RUMI

The experience of falling in love, especially if it happens during mid-life, can reawaken us from a deep sleep. Love can come into our lives unannounced, but welcomed by Spirit. It can shatter our comfortable lives and derail any plans we might have for the future. In Hinduism, the religion of the god Vishnu is that of Love. For Vishnu the highest order of Love is an intoxicating, all-consuming, mystical union with God or the Other. This spiritual ecstasy can also be experienced between two people, and when it is, the divine Voice echoes within each soul.

The great Sufi poet Jalaluddin Rumi was thirty-seven years old and married with children when he fell in love with the wandering mystic and Sufi master Shams of Tabriz. It is said that Shams had been wandering from country to country in search of someone with whom he could share his burning knowledge of God. Rumi was inebriated by a love that few could understand. He said, "What I had thought of before as God, I met today in a human being." Shams eventually disappeared, some say murdered by Rumi's own students, who were jealous of their relationship. The void created by Shams' absence led Rumi to create a vast volume of some of the most celebrated and beautiful love poetry in the world. In the following poem, called "Buoyancy," he speaks of what this love has done to him:

I used to be respectable and chaste and stable, but who can
Stand in this strong wind and remember those things?

A mountain keeps an echo deep inside itself.
That's how I hold your voice.
I am scrap wood thrown in your fire,
And quickly reduced to smoke.[9]

Puzzled by Shams' disappearance, Rumi went out in search of
him. He was unable to find his friend, so he turned back and came
to an important conclusion. He realized that his search had not
been for Shams himself, but for the divine Voice that Rumi could
hear when he was with Shams. He went within himself and there
he found the divine Voice he had been seeking. Eventually Rumi
"influenced thousands of people with his poetry and his vision of
our relationship with God as a path of love."[10]

When my friend K fell deeply in love with the Jesus guy, she
thought her feelings would rip her open and consume her like
fire. When the two finally parted ways, she suffered terribly.
She mourned for the part of her that she felt she had lost. But
she eventually realized that the Jesus guy was not the source of
her connection to God—she was the Source. Like Rumi, she had
to turn inwards and find the divine Voice within her. And when
she did, she learned to love herself unconditionally. That love
seeped into all areas of her life, including her marriage, bringing
with it healing, faith and renewal. Her whole life became more
purposeful and spiritually significant.

Sometimes when people crave a sacred Presence in their
lives, it comes cloaked in Love's embrace. Love taps us softly on
the shoulder like an angel beckoning us to be brave, to open
our hearts wide and let the divine waters cleanse our soul. This

Love can bring us excruciating pain as well as excruciating joy. It's a fire constantly aching to be kindled, stoked and fanned; as it blazes up, it threatens to consume us whole. But it is also a blessing – all of it. "His love is like a warm blanket that covers me all over – in whose presence I feel a holiness I cannot describe," a friend confessed to me. She's a married woman in her thirties who has just woken up to the fact that she is in love with her boss, who is also married. "The ride will be bumpy," I warn her. "Are you up to it?" But I can see that Love had already taken her hostage.

If you are fortunate enough in this lifetime to experience the exultation of Love, have the courage to see it through. Running away from it will not serve your soul. Open your heart to Love and you will open your heart to the Sacred. That's how we come to know God, or the Absolute – through the heart. While another human being might be responsible for opening the door to your heart, remember that you own the key. You have always owned it.

WHEN LOVE SHATTERS US

There are many paths to wisdom,
but each begins with a broken heart.
– LEONARD COHEN

It had been almost two years that I had been counseling my friend "Emilia" through a very turbulent time. She was having a love affair with a married man. Though he loved her and wanted to be with her, he could not bring himself to leave his wife, his kids, his home and his high-profile job in order to be with her. During a particularly difficult time, he stopped communicating with her, and that's when her heart headed for the dungeon. Here is an excerpt from an e-mail she wrote me one night:

How do I forget the love of my life when he is inside me? How do I carry on with all the pieces of my shattered soul? I never imagined this pain existed, not even in my worst nightmares. I have never experienced this darkness. Tell me, why won't he call? Just a few days ago, I was with him in paradise, now he has sent me in exile. What have I done to deserve this? It feels like I've been hit by a huge truck. I'm badly bruised and broken all over. I'm in a body cast. I think it will take me the rest of my life to recover.

When Love disappoints us, it produces drastic consequences. We can become lethargic and depressed, inviting illness or madness to visit us. Those of us who have entered the path of relationship and have emerged unscathed are rare. Nevertheless, the scars of Love make us human – they can either soften us or turn us cold and bitter.

Relationships are like people. They have their own unique lifespans. Like people, no relationship is meant to last forever. When their gift to us has been received, it's time to move on. Never confuse length with quality. The gift of an hour's encounter with an angel is just as worthy of thanksgiving as a lifetime of contact with a friend. People weave in and out of our stories. Let them. Some are meant to remain in our lives and others are meant to move on, but each person comes with a gift.

Why is it that we tend to discount relationships that don't last? Everyone in your life is a stepping stone to growing your soul. Don't beat yourself up over "failed" relationships or "broken" marriages. They were necessary to get you where you are today. Every relationship is unique and possesses its own beauty. We fall in love, we feel, we cherish, we share. We take risks and we grow. Regardless of how relationships end, don't discount the years of happiness or the months of joy or the glimpses of light. Appreciate all the people you've attracted into your life to make you the person you are. All of it is good.

Besides, those we have loved are always inside us. They leave heartprints on our soul. Paul Pearsall says in *The Heart's Code*, "By tapping into the heart's energy and wisdom, we can be energetically 'with' our lover no matter where she or he may be."[11] Tune in to your heart and recover the energy of those who loved us, because that's where they reside in us forever.

A man I once knew, a soulmate, told me he had found in me the "motherlode" and that he finally knew what it was like to be truly loved. It was one of the most beautiful compliments I have ever received. It doesn't matter that I didn't marry him; I'll always cherish his words in my heart. It's your lover's gift you want to hold on to, not your lover, for the gift is of the soul and therefore eternal.

THE INTENSITY OF LOVE

Joy cannot be felt without sorrow, pleasure without pain,
love without emptiness. To have once had one's heart touched
is to carry the scar of love.

– RUMI

When my work took me to different cities, my husband and two young children would drive me to the airport and stay with me until I had to go through security. My kids would hang on to my legs very tightly as I dragged the three of us closer to the gate. I would wait until the last possible minute and then I'd look at my husband and whisper, "I love you. I'll be home in two days," or "I'll see you soon." Those were heart-wrenching moments – to let go, to separate from those whom I loved most in the world, not knowing whether fate would bring me back home safe and sound. Most days my little ones were cool about Mom and her trips. But there were days when I'd hear their sobs and heart-piercing shrieks – "Mommy, Mommy! I w-a-n-t you!" – way past the gate. It would break me in two.

I remember one particular trip to Australia, when I had been away from my children, who were three and five at the time, for nearly two weeks. I had one more seminar to teach, in Perth, on the country's west coast. It might as well have been on the other side of the moon – that's how distant and lonely I felt. On the way to my hotel, a friendly taxi driver, pleased to have a Canadian in his cab, was playing tourist guide, proudly showcasing his city's tourist attractions. Had it been the first or second day of my trip I would have been delighted by the details. But that night I remember feeling cynical and frustrated; all I wanted was for him to shut up. The longing in my heart for my babies was a painful ache. As soon as I got to my hotel I called home, and after I hung up, all I could do was cry and cry.

Who hasn't ached from Love? Whether it's for a child, a lover or a friend, we are not meant to shrink back from the intensity of Love in order to avoid the pain. The ache is part of Love; you can't have one without the other. That's perhaps why Kahlil Gibran says, "Your joy is your sorrow unmasked. And the selfsame well from which your laughter rises was oftentimes filled with tears."[12]

When I was a child, my grandmother Nonna used to tell me, "*Te voglio bene assai.*" I always thought that meant "I love you," but it's different. The literal translation is "I want good for you, a lot of it!" It's different from *"Io ti amo,"* which is what lovers say to each other. *"Te voglio bene"* has an earthy feel to it. It's solid, and it feels like you're being enveloped in God's blanket. I hadn't heard the phrase in years, and then one day I walked into an Italian restaurant where the music of Lucio Dalla was playing. *"Te voglio bene assai,"* the lyrics cried out. His voice was penetrating, powerful, yet tinged with melancholy. The song is his tribute to the late Enrico Caruso, the famous opera singer from Naples. The words were the same, the dialect was the same – everything about the song took me back to the stone house on the hill and the warmth of my grandmother's love. There I was at the takeout counter, unable to move or think, my eyes filled with tears. All I could do was ask for the name of the song.

"You haven't saved one life," my cousin Robbie told the neurosurgeon who operated on his brother Emilio. "You've saved three." The doctor blinked and looked confused. "You saved my parents, too," Robbie added. The doctor still looked confused, but then he smiled. He had to go; someone was paging him. I know the doctor didn't understand what Robbie meant, but I did. That's because we come from the same stock, the same family tree. My grandparents had passed on their intense, burning love for their children to my mother and her brother, Emilio's father.

"How do you explain to people that the reason why my parents aren't here at his bedside is because they would rather die than see Emilio like this?" Robbie asked me through his tears. "How do you explain that kind of love?"

As soon as I heard about Emilio's accident, I was scared for the family. That's one of the reasons why I had to go and help. I instinctively knew that if Emilio didn't survive, something very tragic would befall his parents.

When our love runs deep, life can get messy and unpredictable. It is rapture, and torture at the same time. We can touch the center of our joy but also the core of our sorrow. Mystics have it for God. Some lovers have it for each other. Some parents have it for their children. This love is the fuel, the energy and the passion that makes the planet spin.

CHOOSING THE PATH OF LOVE

Indeed, love heals, but being loved does not. Being loved merely holds the door open for healing, for happiness, for fulfillment, for getting our needs met. But to walk through that door, we must love.
– HUGH PRATHER AND GAYLE PRATHER

Life is a series of human intersections. Every person who crosses our path gives us an opportunity to show our love and make a difference. Every time your life intersects with someone else's life there is a moment of choice. You could make a difference in their life for the better or for the worse. Do you know how to make a fuss over someone? Do you show your love freely and generously? Or do you wait for people to show you love and acceptance first?

I have a rule that I live by: Whatever you want, give it away first. It's the first principle of abundant thinking. There is a real art to knowing how to make people feel good around you. I am trying to instill the importance of this in my kids. I teach my children to be aware of their interactions with people. I tell them, "When you're with your grandparents, let them know how special they are. Be generous with your words and actions. Greet them with love. Every time you enter someone's life, make that life a better place, whether it be with a smile, a hug or a kind word. Never lose an opportunity to show people your love."

Every day we have the opportunity to choose between two paths. One is the path of Love: giving people the benefit of the doubt, opening our hearts to listen empathetically, trying to understand life through their lens. The other is the path of fear and indifference. Only the path of Love will transform us into greater men and women. Only the path of Love brings us closer to our divine genesis. Only Love teaches us our earthly purpose.

As our taxi drove away, my grandfather Nonno Emilio, looking frail and old, called out to my husband and me, "*Voletevi bene*" – "love each other." That was the last time I saw him. We toil and trouble, build castles and bridges to the moon. We study and learn, we invent, we travel. We seek high and low for the answers. Yet the only answer we need, the only answer we've ever needed to know, the one Jesus tried to tell us, is to love each other. How? "I tell you there are a thousand ways to release the joy in the heart of another. Nay, a thousand times a thousand," says Neale Donald Walsch in *Friendship with God*.[13] Here are some ideas on how you can practise Love every day and release the joy in someone else's heart.

PRACTISE LOVE THROUGH TOUCH

**We need four hugs a day for survival,
eight for maintenance, and twelve for growth.**
– VIRGINIA SATIR

A kitten whose eyes are bandaged at birth and left that way for two weeks will never be able to see. Its brain will have no experience of light and without that the visual centers cannot develop; the kitten will be blind for life. If you don't expose a newborn baby to language, it will not learn to speak. In the same way, early deprivation of love and nurturing creates a void that cannot be filled later in life.

Scientists have known for years that maternal deprivation in infancy causes serious behavioral problems in children, often leaving them withdrawn, apathetic, slow to learn and prone to chronic illness. Recent research has revealed that a lack of love in childhood profoundly affects the brain's biochemistry, actually killing off brain cells. Children raised without being regularly hugged, caressed or stroked and who are deprived of the physical reassurance of normal family attention have abnormally high levels of stress hormones in their blood. This was the conclusion of the Harvard University researchers who studied Romanian infants raised in state-run orphanages.[14] Those stress hormones have serious and long-range effects on learning, memory and overall behavior as the child grows and develops. It's obvious that without Love, we shrivel up and die.

Sometimes I feel a burst of joy in my heart for another person and I just want to show them my love. In the past I would repress my feelings and attribute them to the fact that I am a kinesthetic Italian. I would talk myself out of giving someone a hug and instead try to mirror the coldness I saw around me. I've stopped doing that. Now when I'm moved to show my love, I just do it. It's good to remember that when it comes to hugs, you should never assume, always ask. But when I've asked people for a hug, I have never been turned down.

As I am writing this I can hear Jessie, our little pup, whining. He is at the foot of the stairs, and I recognize that his whining is saying, "Mom, I miss you. I need some attention." He was six weeks old when we surprised Jasper on his tenth birthday. Weighing barely two pounds, Jessie was just a tiny ball of black-and-white fur when we brought him home.

I went downstairs and the puppy was ecstatic to see me. He needed my touch, my reassurance. He was wriggling to get closer to me. I picked him up and cradled him, just as I did my babies when I breast-fed them. His eyes rolled back and he let out a sigh of relief, as if to say, "Yes, this is what I was aching for. This is what I wanted." We spent a few moments together in silence, me holding him and stroking his belly, and him staring straight into my soul. I remember the last piece of advice the breeder offered to my husband and me, two novices who had never owned a dog before. "The purpose of your dog's life is to show you unconditional Love. Learn that and you'll understand your dog."

Even though Jessie has wreaked havoc on our house in the past few months and is quite a handful, it is moments like these, when he is in my arms and silently communicating with my soul, that guarantee him a permanent spot in my heart. He can chew all the baseboards he wants – baseboards can never communicate to my soul the way Jessie does.

Diana, Princess of Wales, was right. We are starved for Love, for touch, for a sign that someone cares. Touch is primitive. It's hardwired into our genetics. We need to feel the warmth of contact, skin to skin. Give hugs, get naked, stroke your babies. Reach out and touch your beloved's face. Hold hands. Be demonstrative, hug your friends, hug children. Please hug children; they need to know you love them. Hold your pets. Not touching can become such a habit in this crazy, fast-paced world.

PRACTISE LOVE THROUGH WORDS

None of us has the power to make someone else love us.
But we all have the power to give away love, to love other people.
And if we do so, we change the kind of person we are,
and we change the kind of world we live in.

— RABBI HAROLD KUSHNER

"About ten years ago my son wrote me a Mother's Day card I will never forget," the woman on the plane told me. "I raised this boy on my own, you know. His Daddy died when he was just five years old."

"What did the card say?" I asked her.

"Well, he thanked me for everything I had done for him. For taking him to hockey practice early in the morning and for working two jobs so I could send him to college, and for always believing in him and for loving him and encouraging him to go for his dreams."

"Wow, I bet that must have made you feel appreciated."

"Yes," she said smiling. "He ran out of room in the card, so he wrote three more pages! He described all the things he loved and appreciated about me, little things that I thought he never noticed. He told me he was proud to be my son. Can you imagine?"

"How lovely," I said. "I bet you treasure that." And then I noticed a tear trickling down her face.

"Yes, it was so wonderful to get. At the time I was touched," she said, "but each year that passes, I've come to cherish it more."

"How long ago was that?"

"Oh, almost twelve years ago. My son gave it to me when he was still living at home and going to university. Every

Mother's Day I have a little ritual. I take out the card, make myself a big pot of tea, sit down in my favorite reading chair and reread my boy's letter. And I always have a good cry," she said, wiping away the tear.

We spent a few minutes in silence together, she with her thoughts and I with mine. I thought about all the letters I wanted to write and all the people that needed to hear how much I love them. Then she confided in me that she'd even considered putting her letter in a safety deposit box, just in case of a fire in her apartment. No insurance company in the world could ever replace the sentiments of a son captured in ink for his mother nearly twelve years before.

Have you ever written a letter to someone that they wanted to put in a safety deposit box? The written word is powerful. It makes us immortal. Words have the power to wound or to heal. Do you know how to celebrate someone with your words? Are you generous with your praise and gratitude?

We have opportunities every day to use our words in positive ways. Who needs to hear from you? Who in your life needs to be celebrated, thanked, loved? Do it verbally, but also in writing. Send letters, cards, poems, e-mails or e-greetings. If you're sending a card, don't just sign your name; add your own thoughts. Write something they will cherish – let them know what they mean to you. Let your words flow from your heart. Everyone can use a sentimental card from time to time – and not just on their birthday. To write a card they will cherish forever, close your eyes and connect with the heart of the person. Then answer one or more of these questions: What does this person mean to you? What are you grateful for? How have they made a difference in your life? How have they helped you? How much do you love them? What do you wish for them?

Get into the habit of letting people know when they've made

you happy. Give people feedback. The suggestion boxes we see in restaurants and hotels are not just for complaints. I make a habit of complimenting people who work in the service sector. I know how difficult it is to be in the front line serving customers, so I let them know when I'm pleased. Sometimes I'll even call their boss and sing their praises. I know it makes them feel good, but it makes me feel good too.

I celebrate my children through a game I've invented called "What I Love Best About You." I usually play it with them at night before tucking them into bed, but you can play it any time you feel your children need to reconnect to their magnificence. Sometimes I'll choose things from the day and other times I'll choose general traits I admire about them. It's a wonderful way for your child to drift off to sleep feeling secure and loved by you.

Examples:
- Jasper, I love your brain and how you think deeply about things. I love the way you speak up for yourself. I love your passion when you play sports. I love the way you throw yourself fearlessly into life. I love the way you play with little children and how you have to cuddle me before falling asleep.
- Kajsa, I love your sweet voice. I love your big brown eyes and the way they twinkle at me. I love the way you move with such elegance and grace. I love your genius mind, your kind heart and the way you're soft and gentle with everyone. I love it when you write me love letters and leave them under my pillow.

After you've told them what you love about them, invite them to tell you what they love about you. Teach them this very important skill. When Jasper was younger, he'd always say the same three things, "Mommy, I love your hair, I love the way you love me and I love the way you make food." When it was Kajsa's turn, she'd copy her brother and say exactly the same thing. Now that they're ten and eight, they can better articulate their feelings. They're good at appreciating people and life around them.

You can play this game with your significant other as well; I call it "pillow talk." Play it while lying in bed staring into your beloved's eyes. Wait until the end of a busy week, then light a scented candle and play the game. Reconnect on an emotional level. This game builds intimacy. Not only that, it grows self-esteem. It unfolds our wings and allows us to fly.

PRACTISE LOVE THROUGH APPRECIATION

> Jim continued recognizing and thanking all the people
> who had helped him to succeed, and when his voice cracked
> with emotion, there were tears all around the room.
> - JOHN DEMARTINI

If you look around, you will find many unsung heroes out there. All people want, I find, is a bit of recognition, a pat on the back – at least that's what they tell me during our coaching sessions. In a recent survey, workers listed recognition and feeling valued as two ingredients that were missing from their jobs. That reminds me of the man who followed me up the stairs one day after I had finished a morning workshop.

"Ms. Cirocco, Ms. Cirocco, could I talk to you for just one minute?" he asked. I turned around and saw a man standing before me. He had soft brown eyes.

"Hi, my name is Jason," he said. "I'm the mail boy." He took my hand and began kissing it.

"Hi, Jason," I responded.

"I just want to thank you for your workshop. I'm so glad someone like you came here to tell them they need to appreciate their workers. I've been working here for twenty-five years. I've never made a mistake with their mail, and not once has anyone taken the time to say thank you. They just ignore me like I don't exist, just because of my handicap. But I have feelings too. All I want is to feel appreciated," he said. "All I want is a thank you." And then he began to cry.

Jason's story touched me to the core. I've often thought of him while speaking to managers and leaders and I talk about him to my audiences. People will go the extra mile. They don't even mind doing more for less, but they would like to feel that their efforts are noticed and appreciated. That's all. We all want to be valued, and that's what is missing from so many jobs today. Perhaps it's because there's less time and fewer resources to do the job, but managers who can consistently give their staff positive feedback get the best results. People who know how to make you feel valued and special are the people we want to work for. Yes, Jason lives in all of us. We could all use more appreciation from our families, our friends and our employers.

Perhaps you're thinking, "Why should I appreciate and thank someone else when no one appreciates me?" Practise the rule for abundance: Whatever you want, give it away first. When you praise, celebrate and recognize others, you are teaching them how you want to be treated. It may take a while, but eventually your positive energy will spread. We are mirrors for each other. You get what you give. Take the time to say thank you. Show your love with appreciation, and you'll see how the Love comes back to you.

PRACTISE LOVE THROUGH OUTRAGEOUS ACTS OF KINDNESS

The questions asked at the end of his or her life are very simple ones: "Did I love well? Did I love the people around me, my community, the earth, in a deep way?"

– JACK KORNFIELD

It was a Tuesday afternoon and my daughter and I were returning home after a visit to the dentist. In the subway station there was an old man sitting on the floor, begging for change. He had medals pinned on his chest. People walked by, ignoring him. I too had ignored him on my way downtown; now, on my way home, I couldn't. Why was this man here, begging? I wanted to know the strange twists and turns his life had taken. How did he end up here? My daughter must have picked up my thoughts, because she tugged at my purse and asked for some money. I took out three dollars and gave it to her. We paused and smiled at him. "What are all your medals for?" my daughter asked him. The man shrugged, probably too tired to go into it.

Never wanting to pass up a teaching moment for my daughter, I said, "This man is a veteran. He fought in the war."

"The Second World War," he said.

"That's why we have our freedom now, darling. He's a hero," I told her.

As he looked up at me, I could see tears forming in his eyes. "Bless you, ma'am," he said. As we walked on, he added,

"Keep telling the little ones. Tell them so they don't forget about us. Tell them so we don't have to go through it again."

Martin Luther King is famous for saying that his religion was kindness. So what is kindness? It is synonymous with Love, except that Love is a state of being and kindness is a state of doing. When you can make each human interaction a moment inspired by Love, you are practising kindness – you are taking the step. Love allows us to see the people on our path as the holy creatures they are, and then kindness allows us to bless them with loving acts or deeds.

In my workshops I often do a brainstorming activity called "Outrageous Acts of Kindness." In small groups, the partici-pants come up with practical ideas on how to practise loving kindness at work and at home. The ideas they come up with are amazing, and I love what happens to the energy in the room when they are doing this exercise. They end up energized and determined to try some of the ideas as soon as they leave. Some days I can feel the whole room throbbing with light as they brainstorm and discuss ways to practise loving kindness. People have sent me e-mails and letters telling me how much they enjoyed "Outrageous Acts of Kindness," and what a difference practising them on others has made in their lives.

What is an outrageous act of kindness? One Valentine's Day, when my heart was feeling exuberant, I held the door open for an elderly woman who was dragging a heavy grocery cart. When she smiled to say thank you, I went further. I hugged her and gave her a big kiss on the cheek. She looked at me, a bit stunned, but delighted. Then she asked, "Do I know you, dear?" obviously doubting her mental faculties. "No," I said and shrugged, somewhat embarrassed. And then her expres-sion melted and she muttered something about kindness. I nodded and we stood there for just a few seconds, making that eye contact that is so often missing in our daily exchanges with people. Then we wished each other a happy Valentine's Day and I walked away. When I turned back to look, she was still looking at me and waving. I waved back. I'm sure that my outrageous act of kindness made her day. Her smile sure made mine.

There is a line in Jewel's song "Hands" that says, "In the end, only kindness matters." That line always moves me. If one could distill everything in the world – all the advice and wisdom from the sages, the religions and the philosophies, and everything that mattered to humans – if you could bring it all together and find the common thread, it's kindness. Has a stranger ever blessed you with kindness? Gandhi said, "Be the change you seek in the world." Whatever you want, give it away first. Miracles will begin unfolding as you continue your journey.

PRACTISE LOVE THROUGH FRIENDSHIP

In the Celtic tradition, there is a beautiful understanding of love and friendship. One of the fascinating ideas here is the idea of soul-love; the old Gaelic term for this is anam cara.
- JOHN O'DONOHUE

Kajsa came home one day absolutely jubilant. "Mommy, Mommy," she gasped as soon as she walked in the door. "I have something to tell you."

"Come on up, sweet pea," I called to her. She ran up the stairs, gave me a hug and then plopped herself down on the rug. She took a deep breath and said, "I have great news. Michael told me today that he loves me." She stressed the word "love." "He's loved me for three years, ever since junior kindergarten, but today was the first day he actually told me!"

"What gave him the courage to tell you today?" I wondered out loud.

"I don't know, Mom. But he's been wanting to tell me for a long time. He said he was too scared. He whispered it in my ear right after French."

She waited for my reaction. I had never seen her so animated. "Wow, Kajsa, how wonderful! How do you feel about him?"

"I love him too," she said, somewhat embarrassed. "He's my best friend, Mom." Then, adopting a more serious tone, she told me *the plan*.

"Mom, we want to be in the same class all the way up to university. After university we're going to get married, just like you and Dad." Obviously pleased with herself, she sighed and relaxed in my arms.

That was three years ago. Kajsa's friendship with Michael has continued even though she has switched schools. His mother is deeply touched by the affection her son has for Kajsa and can't quite believe the transformation in him whenever he's around my daughter. Some people bring out the best in us, and I think Kajsa and Michael do that for each other. Their bond is untouched by jealousy, competition or doubt. I think that's because Michael is Kajsa's *anam cara*, or soul friend. "With the anam cara you could share your innermost self, your mind and your heart. This friendship was an act of recognition and belonging," says John O'Donohue, the author of *Anam Cara: A Book of Celtic Wisdom*.[15]

I watch Kajsa and Michael when they're together. They can talk for hours or just sit on the swings side by side in silence. There is a peaceful energy about them, a quiet understanding. They're two pure hearts. An onlooker can sense that they belong together. I'm convinced that Kajsa and Michael have shared many lifetimes; in this lifetime they have been lucky enough to find each other early in their lives.

Who is your *anam cara*? Do you have a soul friend or friends? Do you have people in your life who can listen to you and to your silences, and embrace them all? Friends who understand your deepest longings and who can feel your joy with you? "Friendship is the grace that warms and sweetens our lives," says O'Donohue.[16]

How many relationships do you know in which one person is the talker and the other the listener? Or one is the therapist and the other the client? Or one is the parent and the other the child? Those relationships are not balanced; they can't be called friendship. In those dynamics, one person is at the center of things: one person's health problems are discussed; one person's family troubles are highlighted; one person's marriage is reviewed. That is not true friendship.

Friendship is sacred. Friends add color to life. They bring out the best in us and sometimes they replace family. In addition to improving your quality of life and helping you cope during times of crisis, sharing friendship promotes health and helps protect you against stresses, strains and illnesses.

In Joan Borysenko's book *Minding the Body, Mending the Mind,* we learn about an interesting study done on the Italian-American residents of Roseto, Pennsylvania. Researchers began studying the Rosetans after it was discovered they had a very low death rate from coronary heart disease. The experts expected to find healthy, non-smoking, active people who followed low-fat diets. Instead, they were surprised to discover that the Rosetans had terrible habits. They smoked, ate fatty foods and were overweight. So what was preventing heart disease in these people? It was that in Roseto there was always someone to listen to you or to lend a helping hand. Everyone knew each other. Writes Borysenko, "Social support, the great stress buffer, turned out to be more important than health habits in predicting heart disease."[17] Friendship, it seems, can add years to your life.

Relationships are like porcupines. During a cold winter, porcupines huddle together for warmth. But their sharp quills prick each other, so they pull away. Then they get cold again. They have to keep adjusting their distance to keep from freezing and also from getting pricked by their fellow porcupines. We need to get close to each other to have a sense of community, to feel we're not alone in the world. But we also need to keep our distance, to preserve our independence so that others don't suffocate us. That is our duality. We need to be together and we need to be alone at the same time.

When we meet our *anam cara*, we don't feel alone anymore. We feel understood, appreciated. It's easy to be around them. There is more intimacy in an hour with your soulmate than there is in years with other people. He or she is a friend to your soul. "A pal so fabulous," says Sarah Ban Breathnach, "that we feel like twins separated at birth."

PRACTISE LOVE UNCONDITIONALLY

What would love do now? Go into the heart of love,
and come from that place in all your choices
and decisions, and you will find peace.
- NEALE DONALD WALSCH

American anthropologist Angeles Arrien is famous for her four rules for living, which I talked about in Chapter 5. They are (1) Show up, (2) Pay attention, (3) Tell the truth and

(4) Don't be attached to the results. Of the four, which ones do you practise? Most people confess that Rule number 4 is the most difficult – that's because it's about practising unconditional love.

I remember being hurt by a boyfriend whose only contact with me was a birthday greeting by mail. For a few years after we broke up I sent him beautiful cards telling him how I was and how I wished him happiness on his birthday. Every year on my birthday he'd send a very brief birthday wish on a plain, stark-white sheet, "Grace, Happy Birthday," and then he'd sign his name. I know I should have been happy that he was thinking of me, but that annual unemotional white message containing only four words hurt me. I felt he was doing it out of obligation, not authenticity. Still, as the years passed, I kept practising Rule number 4 and just did what was in my heart. I kept sending him lovely birthday cards, but my patience was wearing thin.

One year I decided to send only a postcard with a few impersonal lines. When my birthday came in the spring, so too came the same cold, dispassionate message on the same white stationery. I figured that our breakup must have hurt him badly and that he must still be feeling it. I stopped acknowledging his birthday, and when spring came around, he had stopped sending me birthday wishes, too.

I wanted something more from him, but that was all he could give. To this day I regret not giving what was in my heart. I let the "quality thing" be an issue. I did not, could not, live according to Rule number 4. I could not practise unconditional love. I withheld my love because it wasn't being returned the way I wanted, the way I expected. We are not meant to think "lack"; we are meant to think "abundance." Some people go to great pains to figure out how much others have spent on them and then try not to spend a penny more. And then there are the types who give *more* in order to make the other person feel guilty.

In the 1970s most doctors and hospital staff were recommending that parents of very sick newborns not get too emotionally close to their children. The thinking was that if the infant should die, it would be less painful for parents who didn't allow the emotional bond to develop than for those who did. In fact, the very opposite was true.

In grief support groups, therapists Hugh Prather and Gayle Prather found that only parents who had "loved without caution" – who had touched, held and cared for their sick offspring, who had prayed and watched over them and had allowed themselves to love – healed quickly from their loss. Contrary to expectations, the moms and dads who had distanced themselves had more difficulty healing. Their feeling of loss was much greater. They had lost not only their children, but also an opportunity to show them their love. The "parents who had loved without caution healed quickly and usually turned immediately to helping other parents. They were also more likely to feel the comforting presence of their child in their daily life."[18]

We must not put conditions on our love. Our hearts must feel unhindered, uninhibited and completely free. Don't let the actions of others influence your expression of Love. Don't hold back who you are because of them. Love freely. Give freely. Let go of expectations. That is what "don't be attached to the results" is about. It means "do it anyway" – try out for the team; apply for that job; ask your friend out for a date – just *live* your precious life.

PRACTISE LOVE THROUGH COMPASSION

The purpose of the journey is compassion.
- JOSEPH CAMPBELL

I was reading the April 2000 issue of *Jane* magazine when I saw a headline that read, "She's a Poster Child for People Who Screw Up." The article was about Monica Lewinsky, the (in)famous lover of President Bill Clinton. The writer reported that after the interview Monica asked for a hug. Something about that request touched me. She must have felt exposed, vulnerable and in need of some reassurance. She's a scared little girl, I thought. All she wants is to be liked and accepted like the rest of us. Instead, all she feels is judgment and hatred.

The media did a good job of bringing Monica down, but that's because there was an appetite for her story. We attacked her for allowing herself to be used, for getting involved with a married man, for "sullying" the office of the presidency and for corrupting the moral fabric of America. There was a lot of judgment and little compassion.

I feel for her story. Monica was America's scapegoat. We mocked her love. We laughed at her naïveté. But Monica did not betray a husband, a friend or a nation. We betrayed her. At twenty-two she had lost her innocence, her confidence and her pride. Monica was crucified by the bureaucrats, grilled about intimate private details and humiliated in front of a nation and the world. Had she been twenty years older, she might have had the confidence to choose what to reveal and what to keep private. But she told all because, she says, she was terrified.

It is the heart of judgment that casts the first stone when it itself is not pure.

The harshest critics of the story had pasts of their own. The truth is, we've all got pasts. We must stop condemning people who make mistakes, and we must stop condemning love. If soul is present in lovemaking, if it is free and tender and kind, it is holy, no matter what anyone says.

Our world cries out for compassion. So many of us have numbed our senses; we've lost the ability to feel for others. We have forgotten that we're all God's children just trying to make our way home. If we are to practise compassion, we must stop judging others by our own self-righteous moral yardsticks. In order to heal our wounds we must wash away our hypocrisy.

We need to step back and see with the eyes of the heart. When French president François Mitterand died, his widow invited his mistress to the funeral and stood beside her as they paid their final respects to the man they had loved. Compassion is not only holy, it is enlightened. It is of God. The Dalai Lama proclaimed compassion the healer of the twenty-first century. Open your heart. Who in your life needs compassion? Practise empathy. Practise looking at life through your neighbor's lens. Activate your imagination. The world needs your compassion.

PRACTISE LOVE AT WORK

The beginning is God. The end is action.
Action is God creating – or God experienced.
– NEALE DONALD WALSH

Theril, a longtime client of mine and someone I admire very much, aims to make one question the focus of his life. This question acts as a lightning rod to keep him centered and focused on what's most important and sacred in his life. The question is "What would Love do now?" He has posted it in various places in his home and office. He's even turned it into a screen saver on his computer so that when he's called away to the telephone, when he returns to his screen he's reminded to consider, "What would Love do now?"

Over his career, Theril has seen his share of cutbacks, backroom politics and toxic personalities scrambling to save their egos, yet he remains unscathed. He meditates, prays and motivates his staff of more than six hundred, while always striving to improve himself. His humility allows him to respect others and to listen to their points of view. This is Love in action. This is the new breed of executive leader. I call these people the gentle giants of the work world. I have been fortunate to have met many such beacons of light in senior management.

Heart is being activated at work. As people change and the revolution of Spirit takes over, it is spreading to the way we do business. But we must continue to play a leadership role in our workplaces if we are to evolve spiritually. If you're a manager, think of how you can help your staff / customer fully realize their potential, not only as members of your team, but as human beings. Keep them motivated by showing how much you value them. If you're not a manager, think about how you can spread sunshine tomorrow when you go to work. How might you surprise someone with an outrageous act of kindness? Leadership is not about position or having some fancy corner office – it's about everyday actions that spring from the heart.

PRACTISE LOVE BY MAKING A DIFFERENCE

I gave my word to this tree and the forest that my feet
would not touch the ground until I had done everything
in my power to stop the destruction.

– JULIA BUTTERFLY HILL

Julia Butterfly Hill lived for two years and ten days in a six-hundred-year-old redwood tree in California in an effort to save its life. The first time she saw the tree, which she named "Luna," she fell to her hands and knees and began weeping. But the lumber company that owned the land didn't care about any sentimental tree-hugger. It was planning to cut Luna down along with several acres of old-growth trees. Julia had to do something. So she took up residence in the tree.

The redwoods grow in the fog belt along the California coast. They breathe in the mist and their bark turns red from the moisture. They absorb water and sunlight and grow to enormous heights. Because the area where these trees grow is high above sea level, they are also exposed to wind and cold. Nighttime temperatures can drop to the freezing point.

Julia's first winter was "merciless" as she swayed in the wind, holding on to branches hundreds of feet in the air.

Her story was broadcast around the world and Julia Hill became an environmental hero. She got a lot of publicity, speaking via a solar-powered cellphone to environmental groups and conferences around the world and receiving hundreds of letters a week. Her friends and supporters came daily to bring her food and collect her waste, but it was she who endured alone in the tree.

Imagine spending 740 days and nights alone up in a tree in the middle of nowhere. What did she do in the darkness, the silence? She was only twenty-five years old, but imagine the spiritual wisdom she must have gained from the experience.

In December 1999 news came that the lumber company had finally decided to spare Julia's tree, as well as a one-hectare buffer zone around it. She had done what she had set out to do. It was time to come down.[19]

Julia's story is one of courage, hope and inspiration and an example of what one person can do to change the world. The first visit to the moon happened over thirty years ago, and yet – as I've heard experts say – Neil Armstrong's footprints are still there today. That's because there's no weather on the moon – no rain, no wind, no snow to wear them away. Imagine! Well, one day it will be our time to go. What footprints will we leave behind? Think about how you want to make a difference. You may not save the life of a six-hundred-year-old tree, but there are thousands of ways to make a difference every day. Leave your footprints – and let them make you immortal.

PRACTISE LOVE BY FORGIVENESS

**When I have forgiven myself and remembered who I am,
I will bless everyone and everything I see.**
– A COURSE IN MIRACLES

The end of a century brings reflection. It makes us think about the past and evaluate history. It connects us to our mortality, to the fact that everything is finite. It softens our hearts and we find the humility to apologize, to let go of the past and embrace the future with a lighter heart and a clearer conscience. I see this happening around me. Many believe we've entered the Age of Forgiveness.

In the year 2000 Pope Paul II made a historic trip to Israel. He apologized to the Israeli nation for the Vatican's silence during the Second World War, when millions of Jewish people were being starved, tortured and slaughtered by the Nazis. Imagine the Pope at the walls of Jerusalem, begging for forgiveness through his tears. I was touched by the event. I know that some may feel that it was too little, too late, but I think this one conscious act had the potential to bring healing to millions. That's what apologies do; they bring reconciliation, forgiveness and healing.

As I was writing this, the world was getting ready for the Olympic Games in Sydney, Australia. I read in the paper how angry the Australian Aborigines are about being treated as second-class citizens, and that they want the world to know about it. The article quoted an Aboriginal community leader who surmised that Australia won the Olympics over Beijing largely because of China's record on human rights. But, she asked, "What about Australia's human rights record? What about the way they treat us? When are they ever going to apologize?" Meanwhile, Australia's prime minister had the power to soothe this ache in their hearts, but he wouldn't. He acknowledged deep personal sorrow and was sorry for the hurt and trauma the Aborigines continue to feel because of practices of past generations. But he said that the bottom line was that today's generation should not be held accountable for the sins of their ancestors. He would not offer an official apology.

Without that apology a reconciliation between the two cultures could not happen – forgiveness cannot be granted. But a healing moment came during the Games when Cathy Freeman, an Aboriginal woman, won the 400-meter race for Australia. During her victory lap she carried both the Australian and the Aboriginal flags. It was an emotional moment for all Australians and for the world that was watching. Here was forgiveness in action. That single loving act helped heal the rift caused by years of silence.

If you truly want to erase barriers between your sisters and brothers, then you must practise forgiveness. How? Just open a space for forgiveness in your life and that space will expand. Make a mental decision that you are ready to forgive, and soon your heart's intelligence will lead you to practise kindness and acceptance. We are all human beings, making mistakes and trying to find our way. We are confused and lost and at times we despair. But we are trying to be found. Forgiveness is the way home. Forgiveness is like a soothing spring that erupts from deep within Mother Earth and bathes everything in its path with Light.

Exchange moccasins. Let go of judgment. We are all works in progress. Past-life expert Brian Weiss says, "We're all connected. We're all the same. We are all rowing the same boat."[20]

WE NEED TO KNOW WE ARE LOVED

The supreme happiness of life is the conviction that we are loved.

– VICTOR HUGO

There is an exquisite scene in the film *The English Patient* when the protagonist, Count Almasy, pulls his beloved, Katharine Clifton, out of a plane wreck and carries her across the desert to a nearby cave. Katharine is wrapped in flowing white garments, and it almost looks as though he is carrying his bride across the threshold after their wedding. As he carries her, he notices her necklace, an ancient thimble hanging from a piece of leather. The thimble was filled with saffron when he bought it for her at a market. For her, wearing the thimble was like having him near her heart. "The thimble," he says, obviously pleased to see it. "Yes," she says. "I have always loved you." The healing power of this truth overwhelms him and he begins to weep.

How awful it is to be ravaged by doubt. How sad not to know the impact we make on people. What a tragedy not to have the faith to know that we matter, that we are cherished. I see examples of this doubt every day between couples, in families and in friendships. Even though you tell them you love them, even though you show them, they don't always receive the message. They need reminding. The heart is like a gas tank that needs to be constantly topped up with fuel if we are to have the necessary energy to move. When our tanks are low, our energy levels drop.

When my children were born, I started a journal for each of them. I'd write stories of what they liked to eat, what games they liked to play and how much I loved them. When I traveled I always took their journals with me so I could write to them on the plane. It helped me feel close to them. I've stopped writing regularly, but every now and then I'll make an entry. They love to read about themselves and they gush with pride when they compare baby stories. The journals will be theirs to take with them when they grow up and move away. They are testaments and reminders of their mother's love.

We need feedback to grow. We need feedback to know we are on the right track. If you don't get enough feedback in your life, ask for it. I am always so grateful when people come up to me after a workshop to give me personal feedback or, years later, to tell me how something has materialized in their life that I may have helped them with.

We also need to find out how the people in our lives receive love. If you're kinesthetic, you need to feel love through touch. You need to *feel* hugs and kisses and lots of physical contact to know you are loved. If you're visual, you need to receive love through the eyes, so that you can *see* you're special. Perhaps you need to be treated to a "dress-up" dinner in a beautiful restaurant; perhaps you need to see your beloved walk through the door with flowers for you. If you're auditory, you receive information through sound. You will need to *hear* words of affection and "I love you" whispered in your ear plenty of times. We're all different, and if we're not loved in the way that we're programmed to receive love, we just don't get it. We lose the faith.

You may need a little bit of all of them, and that's okay. The point is to know yourself and then communicate your style to those closest to you.

My husband used to bring home flowers. Then one day I asked him why and he said, "Because I love you." While I enjoy having flowers around, my husband's act of love was being wasted on me. I did not *feel* loved. Like my children, I'm kinesthetic. I need to be touched in order to feel loved. I love, for example, when he massages my hands and feet in the morning just as I'm waking up, or the way he holds my hand in the car or at the movie theatre, or the long hug he gives me at the door.

If you love someone, let them know – don't let them die not knowing how much they mattered to you. Communicate your preference for receiving Love. We all want to matter. Even when relationships end, we crave to know our effect on people. The gift of Love is the legacy it leaves on our souls.

THE PURPOSE OF LIFE IS TO LOVE

There are only four questions of value in life. "What is sacred? Of what is the spirit made? What is worth dying for? What is worth living for?" And the answer to all four is love.

– DON JUAN DE MARCO

In his book *Life After Death*, Raymond Moody interviews people who have had near-death experiences – those events that happen when the heart monitors go silent and then miraculously start up again. Moody wanted to know what happened to them during those minutes when they were "not alive." He interviewed as many people as he could find, all over the world, who had had these experiences.

As soon as they "died," they could feel themselves leaving their bodies, often seeing their "dead" selves lying below. They felt wonderful because their pain was gone. All of them saw their whole lives before them as they traveled down a tunnel toward a light. Depending on their religious beliefs, at the end of the tunnel people might have seen a golden Christ, a golden Buddha or a white Light. All of them said that the most excruciating part of the journey was revisiting parts of their lives in which they had chosen not to show their love. When they got to the end of the tunnel and merged with the Light, they were asked, "Did you love freely? Did you fulfill your purpose on Earth?" Some of them had such huge regrets that they decided it was too soon for them to die. The next thing they remembered was coming back to consciousness.

When they returned to their bodies and woke up, these "resurrected" people were forever changed. They had renewed vigor, a sharper focus and a clear vision of the true purpose of life. Their priorities had changed. They spent more time with their families and friends. They learned to play and find happiness in the moment. They practised forgiveness. They looked for ways to show their love and appreciation every day. They knew what was important. Imagine if we all had such an experience. How different our lives would be! How would it change your life? Would you have different priorities?

As I mentioned in Chapter 8, Dannion Brinkley was a near-death returnee, not once, but twice. After he was struck by lightning, he was completely paralyzed for six days, and partially paralyzed for seven months. It was two years before he could walk and feed himself. Fourteen years later he had another near-death experience during emergency open-heart surgery. He wrote, "What really becomes important then is realizing the true purpose of our lives. I've found that acts of kindness, and loving and caring for each other, are the most important things in life."[21]

We don't need a near-death experience to learn the truth. But if we were to have experienced that tunnel toward the Light, I imagine it would be a lot easier to let go of petty squabbles, to talk to relatives or friends against whom we hold grudges, and to consciously choose the path of Love every day. I use the image of the tunnel as a way to remind myself of what's important. It helps me to keep focused on what I came here to do – what we all came here to do – and that is to practise Love. Before choosing to withhold love or affection get into the habit of asking: "Will I regret this in my tunnel?"

"ALL I REMEMBER IS THE LOVE"

**When we come to the last moment of this lifetime,
and we look back across it, the only thing that's going to matter
is "what was the quality of our love?"**

– RICHARD BACH

When my maternal grandmother, Nonna, was dying, I found myself wondering about death. Where do we go when we die? Where would Nonna go now? I was hoping that it would be a good place, a beautiful place, to make up for the hardships she had survived on Earth.

My Nonna lived through famine, war and disease. She lost two of her babies to illness. She and my grandfather, Nonno Emilio, devoted most of their life to caring for Barbarella, their youngest, who had been left physically and mentally disabled by childhood meningitis. Now that Nonna was on her death-bed, I wanted so much for her to be taken care of, to go to a nice place.

The night she died, I had a dream. In the dream, Nonno Emilio, who had died ten years earlier, was showing me around the most beautiful, exquisite castle. It was made of pink and white marble and had flowers and lush green plants every-where. In some places, such as over an archway, the marble was carved in such fine, intricate patterns that it looked more like a valance made of white lace. Everywhere I looked I could see white lilies and other, strange flowers I couldn't recognize. The effect was stunning. What a difference, I thought, from the simple stone house on the hill he had lived in for most of his life. Nonno was excited because he was expecting a visitor. I knew immediately that the visitor was his wife, Nonna.

When she arrived she looked just like she did before she got

348

sick, with rosy cheeks and smiling eyes. She cocked her head to one side and looked at me and Nonno with so much love. We baked bread in a big wood-fired oven, just as we used to when I was a little girl. She seemed so happy that I was visiting. When the bread was ready, we dipped pieces in olive oil and ate them. I told them that I worried about them because they had had such a hard life. I looked at Nonna and said how I hoped she wouldn't have to suffer anymore because she had had more than her share on earth. She cocked her head at me with a "wise woman" look in her eyes, a look I will never forget, and said, "Oh, my darling Graziu, all that I remember from my life is the love and the joy." As she said this, her mouth was moving in slow motion: "the l-o-v-e a-n-d t-h-e j-o-y." Then she embraced me, and I was suddenly that little girl back in Italy so many years ago.

When I woke up, I had the most powerful feeling inside me, as if I had the answer to something very important. My Nonna's life had been filled with so much heartache and pain, and yet all that she remembered was the love and the joy. She had come into my dream to tell me that we measure someone's life not by the wealth they've accumulated or the positions they've held, but by their contribution of love. My Nonna's contribution had been enormous, not only in my life but to all who knew her. She and my Nonno Emilio were the embodiment of unconditional love.

All that we do, all that we strive for and all that we want is to love and be loved. Love is the purpose of the journey and the reason we take the step across the bridge. Love can heal the planet. Don't blame the world for the love you lack. *Whatever you want, give it away first.* Commit outrageous acts of love. Give a hug where none is expected, a smile to a stranger, a kind word to a store clerk. Make a fuss over people, listen to their stories, celebrate them. Pay attention to the little things. Love heals the past, gives joy to the present and sends hope to the future.

10

Connect to Spirit

THE SPIRITUAL REVOLUTION

**Authentic spirituality is revolutionary.
It does not console the world, it shatters it.**
- KEN WILBER

What is Spirit? *Spiritus* in Latin means "breath." Spirit is the life force in each of us. The root of "inspiration" is "inspire," which also means "to breathe in." This suggests that when we are inspired, we have breathed in God or the divine Muse. Spirit makes us feel vital, alert and responsive to the moment. It is passion, authenticity and courage. It is God, the divine Voice that calls our name. When we disconnect from Spirit, we disconnect from ourselves and from everything that is meaningful. We lose focus on what is truly important. We go through the motions, but we are not really living. We stop believing in our brilliance and we stop taking action to cross our bridges. Moving your life forward, therefore, depends on your ability to call Spirit into your life and dance with it.

Spirit is all around us. Synchronicities link people, places and events in ways that convince us that the divine Mystery is present in our lives. As spiritual warriors we seek meaning, truth and enlightenment. At our fingertips is an abundance of spiritual wisdom collected from diverse cultures and traditions, from the Dead Sea scrolls to the ancient manuscripts found at Nag Hammadi to the near-death experiences and angelic encounters reported by modern-day mystics. Some people are turning to Native and Aboriginal wisdom, and others to Buddhist texts and practices.

I have noticed in my workshops that people are taking a more spiritual approach to life. This is evident in both their careers and their personal lives. They are working hard to discover who they are and how they fit into the world. For example, one of my clients with whom I was doing "spiritual coaching" decided to quit his six-figure-salary job in the financial industry to open a bookstore with a café. "I realized," he said, "that I want to make a difference to people. I want to nourish their minds, bodies and souls."

This Spiritual Age allows each of us to embrace the Mystery in our own way. We may not be going to church or practising any one religion, but we have, through our spirituality embraced God. "Armed with a vocabulary that was previously restricted to monastics and mystics," says medical intuitive Caroline Myss, "Western culture has broken through the boundaries of religion and begun plunging, largely unescorted, into the realm of the sacred."[1] People not only want to *know* the divine, they want to *experience* it. We sign up for kundalini yoga classes, we go to retreats for the soul, we delve into past lives and we practise meditation. We pray for guidance and wisdom. We are each connecting to the Spirit in our own way.

Spirit has also entered the realm of relationships. There is more sharing and more vulnerability. In business, trust is the tool of the new economy. The deeper the relationship, the more trust there is. And the more trust there is, the more business clients will do with you.

And then there are those who are secretly spiritual but don't want the neighbors, their boss or the secretary to know. These people are still in what I call the "spiritual closet." I've sat beside strangers on airplanes who, after finding out what I do, shared with me their deepest and innermost convictions about God, but told me they would never feel comfortable discussing these ideas with others. One gentleman, the CEO of a large utility company, told me he was on his way home from a religious convention but that his staff thought he was on a golfing trip. A man at one of my seminars, another corporate type, had tears in his eyes when he shook my hand. "I never thought I'd hear the words 'soul,' 'Spirit' and 'God' at a government conference," he said to me, "but it's very refreshing. Thank you."

Spiritual warriors are emerging to find their community and to engage in meaningful conversations about God, the Sacred and Spirit. Spirit has entered our lives. We're evolving, shedding our old skins to emerge renewed, healed and ready to take the step.

CALLING SPIRIT INTO OUR LIVES

Continuous communion with God is the only way
to remain conscious of our spiritual nature in the face
of our constant daily pressures.
– SUSAN L. TAYLOR

Becoming disconnected from Spirit happens subtly. Many of us pay attention to our external lives – where we live, what we buy and what we do – and spend little time focusing on our spiritual growth and inner life. Carl Jung calls this external focus being "horizontal." But our inner world drives our external reality; our external lives reflect the life we have already lived in our thoughts.

Being "vertical" means feeling connected to the wise Voice at the center of our being, our authentic higher Self. Most of us on the spiritual path yearn to stay true to this internal voice, to "walk the vertical path," but we get sidetracked. Other things distract us and demand our time. So we ignore Spirit and slowly shrivel up. "Being the guardian of our inner life must become our highest priority," advises Susan L. Taylor in her book *In the Spirit*, a collection of spiritual writings. "We must never allow people, institutions or social tradition to speak to us so loudly that we cannot hear ourselves."[2]

When we lose the connection to our authentic Self, we lose Spirit too. When we fall asleep to our beauty, we lose Spirit. When we disconnect from our passion and experience psychic absence, we lose Spirit. Calling Spirit into our lives must be done deliberately and consciously and on a daily basis. Calling Spirit into our lives is a commitment to become mature on a deep, inner level, taking full responsibility for whatever shows up in our lives. Calling Spirit into our lives means we surrender to a divine Presence, an Intelligence that brings love and joy and profound peace to our human experience. Calling Spirit into our lives means that we awaken from a long, deep sleep and know our spiritual origin.

There are a hundred ways to connect to Spirit. Here are a few ideas and thoughts for you to reflect on.

PAY ATTENTION TO SPIRITUAL
SYNCHRONICITIES

**The Spirit – whether one uses Christian words such as Holy Spirit
and the Breath of God, the Atman of the Hindus, the Polynesians' Mana, the
Great Spirit of Canadian Indians or the Life Force –
is focused wholly on radical change, on transformation.**

– TOM HARPUR

I was teaching a seminar in Dallas, Texas. At the lunch break a man walked up to me and said, "You have such a beautiful name and you're from Toronto. I have to ask you whether you've heard of the amazing miracles that are happening at a church near the Toronto airport."

"No, I haven't," I responded. "I'd love to hear more. Can you write down a few details for me?"

At the end of the day he handed me a note with details about the so-called miracles that were happening in Toronto: "I have heard that people fall to the ground, sometimes laughing uncontrollably, sometimes weeping and sometimes filled with an overwhelming sense of love, mercy and grace. . . . People have been able to release past hurts, forgive old wounds and heal themselves physically and/or emotionally."

Further down in the note he wrote, "When you said your name this morning and where you're from, I had such a strong impression that God has something very special to give you at that church – if you go with an open, 'thirsty' heart."

That was a synchronicity because three months earlier I had met a lovely family in Sydney, Australia, who were on their way to Toronto to visit the same church. At the time I thought it strange to travel thirty hours with two young children to visit a church. Word of it had obviously spread.

As if that synchronicity wasn't enough, when I got home from Dallas a newspaper article was waiting on my desk. My husband had read about this airport church while I was away and had clipped the article for me. Another synchronicity was that we had just moved from central Toronto to a nearby suburb just fifteen minutes away from the airport. I got the message loud and clear. God wanted me to visit this church, so I did.

At the time I had been looking for a deeper connection with God, but I didn't know how to go about it. Despite my Jesus experience, it had been easy to fall back into my habitual skepticism. What I wanted was a way to bring Spirit into my life without the dogma, the stereotypes and the hypocrisy of organized religion. I thought that God had finally led me to the right place to be on Sunday morning, but it turned out I was wrong. I didn't like the message from the pulpit; there was little humility and too much arrogance. My first visit was also my last.

I eventually figured out that the purpose of that visit was to experience people shamelessly loving God. God was showing me an example of passionate, dynamic faith. Those people were having a love affair with the Divine. There was nothing subdued about their faith, nothing at all like the conservatism of my local Catholic church. I didn't see any miracles that day, but I did see incredible joy on the faces of the people attending. The miracle was faith and it was inside them.

You may have heard the saying "When the student is ready, the teacher will appear." When the message comes from more than one messenger or in more than one way, pay attention. Trust that those synchronicities are being sent to you for a reason. They are not just coincidences. They are *meaningful* coincidences and they are imbued with Spirit. Stay open. Every experience, however subtle, has the power to touch you, to transform you into a higher version of who you are, to take you further along your spiritual journey. The family in the airport, the man at my seminar in Texas, the newspaper article on my desk and the fact that we had just moved closer were all signs that I needed to go and see for myself what that church was all about. Trust that God – or whatever name you choose for the divine Creator, the Beloved, the Great Spirit, your higher Self – will send you teachers and experiences to take you further along your spiritual journey.

Keep a journal and record your spiritual synchronicities. Often we pray for guidance and then when we get it, we discount it as coincidence. According to Julia Cameron, author of *God Is No Laughing Matter*, many of us practise a form of "spiritual amnesia."[3] Pay attention when God is trying to speak to you through the people who weave in and out of your life.

These synchronicities are holy events, proof that divine Spirit is trying to connect with you and touch your life.

OPEN YOUR HEART TO ANGELS AND MIRACLES

There are only two ways to live your life. One is as though nothing is a miracle. The other is as though everything is a miracle.
– ALBERT EINSTEIN

I once gave a workshop in a remote northern community. During the break a woman came up to me, barely able to contain her excitement. "I prayed for you; I know God sent you here," she enthused. And then she told me her story and how my ideas were coming to her at just the right time. I was a vehicle for God. But we're all vehicles for God. God communicates to us all the time and in so many ways.

The founder of the Crystal Cathedral, Robert Schuller, wears a pendant around his neck that reads, "Dear God: Lead me to the person You want to speak to through my life today." I love that. Schuller is dedicating his life to being used by God to bring healing miracles into people's lives. "Grace, you're an angel," a client told me recently. "Thank you," I replied, "but we're all angels." He looked at me, confused. We're *all* angels; we just don't know it.

Spiritual teacher Marianne Williamson says that the traditional drawing depicting the evolution of man – where the ape straightens up in stages to become modern man – is about to change. The man is about to sprout wings![4] Caroline Myss agrees. She says in her book *Why People Don't Heal and How They Can*, "It's a time of transition from Homo sapiens to Homo noeticus – that is, from beings whose perceptions are controlled by the five senses to beings whose perceptions are based on spiritual insight and vision."[5] There are angels amongst us.

In her audio series *The Psychic Pathway*, psychic Sonia Choquette speaks of an encounter with an angel. She was completely exhausted, disconnected and overwhelmed by life. She had been running on empty for over a year and her doctor had suggested she either go into hospital or take a holiday by herself for seven days. She opted for Hawaii. For the first two days all she could do was sleep. On the third day she was walking around town when she found herself being pulled to enter a metaphysical store that carried candles and New Age books. She walked past the store clerk to the back and, all of a sudden, a beautiful black man wearing flowing white robes approached her and said, "Hello, I've been waiting for you." Sonia was surprised. He then took her to a bin of posters and pulled out a picture of an angel who looked tired and worn out.

"That's how I feel," she said. "How did you know?"

Then the white-robed man pulled out another poster, a picture of two angels with the male angel lifting the female into the sky. He said, "You need your partner and you need to slow down. And don't forget to dance." He looked deep into her eyes for a moment and then walked into the back room.

The store clerk, seeing that she was lingering, asked Sonia whether she needed any help. "No thanks," she said. "The man in the back has been quite helpful."

The clerk looked shocked. "What man in the back?"

"The man in white who just helped me."

The clerk ran to the back room and called, "Hello, hello." But no one was there.[6]

Sonia Choquette says that we have a whole team of spiritual guides who help us when we need it most. Angels are assigned to you at birth and their job it is to protect you until your soul's purpose is realized on earth. You also have "runners," who help you find things; "helpers," who help you with projects; "teachers," who guide you through your spiritual evolution; "joy guides," who tickle and amuse you when you need it most and finally a "master guide," who loves you and helps you connect to your Spirit.[7] Angels are everywhere, and many people have had special angel encounters.

My client "Jay" told me how he was saved by his guardian angel one night when he fell asleep at the wheel of his car. He felt two hands grab him by his coat collar and shake him awake. He was so shocked by the event that he stayed awake and alert all the way home. I have heard of other people being "rescued" at the last minute by some unseen force.

Kajsa was only three years old when my grandmother Nonna died, but she has an extraordinary connection with her. Nonna appears in her dreams, and my daughter says she communicates with her through "special feelings." I'm convinced that Nonna is one of Kajsa's Spirit angels. My son never met his paternal grandfather, who died when my husband was seventeen, but as a child Jasper kept talking about "Nonno Frank" as if he lived down the street. I'm convinced that children are closer to that spiritual realm, so it's easier for them to pick up spiritual energy.

Who are your angels? Who has brought healing and understanding into your life? Identify them – both the earthly and the celestial kind – and connect with them when you need their help. How? Close your eyes and talk to them. You can do it through prayer or meditation. Simply breathe deeply and go within. Then ask for their blessing, guidance and protection and thank them when they've shown you miracles. Connect to your angels and they will help you take action toward your life's purpose.

Now think about your life. When did God use you to create a miracle? If you're one of God's messengers, you probably know that you can't deliver a message that you yourself haven't lived and learned first. The message has always been and will always be about Love, because Love is who we are and what God is. When was the last time you brought Love and healing into someone's life? Perhaps you do it every day through your work. Perhaps you recently rescued someone physically or emotionally or spiritually. All lives matter and we're all unique. We all make a difference, whether we realize it or not.

CHERISH MOMENTS OF GRACE

**Grace in a graceless world requires immense personal courage.
Our personal mission is to be in a state of grace, with everyone
with whom we have been in contact, when our souls leave this planet.**

– LANCE SECRETAN

While teaching seminars in England one year, I decided to take a trip to the county of Somerset and visit the spiritual center of Glastonbury. Glastonbury is the ancient Isle of Avalon, nestled at the foot of the Tor, close to its life-giving springs and just above the high-water mark of the Bristol Channel. Some people say it was the birthplace of Christianity in Britain, but Glastonbury has also been a focus for pagan, Arthurian and, lately, hippie and New Age beliefs.

According to legend, the Holy Grail, the chalice used by Jesus at the Last Supper, was buried at the foot of Glastonbury Tor by Joseph of Arimathea. Today the Chalice Well Gardens are just below the Tor, where spring water – once thought to be curative – has flowed since the dawn of time. As soon as I walked into the garden I was intrigued by the very female fountain, which spills into two circular pools, making a *vesica pisces* – a holy symbol that is associated with Glastonbury. The water descends through a series of vulva-shaped bowls of brownish stone that are nestled among rocks and surrounded by beautiful blooms and rich foliage. There was an older woman there, a tourist perhaps, sitting on the edge of the lower pool and dangling her foot in the water. The sounds of the waterfall, the shape of the bowls, the woman whose expression seemed to say "I'm home" – all touched me deeply. It was a moment of grace.

I pressed a hand to my chest, took a deep breath and smiled

back at the woman, who was enjoying my reaction to this unashamedly female fountain. She must have been affected just as I was and had paused to linger for a moment longer. "We are both goddesses," I thought. I was so grateful to be there and able to enjoy it in silence, in the sunshine, with a stranger who was also a kindred spirit. The whole Chalice Well Gardens experience for me was holy. It stands out in my memory as a moment of divine communion.

Moments of grace can arrive in many forms, some subtle and mundane and some powerful and transforming. Grace is any spiritual experience in which you feel the energy of the Divine bubbling up within you. Grace is the energy that suddenly illuminates you with understanding, allowing you to see what you could not grasp before. Grace can be an infusion of holiness in which you are overwhelmed by feelings of love and goodwill for everyone and everything, or an altered state of consciousness in which you feel an indescribable combination of hope, courage and love. Grace is all the extraordinary moments in your life. "For these reasons grace has long been deemed 'amazing,'" says Charlene Spretnak in her book *States of Grace*. "Sometimes the consciousness of grace comes on quite suddenly and so intensely that the moment is never forgotten."[8]

I was driving home one day listening to the car radio when I heard the song "Still Haven't Found What I'm Looking For," by the group U2. I have always loved the song because of its existential message, but I had never heard this version before. It was a live recording with a gospel choir singing the chorus. The effect of so many joyful voices teaming up to sing the lyrics brought me a moment of grace. I was filled with indescribable energy; all I could do was cry.

Often during moments of grace I get an intense flash, a crystal-

clear vision of the meaning of life. In those moments I feel simultaneously detached and connected. I mean detached in the sense
of being able to let go of all the unimportant stuff, the busyness,
the day-to-day worries, the conflicts, the bills – in short, the
material world – and connected in that I feel a oneness with the
spiritual Universe. These moments of grace are like spiritual
orgasms – they last for a short time, but they bring extreme bliss,
happiness and peace.

If you let them, moments of grace can change the way you
look at your life and the way you live each moment. At times,
because of the fast pace of life, I don't stop long enough to
recognize my moments of grace or to properly appreciate their
place in my life. But they are extremely valuable because they
connect us to Spirit and to what nourishes us from the inside.
Those are the times when we "get it" – when we can peel away
the layers of illusion and see what's real. Those are the times
we feel the abundant energy of God's Love, when we feel at
one with our Creator and all of creation. Those are the times
we transcend the mundane details of our lives and experience
the Sacred.

Have you experienced such moments? Have you savored the
serenity of that sweet communion with Spirit? Moments of
grace happen when you're in a state to receive them. They are
opportunities for you to dance with Spirit, and reassurance that
you belong to the divine Mystery. When moments of grace
visit you, when your heart has been softened or when you feel
enveloped by rapture, don't waste that inspiration. Do something with it. Show someone your love, commit a kindness,
paint, write a poem, dance, create.

James Irwin, an Apollo astronaut who walked on the moon,
looked back at Earth from space and said, "Seeing this has to
change a man – it has to make a man appreciate the creation of

God and the love of God."[9] You don't have to leave Earth to experience these holy moments. Look around you, pause and bring your awareness to the present. Using all of your senses, drink in the beauty and the art that surrounds you, and you will be blessed by extraordinary moments of grace.

TAKE A SPIRITUAL PAUSE

If what a tree or a bush does is lost on you, you are surely lost.
Stand still. The forest knows where you are. You must let it find you.
— DAVID WAGONER

I was driving on a busy stretch of highway near my home when I had to come to a screeching stop. Right in front of me a mother goose was crossing the highway with eight or nine goslings in tow. I could tell that the mother was anxious to hurry up her babies as best she could across the three lanes of traffic, but her waddle was painfully slow. I looked around to see the reactions of the other drivers. Everyone had stopped and, amazingly enough, no one behind us was honking their horn. I exchanged looks with the other motorists in the front-row seats. We smiled. We knew we were experiencing something sacred. We realized that those geese were providing us with a much-needed "spiritual pause" in an otherwise hectic day.

I drove off feeling blessed and hopeful – blessed to have witnessed the kindness and gentleness of human beings and hopeful that our planet might actually survive. Spiritual pauses interrupt our busy routines. They make us stop and think about what's truly important to us and about who we are. When was the last time you took a spiritual pause?

Oftentimes people travel through life at such a breakneck speed that they're too busy to take a pause. When we're constantly hurrying to react to stimuli, our awareness of the moment is diminished. We lose our ability to notice Spirit that may be knocking at the window. I know some people who have convinced themselves that if they're not productive, not doing something, then they're not worthwhile. Their self-esteem is tied into *doing* rather than *being*. They may not even be aware of those core beliefs. Ask yourself, why are you so driven to *move*? Why are you a workaholic? Why can't you take a spiritual pause? Ask the mental demons who are sucking joy out of your life what they really want.

It is impossible to connect to Spirit if we're moving at top speed. No one knows this better than me. Keeping still used to be a chore for me. I have had to learn not to get down on myself when I'm not producing or helping someone or solving the world's problems. The older I get, the better I am at carving out my own space and recharging my spiritual batteries. I am now better at noticing other people's energy fields. Some people's energy is scattered in a million directions. It's hard work just to be around them.

When I was in broadcasting, I worked with a senior producer who made me burn calories just by being in the same room. That's because he'd pace back and forth, chew the end of his pencil and repeatedly ask all of us how our stories were coming. His anxiety was contagious and it made us all nervous. These people with frenzied energy are soul polluters. They are addicted to speed. If they're not in a hurry, they don't know who they are. It's become a habit – an addiction, really. They can slow down only if they change their core beliefs about productivity.

With the spiritual pause comes quiet time and an opportunity for your soul to heave a big sigh of relief. Your soul loves the quiet because it is in the quiet that it knows God. Soul and

Ego are constantly battling. Ego wants to do; the soul wants to be. Ego needs constant stimulation; the soul wants quiet contemplation. Ego is addicted to speed; the soul yearns to be still. Which one will you satisfy? Most of us satisfy the Ego, partly because our society programs us to, and partly because we're convinced that Ego will give us a bigger payback. But sooner or later we wake up to the truth and realize that Ego's payback is all illusion. What is real is that we're divine beings on a journey home – back to our spiritual roots.

"The spiritual way home," says Bradford Keeney in *Everyday Soul*, "has less to do with getting knowledge or finding a solution to a problem. It is more directed at removing yourself from the chatter of everyday life and being still in the midst of mystery."[10] Get grounded in your body. Anchor those runaway thoughts. Give yourself permission to recharge and rejuvenate. Try yoga – it teaches you to be aware of your body and your breathing. Stretch into your Spirit. Meditate, sit by a river, gaze at the sky. Rest. Get good at doing nothing, because that's when you learn how to just *be*.

RECOGNIZE AND APPRECIATE BEAUTY

The beautiful creates a sense of the sacred.
Beauty remains a gateway to God.
– JULIA CAMERON

One day last fall I was bursting with creativity. Words flowed freely onto the page. After a wonderful day of writing, I went for an evening walk with my family and saw the most exquisite, stunningly beautiful full moon that I had ever seen. It was bright orange and bursting with ripeness. My heart felt like it was going to burst. Later that night I talked with a client whom

I was coaching by telephone once a week. We had a great session. Then just before she hung up, almost as an afterthought, she told me, "It's a harvest moon tonight. That's when the moon is closest to the earth. Look for it; it should be extra bright and extra big."

A harvest moon — what a wonderful concept! I smiled and thought, "That explains it."

"Oh," she added as an afterthought, "It's rising in Pisces." (She's an astrologer.)

"What does that mean?" I asked.

"Well, it's a time for high creativity," she said.

Hmmm, another piece of the puzzle had been found. There was magic in the Universe. There was beauty unfolding in my life.

When does beauty unfold in your life? While watching a sunset? Enjoying a good novel? Holding your children? Beauty is seeing through the eyes of the soul. If the soul finds it sacred, meaningful and reverent, then it's beautiful. It is your attitude toward life that brings beauty to your experience. When you see life through the eyes of your soul, you not only see beauty all around you, you see God, too. Smell a rose, watch a hummingbird, study a column of ants carrying scraps of bread or a colony of bees building a honeycomb — these are expressions of God's intoxicating joy.

The older we get, the easier it is to become disconnected from beauty. It's not because of age — very old people are often strongly connected to beauty. It's the busyness of middle age that disconnects us. Look at the world through a child's lens. It's so simple. They see the wonder, the awe, the uniqueness. "How does God make clouds?" Kajsa asked me one day. How indeed? Have you ever stared at clouds long enough to see them change shape? When I lived in the foothills of the Rocky

Mountains, every morning I awoke to a big sky. It seemed vast, endless, uniquely beautiful. Why was there so much room up there? The sunrises and sunsets out west were the most spectacular I've ever seen. God had, after all, a huge canvas with which to work.

Beauty is subjective. The award-winning movie *American Beauty* explores the concept of beauty in the ordinary. The idea for the film was born as the screenwriter watched a plastic bag dancing in the wind in New York City. He found the experience so moving and so beautiful that it inspired him to write the script. One moment of beauty can be healing. It can awaken our creativity. It can, in Leonard Cohen's words, "dance us to the end of time."

Pull out your journal and write down ten things you find beautiful. Now think about something that you're indifferent to. Practise looking at it with new eyes – the eyes of your soul. Can you bring more beauty to it? Beauty is in the eyes of the beholder. Can you behold more generously and look at the world through a softer lens?

Beauty is sacred. It is of Spirit. The more you connect to beauty, the more you welcome Spirit into your life.

Start today. Go for a walk at lunch. Watch two squirrels do their mating dance in the park. See lovers kissing under the bridge. Smell fresh-cut grass. Visit an art gallery. Stroll through a public garden. Visit a bird sanctuary. Experience the stillness of a winter wonderland after a snowfall. Stand by the water's edge. My children have learned that when brilliant sunshine follows a summer shower, a rainbow appears. After it rains, they run outside looking for rainbows. When I hear "Mom, Mom!" I know they've found one. Perhaps if you look, you too will find a rainbow.

HAVE REVERENCE FOR NATURE

Rather than chairs and tables, I preferred the ground, trees, and caves, for in those places I felt I could lean against the cheek of God.

— CLARISSA PINKOLA ESTES

I'm a spring girl, born in April. My soul comes alive when I see new life bursting from its winter sleep. Spring is the season when I am most mindful. When I'm outside I notice that the ground smells different. I see tiny shoots making their way up through the snow and the mulch of old leaves. I love watching the buds. I notice the tender green that bursts first from the shrubs, gradually spreading over the trees and landscape – and I get all happy inside. When I see my first tulips, I am at peace with the world.

Last spring I saw tulips pushing themselves up and around some stones. I had put in a rock garden and mistakenly placed some of the stones above the bulbs. When I saw the twists and turns those flowers took to greet the sun, I was humbled. I felt God's intoxicating joy in that moment and knew how Spirit manifests itself in nature. Deep reverence for what grows, for rivers and mountains, for the earth and the sky, awakens the Sacred in us and connects us with Spirit.

Immerse yourself in nature. The fruit farm I grew up on was in the Niagara region near Lake Ontario. I have wonderful memories of walking through the orchards when the peach and cherry trees were in full bloom. I think that's where my love of nature was nurtured. It's that way for many of us; teaching children respect for and awe of nature is one way we can help them connect with Spirit. Clarissa Pinkola Estes' love of the outdoors began as a child, too. A *cantadora* storyteller and the author of *Women Who Run with the Wolves*, she too was raised surrounded by woodlands, orchards and farmland near the Great Lakes. She writes, "There, thunder and lightning were my main nutrition. Cornfields creaked and spoke aloud at night. Far up in the north, wolves came to the clearings in moonlight, prancing and praying."[11]

I get excited when I discover pockets of green in a city, places where we have been able to preserve something alive amidst construction, progress and commercial rezoning. My old house in Toronto's east end was in such a pocket. I used to love driving up the hill where hundred-year-old trees lined both sides of my street. In the spring and summer I was greeted by dappled sunlight dancing among the branches, the canopies of leaves touching and kissing each other. I used to see it every day, and every day, regardless of the season or my mood, it would give me a thrill. Like beauty, nature is all around us.

Bill Leishman, the iconoclastic Canadian inventor who adopted a family of geese, made history when he led them south to migrate. There he was, Papa Goose, flying in his ultra-light glider with the young geese right beside him. (The movie *Fly Away Home* was based on his story.) Leishman said that when the geese were flying next to him, accepting him as their mother and guide, he felt an incredible identification, a surge of emotion that made him feel at one with the birds and with the whole Universe.[12] It was nature at its most sacred.

You must find ways to carve out your own living sanctuary. The sounds, sights and scents of nature are healing; they will soothe your Spirit. Who hasn't been healed by the scent of sweet spring lilac, the glory of a sunset or the ripple of a babbling brook? If we spend all our time working and living in skyscrapers, driving on highways and breathing exhaust fumes, our soul can't receive Spirit. Go to the woods, climb a tree, hike. Take in the colors of the landscape. Pray and give thanks; have reverence for the gifts of nature.

PRACTISE MEDITATION

Stop talking! What a shame you have no familiarity with inner silence! Polish your heart for a day or two; make that mirror your book of contemplation.

- RUMI

Meditation will help you connect to Spirit and to your authentic Voice. It's also one of the best ways to get grounded. It's a harness for the mind. It helps you do some mental housecleaning so that you can restore your focus on what's important. A state of meditation is reached when we are fully engaged in the moment. It is aerobics for the mind. Being mindful during meditation can clear your mind of clutter so that you can journey within and enjoy the present moment.

There are different types of meditation. The more traditional ones focus on the breath, and sometimes a word or a phrase is repeated silently over and over to focus the mind. In the East it is common to use mantras, which are focus words or phrases. The Sanskrit *om* is particularly popular. You breathe in and then on the out breath you say *ommm* or simply *mmmmm*. These sounds are very effective.

You can meditate lying down, but most people fall asleep. I recommend that you sit on a chair, preferably straight-backed, or on the floor with your legs crossed. Create a ritual. Perhaps you will always use the same chair and light a candle. Perhaps you will dim the lights. The ritual prepares the mind for meditation.

Close your eyes and begin by concentrating on your breath.

Notice how you are breathing. Are you a chest breather or an abdomen (diaphragm) breather? Breathing from the chest is shallow breathing, and it actually makes your body work harder. Chest breathers take sixteen to twenty breaths per minute, while diaphragm breathers take only six to eight breaths per minute. In one day chest breathers take between 22,000 and 25,000 breaths, while those who breathe using their diaphragm muscle take between 10,000 and 12,000 breaths per day. That's a big difference. For deep breathing, your belly must expand as you take in air. If it doesn't, you are breathing from your chest.

Now take four seconds to inhale a deep breath into your abdomen, not your chest. Hold the breath for four seconds (this is very important) and then take four seconds to release the breath. Gradually move up to six seconds and then eight seconds. With each breath, let go of any tension you may be holding in your jaw or your face or your body. If you've chosen a word or phrase, repeat it just on the out breath. You may also want to imagine a healing white light washing over your body as you breathe out. Be creative.

Breathing is the single most important technique for centering yourself and learning to relax deeply. "Texts linking proper breathing to peace of mind and well-being were written over three thousand years ago."[13] When my father was critically ill from a pancreatic attack and his heart rate was all over the map, I helped him stabilize with deep-breathing exercises. With my hand on his belly, I helped him focus on his breath for one hour. The nurses were amazed that I was able to calm him down so quickly. I learned later that belly breathing is the most common stress-reduction tool used in hospitals today. When you are in control of your breath, you are in control of your mind.

One of the biggest reasons that people don't stay with meditation – and why I didn't at first – is because of performance anxiety. I didn't think I was doing it right. The truth is, there is no right way. Your mind is like a wild stallion. It doesn't want to be told what to think; it wants to run wild. In order to tame your thoughts, you must be gentle. You won't get anywhere with anger, frustration or judgment. Stop judging yourself. Be gentle. What your mind is doing is perfectly natural.

"The primary goal of meditation is not relaxation," says Joan Borysenko. "It is awareness."[14] Relaxation is a side effect of learning how to meditate. When I learned that about meditation, I had a breakthrough. I had always thought meditation had to be a peaceful experience, so when I was fighting with my thoughts during my mediations, I thought I was doing it all wrong. Borysenko says, "restless meditation is usually a better learning experience than one where the mind becomes peaceful."[15]

Training your mind is much like training a new puppy – it takes a lot of patience. If you get distracted, be aware of where your mind wants to go and then say, "Not right now." If you hear your inner critic, give it a name and then address it briefly: "Okay, Harriet/Harry, I know you hate doing this, but please park your criticism for just a few minutes."

Meditation is a mental discipline. Its goal is to bring you to a closer relationship with your divine Self. When you can finally silence the chatter, your soul can give you the guiding wisdom you need to hear.

If you're just starting, meditate daily for ten to twenty minutes a day. As you get better, do it twice a day. Choose a positive place that is conducive to quiet. Make sure you won't be interrupted.

The thirteenth-century theologian and philosopher St. Thomas Aquinas spent years trying to know God through his rational defenses of Christian doctrines. He filled volumes and volumes with his thoughts. But once he had attained a meditative union with God, he stopped writing. When asked why, he said that what he had been shown in meditation made everything that he had written "only straw."

If prayer is talking to God, meditation is when God talks back. Meditation is listening to God. The biggest challenge for most people is to stay with it – to practise meditating every day. I know it is for me. "Don't allow your ego to convince you that you haven't the time to pray and meditate," advises Joan Gattuso in her book *A Course in Love*. She says it's the most important thing you'll ever do for yourself.[16]

CULTIVATE HEALING WORDS

Words are merely manipulated energy pulled from various frequencies of expression. These expressions are materialized on an emotional level and conveyed as forms of encouragement, guidance, humor and sadness. [They] awaken each being to the divine.

– JAMES VAN PRAAGH

What are healing words? Healing words can be prayers, but they can also be songs, poems, stories and inspirational quotations that have touched your heart and brought you wisdom or healing. Any time words affect you, they are connecting you to Spirit. Make a file of healing words. Today even the Internet is a rich source of inspiration. One day I found this beautiful anonymous poem on my e-mail:

May today there be peace within you.

May you trust God that you are exactly where you are meant to be.

May you not forget the infinite possibilities that are born of faith.

May you use those gifts that you have received, and pass on the love that has been given to you.

May you be content knowing that you are a child of God.

Let His presence settle into your bones, and allow your soul the freedom to sing, dance, and to bask in the sun.

I had been restless and agitated that day, but as soon as I read those words I felt a calmness sweep over me. Words have power to enter our souls and heal our hearts. And words in the shape of prayers are perhaps the most powerful of all. I wrote about the power of prayer in Chapter 6, in Emilio's story. Prayer can be used to help us establish a conscious connection to the spiritual world.

All you need to know is that there is no right or wrong way to pray. Just follow your heart. Create your own words and speak them or write them. Have a conversation with your divine Creator. During those days when you seem inundated with the concerns and petty problems of the physical world, escape into prayer.

My naturopathic doctor, Sat Dharam Kaur, is an expert on cancer prevention and the author of *A Call to Women*. She has been teaching prayer as a way to help her patients deal with illness and disease. At a recent workshop she held at the Naturopathic College, she encouraged all of us to write our own personal prayers as a pathway to healing. As each person got up to share their individual prayers, I could feel an energy-shift in the room. It was intimate and profound; we were surrounded by God's grace. Here are a few I wrote that day and that you can borrow:

Dear God: Help me keep my eyes, ears and heart tuned to your frequency. My mind is open. Fill it with pure thoughts. My heart is open. Nurture it with unconditional love. My soul is open. Rekindle the fire within me. Continue to give me the wisdom I need to bring healing and love to my world. Amen.

Dear Great Spirit: My heart is overflowing with gratitude at the abundance you have created in my life. Thank you, thank you, thank you for blessing me in every way. Thank you for my family and friends and the love they have showered on me. Thank you for this work that I love. Thank you for planet Earth, and the sunshine and rain that nourish us all. What bounty there is to enjoy! Help me see the beauty every day. Continue to shine your Light deeply into me so that I may radiate it to others. Let my words, thoughts and actions carry out the highest ideals of Love. Amen.

If you don't feel comfortable communicating with "God," then choose another focus. There are all sorts of deities, saints, enlightened spirits and teachers you can pray to. You can pray to the feminine creative power of the Universe, known as Adi Shakti in India or the Virgin Mary in Christianity. You can pray to your angels or Spirit guides. You can pray to Jesus, the Buddha, Mohammed or Krishna. You can choose a Greek or Norse god or goddess such as Zeus, Athena or Odin.

My friend Wally prays to his grandma. He had a sacred connection to her when she was alive and now that she has passed away, he believes she is one of his angels. He has felt her presence on more than one occasion, and during times of crisis, he takes out her picture and prays to her.

Recently my friend Addie scratched the cornea of her eye. After she told me about her excruciating pain and how the doctors said there could be permanent damage, I spontaneously said, "Addie, I will pray to Santa Lucia for you. Santa Lucia is the patron saint of the eyes."

When I was young, my grandmother taught me a who's who of the saints. Any time anyone was sick or needed a prayer, Nonna would invoke the appropriate saint for the situation. I had turned my back on saints during my skeptical phase, but now I realize that help and guidance can come from many sources.

Write down your healing words and put them by your bed. Repeat them before you go to sleep. Share them at mealtimes. Keep your healing words in your wallet and take them out when you're stuck in traffic. I carry the prayer of St. Francis of Assisi and the poem "Footprints" in my wallet and pull them out from time to time to remind myself of their healing words.

Prayer of St. Francis of Assisi
Lord, make me an instrument of thy peace.
Where there is hatred, let me sow love.
Where there is injury, pardon.
Where there is doubt, faith.
Where there is despair, hope.
Where there is darkness, light
And where there is sadness, joy.
O, Divine Master, grant that I may not
So much seek to be consoled as to console;
To be understood, as to understand;
To be loved, as to love;

For it is in giving that we receive,
It is in pardoning that we are pardoned,
And it is in dying that we are born to eternal life.

Footprints
One night I dreamed a dream.
I was walking along the beach with my Lord.
Across the sky flashed scenes from my life.
For each scene, I noticed two sets of footprints in the sand,
one belonging to me and one to my Lord.
When the last scene of his life shot before me
I looked back at the footprints in the sand
and to my surprise,
I noticed that many times along the path of life
there was only one set of footprints.
I realized that this was at the lowest
and saddest times of my life.
This always bothered me
and I questioned the Lord
about my dilemma.
"Lord, you told me when I decided to follow You,
You would walk and talk with me all the way.
But I'm aware that during the most troublesome
times in my life, there is only one set of footprints.
I just don't understand why, when I needed You most,
You leave me.".
He whispered, "My precious child,
I love you and will never leave you
Never, ever, during your trials and testings.
When you saw only one set of footprints
it was then that I carried you."

— Margaret Fishback Powers[17]

BE GRATEFUL FOR YOUR LIFE

The biggest lesson I learned was that if you have all the fresh water you want to drink and all the food you want to eat, you ought never to complain about anything.

– EDDIE RICKENBACKER

Eddie Rickenbacker uttered the words above after being rescued during the Second World War. He and his buddies had spent twenty-one days at sea drifting on life rafts in the Pacific Ocean. That experience gave him a perspective of gratitude for his life that he never lost. Why is it that we must come face to face with adversity or death before we appreciate the many blessings of our lives?

Feeling truly grateful for one's blessings and appreciative of being on the journey called life is the ultimate wisdom and the pinnacle of happiness. Only those who are sufficiently enlightened have this "gratitude attitude," and it often comes, sadly enough, after some adversity or tragedy. The gift that gratitude brings is a deeper connection to Spirit, a more intimate relationship with God.

At the end of the film *City of Angels*, the fallen angel Seth is asked whether leaving eternity for his beloved, Maggie, was worth it now that she had tragically been taken away from him. Seth replies, "Just to feel the touch of her lips, the feel of her skin on mine, the scent of her hair – yes, it was worth it." As an angel Seth hadn't been able to experience the physical sensations that humans take for granted, like relaxing under a hot shower, biting into a ripe pear, riding a wave in the ocean, touching someone's hand or twining bodies together in the act of lovemaking. In the movie these human experiences are coveted by the angels. "What was it like?" another angel asks enviously after Seth "takes the fall."

Taking our lives for granted is a bad habit. We don't mean to, but we do, and nothing is immune. We take our partners for granted, our kids, our jobs, our health, our parents, the government, even technology. Everything becomes routine and predictable.

One thing I cannot take for granted is the experience of flying in an airplane. How is it that a metal machine filled with hundreds of people and many thousands of pounds of cargo stays aloft in nothingness? Regardless of how many planes I've taken, when I look out over the wing and beyond the horizon, I give thanks to the God who gave human beings the capacity to conceive of powered flight. I will never take flying for granted – it's too much of a miracle for me. Maybe it comes from my ancestry. On Alitalia flights everyone applauds when the plane touches down. Perhaps they're applauding the crew and saying thanks. But I think they're applauding God, appreciating the miracle of flight even more now that it's over and they are again on solid ground.

What if we looked at our lives as miracles? Would we stop taking them for granted?

THE MOSAIC OF HAPPINESS

To see a world in a grain of sand,
And a heaven in a wild flower,
To hold infinity in the palm of your hand,
And eternity in an hour.

— WILLIAM BLAKE

Many of us can't be grateful for our lives because we don't see the miracles that we are. Gratitude leads to happiness and happiness is an attitude, a state of mind. We have the power to feel happy through the way we look at our lives. It's a feeling of being alive, engaged and responsive to the moment. And we do not seek happiness because it will give us something else. Happiness itself is the ultimate feeling we desire – nirvana, tranquility, the bottom line of human existence. "Happiness is not a cure-all, it is an antidote . . . something that will enable us to handle and deal with our problems and still maintain our self-esteem, so that we do not resign from the human race," says Simon the ragpicker.[18]

But we tend to associate happiness with material success, so we buy lottery tickets. Micheline Gravel won four million dollars in a lottery, and she didn't get one moment's peace out of it. In fact, she lost her husband and all her winnings and then almost died when she attempted suicide in a fit of despair. When Gravel contacted fifteen other lottery winners, they told her similar stories of their lives falling apart after winning huge sums of money.[19]

So what does it mean to be happy? What will it take for you to be happy? When are you most happy and how long does it usually last? What is the ingredient that guarantees perpetual happiness? Is there such a thing? We've all met people whose problems are completely unnecessary, yet they lack the insight to find solutions. We find things to complain about; we focus on lack rather than abundance in our lives.

What if life were a series of moments and the way to achieve happiness in life was to have as many "holy" or "sacred" or "perfect" moments as possible? And what if those moments could be represented by small, colorful pieces of glass to be added to a huge mosaic? The mosaic represents your life. Try thinking of happiness as a collection of perfect moments to be savored – little pieces of bliss here, a few highs there, moments of grace scattered about – all to be added one by one to the masterpiece mosaic called *My Life*. Instead, most people think happiness must be constant and continuous or else it's not happiness. They don't want little pieces of broken tile in their mosaic; they want one giant, uniform piece of happy carpet.

But this uniformity is not possible. Constant happiness wouldn't *be* happiness, because you'd have nothing to compare it with. You've just had a beautiful day at your annual family reunion when another driver forces you off the road. You say, "What a lousy world!" You've had a perfect afternoon with your beloved and then come home to a flooded basement. You think, "Why is my life falling apart?" You get a speeding ticket, burn dinner or have a fight with a friend and you announce to the world that your life is in the toilet and happiness will never be yours.

The tragedy of life is when we toss away our sacred pieces of priceless tile – our "holy moments" – because we think them too insignificant to qualify as happiness. We throw them away every time we lose faith, experience failure or get angry. Why is it that one negative experience can erase ten positive ones?

Why do we let the negative take over our lives? We need a new attitude toward happiness.

We must let go of the idea of happiness as constant, unbroken and permanent. That version of happiness doesn't exist, and *that's okay*. We must not feel like failures if we haven't achieved that kind of happiness. Instead we must collect and protect the thousands of pieces of tile, each one representing one holy moment, each moment carrying its own unique story and sentiment, each one an expression of Spirit in our lives. In the end, this is what we've lived for. This is happiness – moments so real and so beautiful that they leave an ache in our souls, memories of love and kindness locked within our hearts, moments of grace so overwhelming that you swear you've seen the face of God. These treasured fragments are what make each life unique and truly worth living.

Don't let life steal away your perfect moments. Recognize them and protect them and store them in your heart. And when you're ready, add them to your mosaic one by one. In your twilight years you'll be able to stand back and admire your masterpiece. You will look up at your giant work of art and tell the world with pride, "That's my life!"

THE PERFECTION OF EVERYTHING

The world, Govinda, is not imperfect or slowly evolving along a long path to perfection. No, it is perfect at every moment; every sin already carries grace within it, all small children are potential old men. . . . Therefore, it seems to me that everything that exists is good – death as well as life, sin as well as holiness, wisdom as well as folly. Everything is necessary, everything needs only my agreement, my assent, my loving understanding; then all is well with me and nothing can harm me.

– HERMANN HESSE, *SIDDHARTHA*

I began this book with the question "Who are you?" and I am ending it by reminding you that who you are is Spirit. But Spirit goes by many names. Connect to Spirit and you connect to your higher Self – the part of you that has dreams, and desires to cross the bridge toward a potential not yet known. Connect to Spirit and you connect to God or your divine Voice – the part of you that whispers what is true, beautiful and ever-lasting in your life. Connect to Spirit and you connect to that well of unconditional Love – that part of you that can forgive and see your neighbor's story with compassion.

Between the year of your birth and the year of your death – between those two sets of four numbers – there is a hyphen, a space. That space is your life. What will you do with it? How will you let God use your life? What words will flow from your lips? What steps will you take? How will you define "move forward"? Will you have the courage to embrace faith and continue your spiritual journey? Or will you let fear turn you away from your soul's calling?

Find your own way to connect to Spirit and belong to the Mystery. Your soul knows that everything that happens to you, whether positive or negative, is necessary for your spiritual evolution. Stop fighting yourself. Stop feeling so alone. People say that we enter the world alone and we exit the same way, but we're not really alone. Spirit is there. It has always been there, guiding us, nurturing us and holding our hand.

In the enchanted land of Hawaii, the traditional greeting is *aloha. Alo* means "go with" and *ha* means "breath." When Hawaiians greet you, they're really saying, "My breath goes with you." As you continue your spiritual journey, as you continue to grow, expand and stretch into a fuller expression of yourself, may God's breath go with you. May divine Light be a beacon of inspiration as you dance across your bridge. Take the step toward your future. Take the step toward your dreams. Your bridge *is* there. *Aloha.*

Acknowledgements

I am the person I am today because of the people who have loved me. I would like to celebrate them for helping me become a fuller version of myself.

Thanks first to my parents, Matteo and Concetta Cirocco, who gave me life and who always gave me bigger shoes to wear. Their confidence and belief in me made me want to climb to higher peaks. *Vi voglio sempre bene.* To my brothers, John and Tony, with whom I share a name, a heritage and precious memories, and their families—thank you for your love and support.

To Nonna Antonia and Nonno Emilio, who are on the "other side" now, but who continue to watch over me—your love and kindness were the purest I'll ever know. I am who I am because of you.

To my aunts, uncles and cousins in Canada, Australia, France and Italy. Thank you for welcoming me with open arms and always showering me with love.

To my husband's brother and sisters and especially his mother, Lucy D'Agostino, thank you for your love and support over the years.

Brian Weiss says friends make up our spiritual family. I am particularly blessed with a large spiritual family. I would like to acknowledge and celebrate some special people:

Nesrin Berrak, Leslie Chambers, Janet Clark, Caroline Cobham, Filomena and Joseph Costa, Annika Daley, Monique Danis, Lara D'Avilar, Tina DiPietro, Bea Doyle, Rosemary French, Ellen Goldhar, Addie Greco-Sanchez, Katalin Eszterhai, Joanne Harrington, Jill Hewlett, George Lajtai, Lorna Langford, Jeanne Ma, Linda Moras, D'Arcy MacKenzie, Linda Montgomery, Wally Morgado, John McCormick, Trisha Naylor, George Novak, Peri and Tom Ongarato, Nick and Gloria Olenick, Lucy Rinaldi, Mary and Jim Slominski, Yulia and Ed Sternin, Fatih Tinaz, Melody and Ron Vahrmeyer, Owen Williams, and Sara and Mayer Yashar. All of you are threads in my tapestry—you have contributed to my story, and for that I am grateful.

I am grateful to my clients, especially my community of "Goddesses" who have let me into their hearts and whose generous feedback over the years has fuelled my faith to stay true to my calling. Thanks also to the thousands of people in the United States, Canada, Australia and the UK who have attended my workshops, seminars and retreats and shared their thoughts and feelings with me. Ultimately it is the Divine Voice expressing itself to you through me that I credit for the courage to take the step and write this book.

To the many corporate leaders who have hired me to lead workshops or give keynotes, I thank you for the privilege of being able to serve you. You are the brave hearts our world needs today.

Thank you to my assistants, Barb Marks and Leah Taylor. I so appreciate your professionalism, dedication and loyalty. I am grateful to Susan Lilholt for the contact at HarperCollins, and Dawn McKinney Maxwell at Fred Pryor Seminars, who was the first to recognize and celebrate my speaking gift.

A special thank you to Neale Donald Walsch, Wayne Dyer, Blaine Lee, Brian Tracy, Daphne Rose Kingma, Denise Bisonnette, and Michelle Tocher for their very kind endorsements of *Take the Step* and for writing books that have inspired me along my journey.

Finally, I would like to acknowledge my editor, Don Loney, at HarperCollins. Thanks, Don, for supporting my vision and for making this process not only painless but joyful. Your faith in this project helped me across the bridge. Don was supported by an extraordinary team of professionals at HarperCollins, and I am grateful to them all. Special thanks to Iris Tupholme, Yvonne Hunter, Greg Tabor, and Neil Erickson. Thanks also to Kate Cassaday, who helped produce the 10th anniversary edition.

I could not have done this work without the love and support of my family. To my two precious children, Jasper and Kajsa, your energy and passion for life inspire me. Your innocence renews me and your love completes me. Thank you for choosing me as your mother and for constantly teaching me to take the step.

To my life partner, editor and best friend, Santo D'Agostino, your love is the rock I hold onto in the storm and the wind that carries me to seek higher versions of myself. I feel blessed that our stories intertwined in this lifetime. Everything makes sense because you're in the world.

And last but not least, I want to acknowledge the Great Spirit that speaks through me and allows me to do this work with so much passion and joy. As William Blake says, "I myself do nothing. The Holy Spirit accomplishes all through me."

Endnotes

Chapter 1: Authenticity

1 Mark Albion, *Making a Life, Making a Living* (New York: Warner Books, 2000), p. 9.
2 Georgia Witkin, *The Female Stress Syndrome* (New York: Newmarket Press, 1991) and *The Male Stress Syndrome* (New York: Newmarket Press, 1996).
3 Robin Norwood, *Why Me, Why This, Why Now?* (Toronto: McClelland & Stewart, 1994), p. 12.
4 Caroline Myss, *Why People Don't Heal and How They Can* (New York: Three Rivers Press, 1997), p. 12.

Chapter 2: Truth

1 Sam Keen, *To Love and Be Loved* (New York: Bantam Books, 1997), p. 6.
2 Oriah Mountain Dreamer, *The Invitation* (San Francisco: HarperSanFrancisco, 1999), p. 1.
3 Neale Donald Walsch, *Conversations with God*, Book 2 (Charlottesville, VA: Hampton Roads, 1997), pp. 95–97.
4 Shakti Gawain, "The Path of Relationship," public lecture given at the Learning Annex, Toronto, March 1994.
5 Nag Hammadi Codices 11.33.18–21.

Chapter 3: Destiny

1 Stephen Covey, *The Seven Habits of Highly Effective People* (New York: Simon & Schuster, 1989), p. 108.
2 Mitch Albom, *Tuesdays with Morrie* (New York: Doubleday, 1997), p. 82.
3 David Spangler, *The Call* (New York: Riverhead Books, 1996), p. 13.

Chapter 4: Passion

1 Sarah Ban Breathnach, "A Gift for Giving," *People* magazine (September 22, 1997), pp. 101–102.
2 Marianne Williamson, *A Woman's Worth* (New York: Random House, 1993), p. 14.
3 Toni Morrison in an interview by Oprah Winfrey, *O* magazine (March 2001), p. 185.
4 Og Mandino, *The Greatest Miracle in the World* (New York: Bantam Books, 1975), p. 91.
5 Barbara De Angelis, *Passion* (New York: Delacorte Press, 1998), p. 20.
6 *The Essential Rumi*, Coleman Barks, trans. (New York: HarperCollins, 1995), p.105.
7 Robert Fritz, *The Path of Least Resistance*, quoted in Barbara J. Braham, *Finding Your Purpose* (Menlo Park, CA: Crisp Publications, 1991), p. 4.
8 Barbara J. Braham, Finding Your Purpose (Menlo Park, CA: Crisp Publications, 1991), p. 5.
9 Robert Hopcke, *There Are No Accidents: Synchronicity and the Stories of Our Lives* (New York: Riverhead Books, 1997), p. 14.
10 Brian Weiss, *Messages from the Masters: Tapping into the Power of Love* (New York: Warner Books, 2000), pp. 108–109.
11 Sam Keen, *The Passionate Life* (San Francisco: HarperSanFrancisco, 1992), p. 254.
12 Sarah Ban Breathnach, *Something More* (New York: Warner Books, 1998), p. 156.
13 Diane Ackerman, *A Natural History of the Senses*, quoted in "Diane Sawyer Shares a Great Read," *O* magazine (September 2000), p. 274.
14 De Angelis, p. 4.

Chapter 5: Courage

1 Mountain Dreamer, *The Invitation*, p. 91.
2 Theodore Roosevelt, "Citizenship in a Republic," speech delivered at Sorbonne, Paris, April 23, 1910. (U.S. History Interactive 1999, www.geocities.com/Heartland/Pointe/3048/bio/TR/TR.html).
3 Weiss, p. 95.
4 Paul Ferrini, *Love Without Conditions* (Greenfield, MA: Heartways Press, 1994), p. 49.
5 Ferrini, p. 33.
6 Bradford Keeney, *Everyday Soul: Awakening the Spirit in Daily Life* (New York: Riverhead Books, 1996), p. 30.
7 Angeles Arrien, *The Four-Fold Way* (New York: HarperCollins, 1993), pp. 7–8.
8 Weiss, p. 101.

Chapter 6: Embrace Faith

1 Marilyn Snell, "The World of Religion According to Huston Smith," *Mother Jones* (November/December 1997), p. 42.
2 "Social Studies," *Globe and Mail* (9 May 2001), p. A20.
3 Keeney, inside front flap.
4 James Hillman and Michael Ventura, *We've Had a Hundred Years of Psychotherapy and the World Is Getting Worse* (San Francisco: HarperSanFrancisco, 1992), p. 12.
5 Hillman and Ventura, p. 151.
6 Ken Blanchard, *We Are the Beloved* (Grand Rapids, MI: Zondervan Publishing, 1994), p. 6.
7 Idries Shah, *The Exploits of the Incomparable Mulla Nasrudin* (London: Octagon Press, 1983), p. 9.
8 Deepak Chopra, *How to Know God* (New York: Harmony Books, 2000), p. 203.
9 Neale Donald Walsch, *Conversations with God*, Book I (Charlottesville, VA: Hampton Roads, 1995), back cover.
10 NHC 11.32.25–33.5.
11 George Fowler, *Learning to Dance Inside* (New York: Addison-Wesley, 1996), p. 92.
12 "This Is Brain Surgery," *Globe and Mail* (28 March 1998), p. D5.
13 Julia Cameron, *God Is No Laughing Matter* (New York: Jeremy P. Tarcher/Putnam, 2000), p. 278.
14 Cameron, p. 280.
15 Jeffrey Klein, Editorial, *Mother Jones* (November/December 1997), p. 5.

Chapter 7: Heal the Past

1 Gabriele Rico, *Pain and Possibility* (New York: Jeremy P. Tarcher/Perigee Books, 1991), p. viii.
2 Thomas Moore, *Care of the Soul* (New York: Harper Perennial, 1992), p. 136.
3 Debbie Ford, *The Dark Side of the Light Chasers* (New York: Riverhead Books, 1998), pp. 24–25.
4 Rico, p. xii.
5 David Whyte, *The Heart Aroused* (New York: Currency Doubleday, 1994), p. 109.
6 Joan Borysenko, *Fire in the Soul: A New Psychology of Spiritual Optimism* (New York: Warner Books, 1994), pp. 9 & 58.
7 Christiane Northrup, *Women's Bodies, Women's Wisdom* (New York: Bantam Books, 1998), p. 760.
8 Norman Cousins, quoted in Rico, p. 7.
9 Alice Miller, *The Drama of the Gifted Child* (New York: Basic Books, 1994), p. 35.

10 Julia Cameron, *The Artist's Way* (Jeremy P. Tarcher/Putnam, 1992), p. 61.

Chapter 8: Esteem the Self

1 Nathaniel Branden, *The Power of Self-Esteem* (New York: Health Communications, 1992), p. viii.
2 Dan Millman, *Everyday Enlightenment* (New York: Warner Books, 1998), pp. 14–15.
3 Mandino, p. 97.
4 Dannion Brinkley, "We Are All Great, Awesome, Powerful, Spiritual Beings," in *Experiencing the Soul*, Eliot Jay Rosen, ed. (Carlsbad, CA: Hay House, 1998), p. 103.
5 NHC 11.45.29–33.
6 John K. Williams, *The Knack of Using Your Subconscious Mind* (New Jersey: Prentice-Hall, 1980), p. 27.
7 Walsch, *Conversations* 3, p. 61.
8 Walsch, *Conversations* 3, p. 60.
9 Gary Zukav, *The Seat of the Soul* (New York: Simon & Schuster, 1990), p. 96.
10 All examples from Williams.
11 Williams, p. 26.
12 See Thomas Verny, *The Secret Life of the Unborn Child* (Toronto: Collins, 1981).
13 in Elaine Dember, *Use the Good Dishes: Finding Joy in Everyday Life* (Toronto: Macmillan, 2000), p. 85.
14 Kahlil Gibran, *The Prophet* (New York: Alfred A. Knopf, 1991), p. 61.

Chapter 9: Practise Love

1 John O'Donohue, *Anam Cara: A Book of Celtic Wisdom* (New York: HarperCollins, 1997), p. 15.
2 Carolyn Hillman, *Recovery of Your Self-Esteem* (New York: Simon & Schuster, 1992), p. 24.
3 Gabriele Roth, "The Dance of the Wounded Heart," in *Handbook for the Heart*, Richard Carlson and Benjamin Shield, eds. (Little, Brown & Co., 1996), p. 140.
4 Leo Buscaglia, *Loving Each Other* (Thorofare, NJ: Slack Publishing, 1984), p. 20.
5 See Dean Ornish, *Love and Survival: The Scientific Basis for the Healing Power of Intimacy* (New York: HarperCollins, 1998).
6 See Paul Pearsall, *The Heart's Code* (New York: Broadway Books, 1998).
7 Williamson, p. 89.
8 O'Donohue, p. 28.

9   *The Essential Rumi*, p. 104.
10 Manuela Dunn Mascetti, *Rumi: The Path of Love*, Camille Helminski and Kabir Helminski, trans. (Boston: Element Books, 1999), p. 9.
11 Pearsall, p. 181.
12 Gibran, p. 32.
13 Neale Donald Walsch, *Friendship with God* (New York: Putnam, 1999), p. 267.
14 "Brains Shaped by Touch," *Toronto Star* (29 October 1997), p. A28.
15 O'Donohue, *Anam Cara* (Cliff Street Books, 1997), p. 15.
16 O'Donohue, *Anam Cara* (Cliff Street Books, 1997), p. 9.
17 Joan Borysenko, *Minding the Body, Mending the Mind* (New York: Bantam Books, 1987), pp. 25–26.
18 Hugh Prather and Gayle Prather, "God Is Love," in *Handbook for the Heart*, Richard Carlson and Benjamin Shield, eds. (New York: Little, Brown & Co., 1996), p. 84.
19 "The Height of Commitment," *Globe and Mail* (10 December 1999), p. A20; and "Deal to Spare Redwood Knocks Environmental Activist from Perch," *Globe and Mail* (20 December 1999), p. A14.
20 Weiss, p. 91.
21 Brinkley, p. 103.

Chapter 10: Connect to Spirit

1   Myss, pp. 86–87.
2   Susan L. Taylor, *In the Spirit* (New York: Amistad, 1993), p. 2.
3   Cameron, *God is No Laughing Matter*, p. 120.
4   Marianne Williamson, Public lecture at the Learning Annex, University of Toronto, May 27, 1999.
5   Myss, p. 88.
6   Sonia Choquette, *The Psychic Pathway* (Nightingale Conant Audio), side 4.
7   Sonia Choquette, *The Psychic Pathway Workbook* (Nightingale Conant Audio), pp. 30–31.
8   Charlene Spretnak, "States of Grace," in *God in All Worlds*, Lucinda Vardey, ed. (Toronto: Alfred A. Knopf Canada, 1995), pp. 504–505.
9   James Irwin, "Going to the Moon," in *The Home Planet*, Kevin Kelley, ed. (New York: Addison-Wesley, 1988), p. 38.
10 Keeney, p. 15.
11 Clarissa Pinkola Estes, *Women Who Run with the Wolves* (New York: Ballantine Books, 1992), p. 4.
12 Bill Leishman, public lecture. Jan. 26, 2000 Ottawa.
13 Joan Borysenko, *The Power of the Mind: Renewing Body, Mind and Spirit* (Nightingale Conant Audio), Accompanying Booklet, "Dr. Joan Borysenko's Guide to Meditation and Inner Peace," p. 3.

14 Borysenko, *Minding the Body*, p. 50.
15 Borysenko, *Minding the Body*, p. 50.
16 Joan Gattuso, *A Course in Love* (San Francisco: HarperSanFrancisco, 1996), p. 137.
17 Margaret Fishback Powers, *The Footprints Book of Prayers* (Toronto: HarperCollins, 1996), p. 5.
18 Mandino, p. 57.
19 "Lottery Windfall Dragged Woman 'Through Hell,'" *Globe and Mail* (4 March 2000), p. A11.

Suggested
Reading Resources

Albion, Mark. *Making a Life, Making a Living*. New York: Warner Books, 2000.

Albom, Mitch. *Tuesdays with Morrie*. New York: Doubleday, 1997.

Arrien, Angeles. *The Four-Fold Way*. New York: HarperCollins, 1993.

Ban Breathnach, Sarah. *Something More: Excavating Your Authentic Self*. New York: Warner Books, 1998.

Blanchard, Ken. *We Are the Beloved*. Grand Rapids, MI: Zondervan Publishing, 1994.

Bly, Robert. *A Little Book on the Human Shadow*. New York: HarperCollins, 1988.

Bolen, J. S. *Crossing to Avalon*. San Francisco: HarperSanFrancisco, 1994.

Bolles, Richard N. *How to Find Your Mission in Life*. Berkeley, CA: Ten Speed Press, 1991.

Borysenko, Joan. *Fire in the Soul: A New Psychology of Spiritual Optimism*. New York: Warner Books, 1994.

———. *Minding the Body, Mending the Mind*. New York: Bantam Books, 1987.

Burnham, Sophy. *A Book of Angels: Reflections of Angels Past and Present and True Stories of How They Touch Our Lives*. New York: Ballantine Books, 1990.

Buscaglia, Leo. *Loving Each Other*. Thorofare, NJ: Slack Publishing, 1984.

Cameron, Julia. *The Artist's Way*. New York: Jeremy P. Tarcher/Putnam, 1992.

———. *God Is No Laughing Matter*. New York: Jeremy P. Tarcher/Putnam, 2000.

Campbell, Joseph. *Reflections on the Art of Living: A Joseph Campbell Companion*. Edited by Diane K. Osborn. New York: HarperCollins, 1991.

Carlson, Richard, and Benjamin Shield, eds. *Handbook for the Heart*. New York: Little, Brown & Co., 1996

Chopra, Deepak. *How to Know God*. New York: Harmony Books, 2000.

Choquette, Sonia. *The Psychic Pathway*. New York: Crown Trade Paperbacks, 1994.

———. *The Psychic Pathway*. Nightingale Conant Audiocassette and workbook.

Collinge, William. *Subtle Energy: Awakening to the Unseen Forces in Our Lives*. New York: Warner Books, 1998.

Cousineau, Phil. *Soul Moments*. Berkeley, CA: Conari Press, 1997.

Covey, Stephen. *The Seven Habits of Highly Effective People*. New York: Simon & Schuster, 1989.

De Angelis, Barbara. *Passion*. New York: Delacorte Press, 1998.

Demartini, John. *Count Your Blessings*. New York: Element Books, 1997.

Dossey, Larry. *Be Careful What You Pray For*. New York: HarperCollins, 1997.

Dyer, Wayne. *There's a Spiritual Solution to Every Problem*. New York: HarperCollins, 2001.

———. *10 Secrets for Success & Inner Peace*. Carlsbad: Hay House, 2002.

Dyson, Brian. "Life as a Juggler." Available online at <www.ramgo.tripod.com/juggler.html>

Estes, Clarissa Pinkola. *Women Who Run with the Wolves*. New York: Ballantine Books, 1992.

Ferrini, Paul. *Love Without Conditions*. Greenfield, MA: Heartways Press, 1994.

Ford, Debbie. *The Dark Side of the Light Chasers*. New York: Riverhead Books, 1998.

Fowler, George. *Learning to Dance Inside*. New York: Addison-Wesley, 1996.

Gattuso, Joan. *A Course in Love*. San Francisco: HarperSanFrancisco, 1996.

Gibran, Kahlil. *The Prophet*. New York: Alfred A. Knopf, 1991.

Hawker, Paul. *Secret Affairs of the Soul*. Kelowna: Northstone Publishing, 2000.

Helmstetter, Shad. *What to Say When You Talk to Yourself*. New York: Pocket Books, 1987.

Hesse, Hermann. *Siddhartha*. Translated by Hilda Rosner. New York: New Directions, 1951.

Hillman, Carolyn. *Recovery of Your Self-Esteem*. New York: Simon & Schuster, 1992.

Hillman, James, and Michael Ventura. *We've Had a Hundred Years of Psychotherapy and the World Is Getting Worse*. San Francisco: HarperSanFrancisco, 1992.

Hopcke, Robert. *There Are No Accidents: Synchronicity and the Stories of Our Lives*. New York: Riverhead Books, 1997.

Hybels, Bill. *The God You're Looking For*. New York: Thomas Nelson, 1997.

Kabir. *A Touch of Grace: Songs of Kabir.* Translated by Linda Hess and
  Shukdev Singh. Boston: Shambhala, 1994.
Kaur, Sat Dharam. *A Call to Women.* Kingston: Quarry Health Books, 2000.
Keating, Thomas. *Open Mind, Open Heart.* New York: Continuum, 1995.
Keen, Sam. *The Passionate Life.* San Francisco: HarperSanFrancisco, 1992.
———. *To Love and Be Loved.* New York: Bantam Books, 1997.
Keeney, Bradford. *Everyday Soul: Awakening the Spirit in Daily Life.* New
  York: Riverhead Books, 1996.
Kelley, Kevin, ed. *The Home Planet.* New York: Addison-Wesley, 1988.
Mandino, Og. *The Greatest Miracle in the World.* New York: Bantam Books,
  1975.
Mascetti, Manuela Dunn. *Rumi: The Path of Love.* Translated by Camille
  Helminski and Kabir Helminski. Boston: Element Books, 1999.
Mayes, Frances. *Bella Tuscany: The Sweet Life in Italy.* New York: Broadway
  Books, 1999.
Miller, Alice. *The Drama of the Gifted Child.* New York: Basic Books, 1994.
Millman, Dan. *Everyday Enlightenment.* New York: Warner Books, 1998.
Moore, Thomas. *Care of the Soul.* New York: HarperPerennial, 1992.
Mountain Dreamer, Oriah. *The Invitation.* San Francisco:
  HarperSanFrancisco, 1999.
Myss, Caroline. *Why People Don't Heal and How They Can.* New York: Three
  Rivers Press, 1997.
Northrup, Christiane. *Women's Bodies, Women's Wisdom.* New York:
  Bantam Books, 1998.
Norwood, Robin. *Why Me, Why This, Why Now?* Toronto: McClelland &
  Stewart, 1994.
O'Donohue, John. *Anam Cara: A Book of Celtic Wisdom.* London:
  HarperCollins, 1997.
———. *Eternal Echoes: Celtic Reflections on Our Yearning to Belong.* New
  York: HarperPerennial,1999.
Ornish, Dean. *Love and Survival: The Scientific Basis for the Healing Power of
  Intimacy.* New York: HarperCollins, 1998.
Pagels, Elaine. *The Gnostic Gospels.* New York: Vintage Books, 1989.
Pearsall, Paul. *The Heart's Code.* New York: Broadway Books, 1998.
Powers, Margaret Fishback. *The Footprints Book of Prayers.* Toronto:
  HarperCollins, 1996.
Rico, Gabriele. *Pain and Possibility.* New York: Jeremy P. Tarcher/Perigee
  Books, 1991.
Rosen, Eliot Jay, ed. *Experiencing the Soul Before Birth, During Life, After
  Death.* Carlsbad, CA: Hay House, 1998.
Rumi. *The Essential Rumi.* Translated by Coleman Barks. New York:
  HarperCollins, 1995.
———. *In Praise of Rumi.* Introduction by Regina Sara Ryan. Prescott, AZ:
  Hohm Press, 1989.

Secretan, Lance H. K. *Reclaiming Higher Ground*. Toronto: Macmillan Canada, 1997.

Shah, Idries. *The Exploits of the Incomparable Mulla Nasrudin*. London: Octagon Press, 1983.

Spangler, David. *The Call*. New York: Berkeley Publishing Group, 1998.

Taylor, Susan L. *In the Spirit*. New York: Amistad, 1993.

Van Praagh, James. *Reaching to Heaven*. New York: Dutton, 1999.

Vardey, Lucinda, ed. *God in All Worlds*. Toronto: Knopf Canada, 1995.

Walsch, Neale Donald. *Conversations with God*, Books 1–3. Charlottesville, VA: Hampton Roads, 1995–98.

———. *Friendship with God*. New York: Putnam, 1999.

Weiss, Brian. *Messages from the Masters: Tapping into the Power of Love*. New York: Warner Books, 2000.

———. *Only Love is Real*. New York: Warner Books,1996.

Whyte, David. *The Heart Aroused: Poetry and the Preservation of Soul in Corporate America*. New York: Currency Doubleday, 1994.

Williams, John K. *The Knack of Using Your Subconscious Mind*. New Jersey: Prentice-Hall, 1980.

Williamson, Marianne. *Enchanted Love*. New York: Simon & Schuster, 1999.

———. *A Return to Love*. New York: HarperCollins, 1993.

———. *A Woman's Worth*. New York: Random House, 1993.

Zukav, Gary. *The Seat of the Soul*. New York: Simon & Schuster, 1990.

Index

Dear friends:

Thank you for making this book a "classic" bestseller in Canada. I am grateful for all your support in the past ten years. If you're new to *Take the Step* . . . I thank you for adding it to your library. I hope it will give you inspiration and encouragement as you journey forward. If you have any feedback for me, drop me a line at *grace@gracecirocco.com*. I would love to hear from you.

With light and love,

GRACE CIROCCO is a professional speaker, personal development expert and marriage coach. A celebrated healer and free Spirit, Grace has delivered her inspirational business keynotes and seminars to hundreds of thousands of people on three continents. Grace specializes in personal mastery, resilience and wellness in the workplace and is a leading authority on relationship intervention and women's mental and emotional health. Her intensive retreats for couples and individuals produce lasting transformational shifts and are recommended by therapists. A former broadcast journalist with CBC Radio, Grace has appeared on television and radio, and her work has been published in newspapers and magazines. She lives with her husband and two children in the Niagara Peninsula. Visit Grace Cirocco at *www.gracecirocco.com*.